IMAGES
of America

HOWEY-IN-THE-HILLS

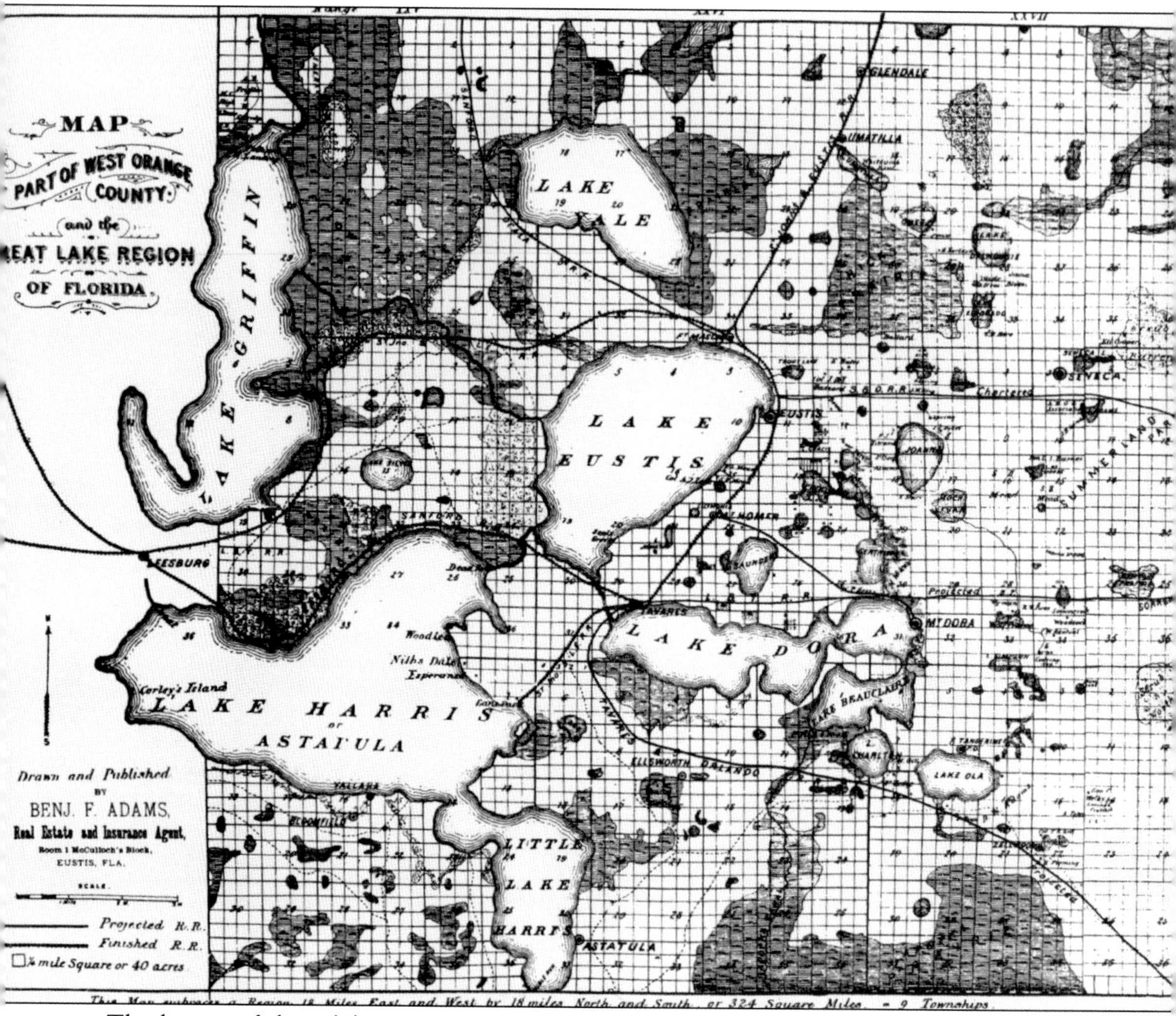

The largest of these lakes was once known by the indians as Lake Astatula or "lake of the sunbeams." Area settlers called it Lake Eustis from 1823 until 1850, when the name Lake Harris was finally etched in stone. Little Lake Harris (bottom center), on the eastern border of Howey-in-the-Hills, first appeared as a named lake in this 1880s West Orange County and Great Lake Region of Florida map. In 1887, Lake County was carved from Sumter and West Orange Counties, including this vital network of waterways. Prior to railroads, towns grew from landing stages in the wilderness to important sightseeing wharfs and shipping ports. The success of Howey's citrus enterprise depended on the Harris chain of lakes. (Lake County HIstorical Museum.)

ON THE COVER: On November 28, 1925, Howey's town council signed an $8,000 contract for a triple combination pumper fire apparatus to be built by the renowned American LaFrance Fire Engine Company's Elmira, New York, plant. Much to the delight of these children, the truck was delivered in April 1926, equipped with a brass test nozzle on the back. This model was the same modern type in use in Orlando and other larger cities. Howey had ample protection for a number of years with its volunteer fire department and this custom fire engine. (Howey-in-the-Hills Historic Preservation Board.)

IMAGES
of America

HOWEY-IN-THE-HILLS

Peggy Beucher Clark

ARCADIA
PUBLISHING

ISBN 978-0-7385-8815-5

Published by Arcadia Publishing
Charleston, South Carolina

Printed in the United States of America

Library of Congress Control Number: 2011933053

For all general information, please contact Arcadia Publishing:
Telephone 843-853-2070
Fax 843-853-0044
E-mail sales@arcadiapublishing.com
For customer service and orders:
Toll-Free 1-888-313-2665

Visit us on the Internet at www.arcadiapublishing.com

For my mom and dad, Margaret and Nick Beucher; my husband and son, John and Matt Clark; and my entire family, I dedicate this history of Howey-in-the-Hills.

Contents

ACKNOWLEDGMENTS

Memories such as those collected and preserved in the following pages are only made possible because someone thought a moment so cherished that a snapshot was taken. Vivid or faded, every image detail tells a unique story or solves an elusive mystery. And while names and places may lose their identity over time, those images that were turned over for notations have become puzzle solvers to our past. I am grateful to so many for being stewards of these timeless, vintage photographs, whether in a personal or official capacity.

To the museum historical collections guardians Bill Streeper and Edith Mordini, who serve with me on the Howey-in-the-Hills Preservation Board, of which it has been my privilege and pleasure to chair in recent years; Lovonda Morris, Lake County Historical Museum, Tavares; Stephanie Gaub Antequino, Orange County Regional History Center, Orlando; and Burt Altman, Florida State Archives, Tallahassee; I thank each of you for your commitment and assistance in gathering images for this remarkable preservation project.

To photographer Britt Runion, thank you for giving your time and talent to help preserve the history of Howey-in-the-Hills. Clayton Bishop, an avid collector of antique Lake County postcards, was a fountain of information. Longtime resident Al Schilling contributed photographs from his days with the Griffin Company. To Chester Wrobel and his son Kerry, thank you for sharing your family and business memories from the day you arrived in Howey. Thank you, Ann and Rodney Griffin, for being such good storytellers and for sharing family photographs. Thank you, Les Deathredge, for contributing the background of the Community Church and its founding members. Special thanks go to Suzanne Gray for proofreading this project and to Ginny Livingston Tackett for sharing photographs and tales of growing up in town.

I am especially grateful for the following people: my husband and son, John and Matt Clark, who are deserving of very special thanks for their love, support, and encouragement; and my siblings, Bob, Donna, Carol, Michelle, and Bud, and our entire Beucher family for decades of accomplishments in Howey-in-the-Hills.

Key to Photograph Courtesies

Howey-in-the-Hills Historic Preservation Board (HH)
Lake County Historical Museum (LCHM)
Orange County Regional History Center (OCHC)
Florida State Archives (FSA)
Peggy Beucher Clark (PBC)
Mission Inn Resort (MIR)
Clayton Bishop (CB)
Chester and Kerry Wrobel (CW)
Edith Mordini (EM)
Ann and Rodney Griffin (ARG)
Al Schilling (AS)
Britt Runion Photography (BRP)
Ginny Livingston Tackett (GLT)

INTRODUCTION

The record of William John Howey (a builder of cities, a visionary of Florida's greatest citrus community in the frost-proof highlands of Lake County, an overseer of 60,000 acres of groves that surrounded and poured a golden wealth into a greater and finer city, and a pursuer of unceasing endeavors that made his vision a reality) is a story unto itself. Valued at $50 million, Howey-in-the-Hills was the greatest homebuilding and income-making opportunity of its day.

Located in the geographical center of Florida, Lake County is found midway between Jacksonville and Tampa and between the Atlantic Ocean and the Gulf of Mexico, and it is on top of the highest hills found in Central Florida in what is sometimes called the Lake Region or "the Alps of Florida."

On May 8, 1925, Florida governor John W. Martin signed the town charter of Howey, the surname of the community's founding father, William J. Howey. The town's name was then officially changed to Howey-in-the-Hills, the legacy of this influential businessman made everlasting.

The son of a circuit-riding United Brethren minister, Howey was born on a farm on January 18, 1876, in Odin, Illinois. His journey to the Sunshine State was an adventurous trek that was dotted with financial success as an established insurance salesman in several states by the age of 24, a land developer for the railroad in Oklahoma, and an automobile manufacturer in Kansas City.

In 1903, Howey moved to Mexico with hopes of developing large pineapple plantations aided by US capitalists. The country's revolution forced him to return to the States and try his hand at another form of fruit farming. In nearby Polk County, Florida, Howey received his first taste of the citrus industry. He perfected his farming and sales techniques in Winter Haven and Lake Hamilton.

Howey traveled to central Lake County in 1914 for his largest land venture ever. Less than six years later, he had amassed 60,000 acres to attract citrus investors. He originally purchased the land parcels for an average of $9 per acre and resold portions for a stout 10,000- to 20,000-percent profit.

To celebrate the completion of the five-bedroom Howey Mansion in 1927, he hosted the New York Civic Opera Company, drawing a crowd of 15,000 to a free outdoor performance. Located on the north end of town, the mansion was listed in the National Register of Historic Places in 1983. Howey served as the town's first mayor, holding that office from 1925 to 1936. After the 1929 stock market collapse, the discovery of the Mediterranean fruit fly in Florida (though Howey's properties were not infested), and bad publicity from the 1926 and 1928 hurricanes, all investors were discouraged.

When Howey died on June 7, 1938, many considered him Florida's greatest citrus developer, but the Securities and Exchange Commission thought otherwise. After Howey's death, the commission ruled that Howey's method of selling orange groves and land amounted to selling unregistered securities, which was illegal.

In 1940, the town defaulted on its bond obligations. C.V. Griffin came to the rescue of the town and purchased the disappearing Howey Company assets. Saving both from certain demise, Griffin and Dodge Taylor took years to reestablish financial security after assuming the debts. To stimulate new home sales, Griffin held four auctions. He worked with his friend Florida governor Fuller Warren to replace the wooden bridge in 1950 with the Memorial Bridge and helped to establish the Howey Academy. Griffin was a citrus industry leader who served four years on the Florida Citrus Commission and helped to facilitate the Florida Citrus Code of 1949.

Nick Beucher, after riding the length of Mexico on horseback in 1939, married Margaret Fortmann in 1940 and opened his commodities brokerage business, Packing House By-Products Company, in Chicago in 1942. Beucher served on numerous boards of directors, including Stark & Wetzel of Indianapolis, Indiana, and two consecutive terms as president of the National Hide and Leather Association. For years, the brokerage business flourished and expanded, with new company offices in Boston and Jersey City. By the mid-1960s, the industry changed, and a classified advertisement for the sale of an 18-hole golf course near Orlando caught his eye. Beucher inspected the 168-acre property in May 1964 and, by September, was in the golf business. The property has since evolved from a distressed golf layout and dated 1940s clubhouse to a beautiful golf resort and home development that sprawls over 1,000 verdant acres.

The initial investment included planting hundreds of trees and installing irrigation. By 1970, Beucher added lodging and dining facilities to sell overnight golf package plans. Additional facilities included the following: a marina, clubhouse, second golf course, restaurants, golf academy, spa, and more. Just as Howey laid the groundwork for those who followed, Nick Beucher laid the foundation on which his family of six children would build an award-winning resort.

The land was the bond between visionaries, Howey, Griffin, and Beucher, luring them to the same location for different reasons. The natural advantages of Howey-in-the-Hills were obvious when compared to other areas of the state. For citrus development, soil conditions were ripe for W.J. Howey. For shipping fruit, the central location was ideal for C.V. Griffin. And for attracting golfers and homebuyers, Howey-in-the-Hills was a hole in one for Nick Beucher. These three men dominated a century of progress, established a city and resort from nothing but opportunity, and successfully marketed their life work to the world. Their supporting cast of thousands, including family, customers, business associates, and employees, helped make Howey-in-the-Hills possible. Few places in the world are as rich in history and as blessed by their founding fathers as Howey-in-the-Hills.

One

The Story of a Great Enterprise

Success was a habit with W.J. Howey, and his secret was in his enthusiasm, integrity, vision, energy, and unbounded faith in the ridge of Florida. As a result of large practical experience and intensive study, he acquired a thorough knowledge of soils, cultural methods, and merchandising principles as they related to citrus fruit.

Widely considered the foremost citrus developer in Florida, Howey's achievements resulted from years of patient concentration on a single dominant idea. When he first arrived from Mexico, he was a pioneer of citrus, breaking his way though a wild country that was practically uninhabited except for a few scattered lumber and turpentine camps.

Howey started his first citrus development at Winter Haven in 1908 before moving to Lake Hamilton in 1910 with a colony of tents on scrub oak land. In 1912, Dundee became his third development, followed by Starr Lake in 1914. When word of his success reached Lake County citrus leaders attorney Harry Duncan and Sheriff Balton A. Cassady, the two extended an invitation to Howey to consider development in their county. After seeing the rolling hills, lakes, and soil, Howey sold his holdings near Starr Lake, where Bok Tower now stands, and began to purchase land at Yalaha in 1914.

By 1920, Howey had accumulated 60,000 acres for his land development project, and a town called Howey was taking shape. Creet Hosler Kenmuir, wife of sales manager W.A. "Bill" Kenmuir of the Howey–St. Petersburg office, suggested to W.J. Howey that the town name be changed to "Howey-in-the-Hills," and so it was in 1925 by state officials when the town was incorporated.

During his tenure, Howey made unfathomable strides in the citrus and hospitality industries and established a mark on every map for a new town called Howey-in-the-Hills. Signs of success were everywhere after a municipal bond of $300,000 was passed to fund ambitious city improvement projects. The town and company's future looked sun-kissed until the 1929 stock market crash, when sales imploded, and at 62 years old on June 7, 1938, William J. Howey died, changing everything.

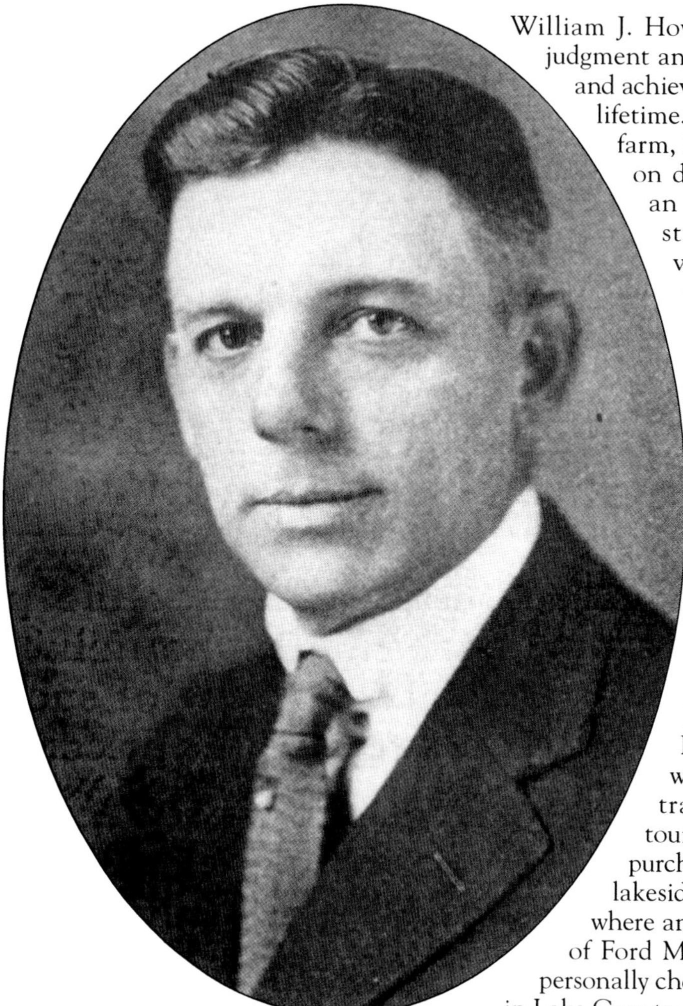

William J. Howey possessed sound business judgment and a high degree of imagination and achieved big, lasting results during his lifetime. Born and raised on an Illinois farm, his chief interest was centered on developing Mother Earth from an agricultural and horticultural standpoint. Howey's broadest vision, which became his life's work, came at a young age when he discovered the greatest of all Florida's natural resources, the citrus industry. (LCHM.)

In the early 1920s, the W.J. Howey Land Company chartered whole trains at excursion rates to transport "Land Seekers." The tour fare was refunded if land was purchased. Guests were housed at the lakeside Highlands Hotel in Dundee, where an escorted, organized motorcade of Ford Model Ts departed for Howey's personally chosen points of great opportunity in Lake County. (FSA.)

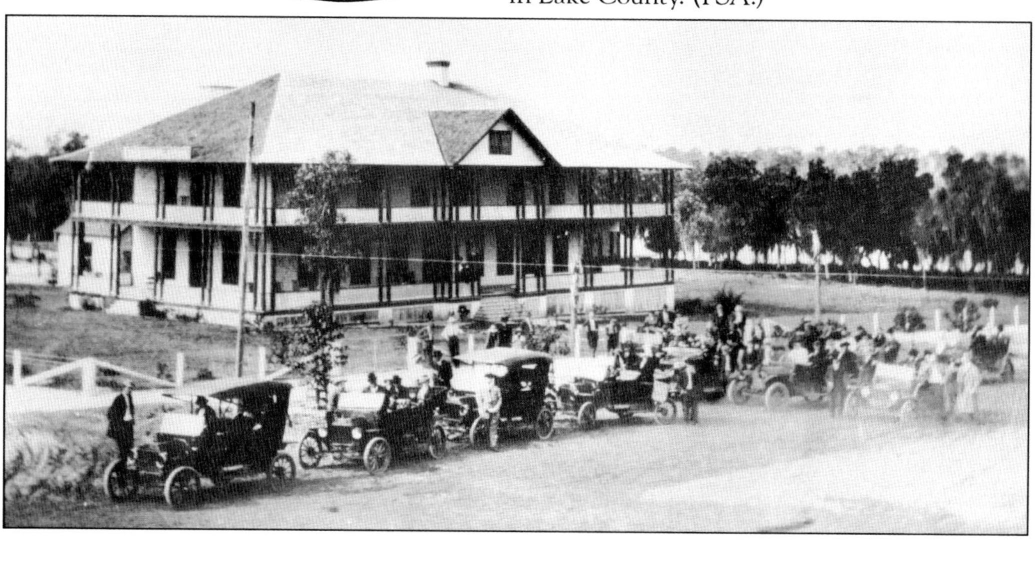

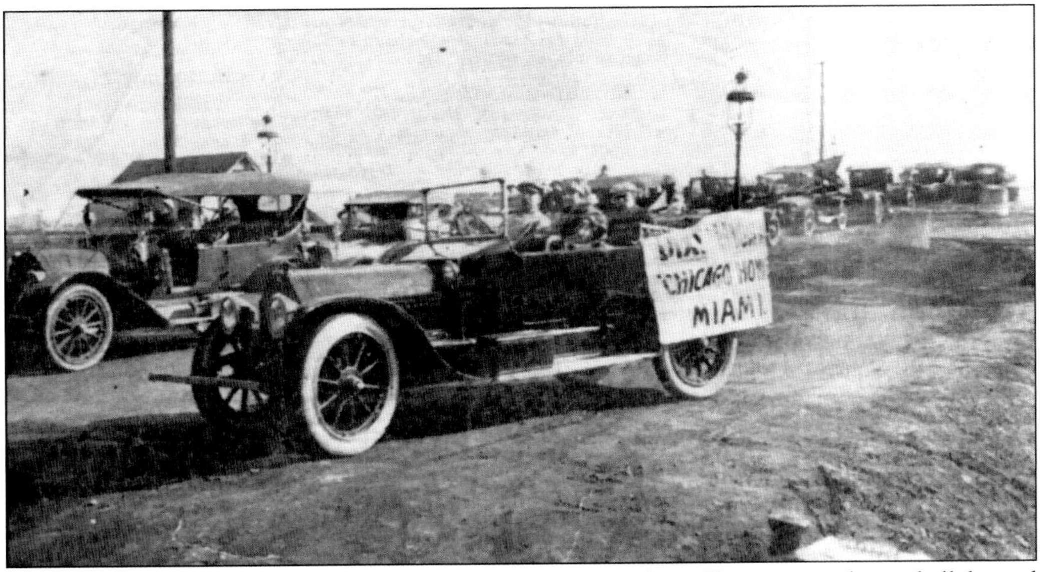

On October 6, 1917, this scouting party left from Grant Park in Chicago, goggles and all, bound for Miami via the new Dixie Highway. The open-air pilot car was that of W.J. Howey, who was largely interested in the development of Florida and his citrus empire in Howey. The caravan of "scouts" was scheduled to arrive in Jacksonville on October 20, 1917, bearing the banner "Dixie Highway-Chicago-Howey-Miami." (PBC.)

The elevated Howey grove lands with frost protection from Lake Harris to the north and surrounding lakes saved territory grove owners thousands of dollars in lost crops, guaranteeing the highest market prices. All Howey tracts benefited from these exclusive features and were certain of success, as delicate January blooms were retained and full yields of fruit were assured. This 1919 map illustrates railroad, waterway, and shipping dock access to Howey. (LCHM.)

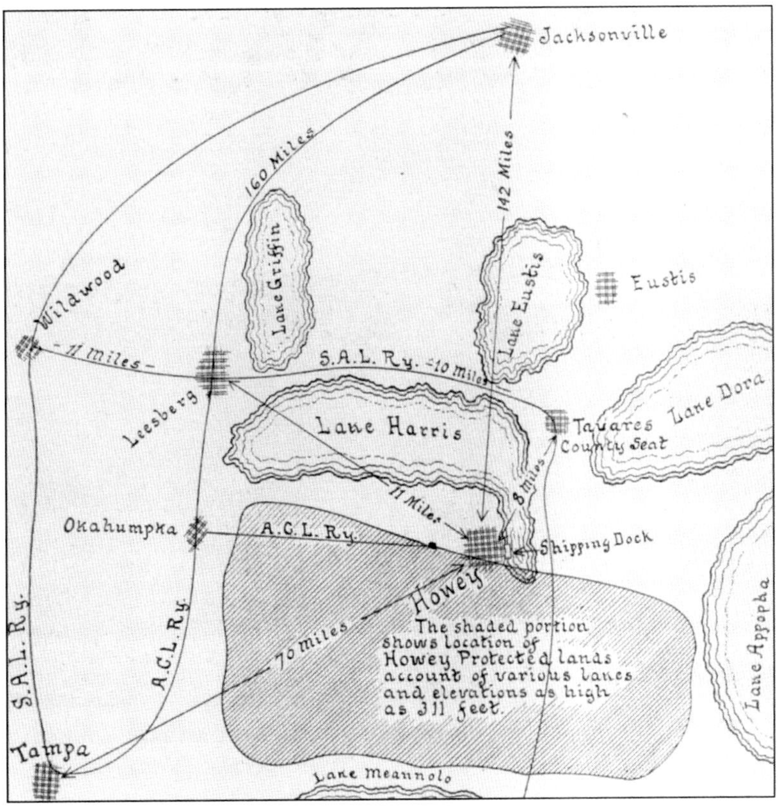

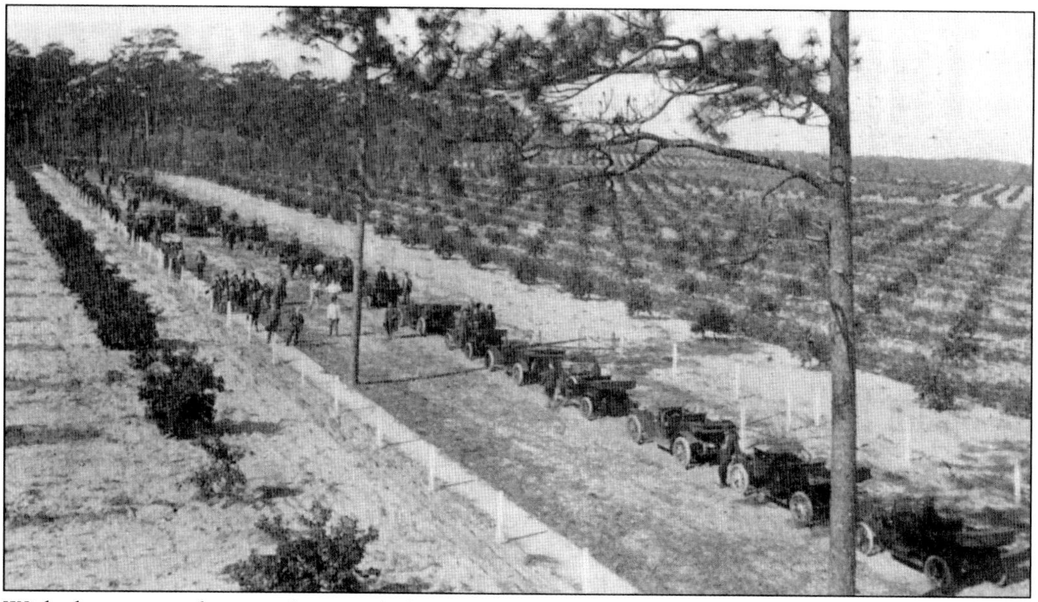

With the return of peace after nearly five years of war and its influence, there was a rush toward grove development such as the world had never known. Global demand for citrus fruits was never so great or supplies so limited, resulting in the highest crop prices in history. A caravan of 57 automobiles transported an inspection party to this 1,000-acre Howey grove owned primarily by eastern bankers and executives. (LCHM.)

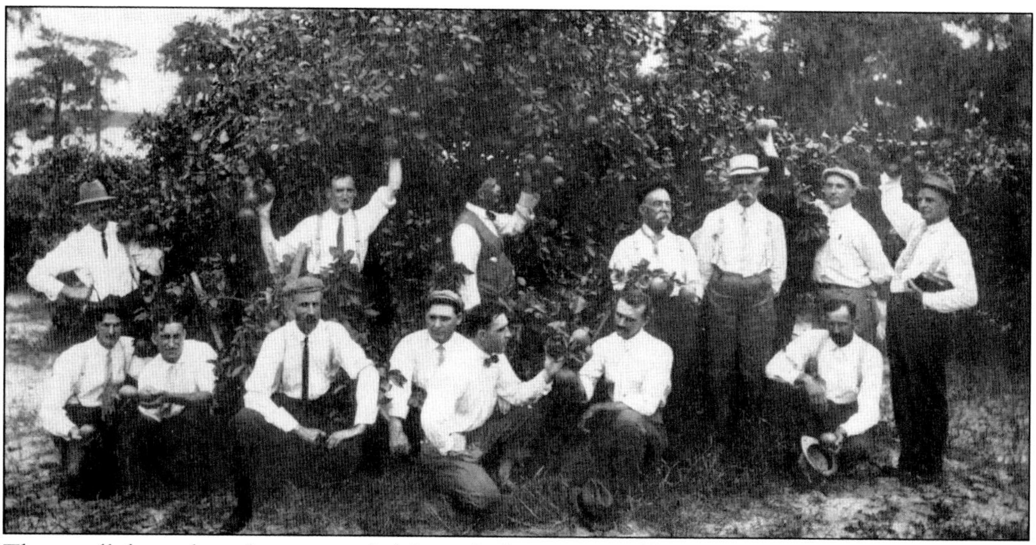

These well-dressed gentlemen traveled through the scenic and beautiful highlands of Lake County, Florida, on the 100-mile inspection tour of Howey groves, where they gathered examples of the golden harvest, oranges. Their experience of Howey far exceeded their most vivid anticipation, never dreaming there was such scenery or prospects of accumulating wealth and independence. In 1920, the "Switzerland of Florida" boasted an altitude of 362 feet above sea level. (LCHM.)

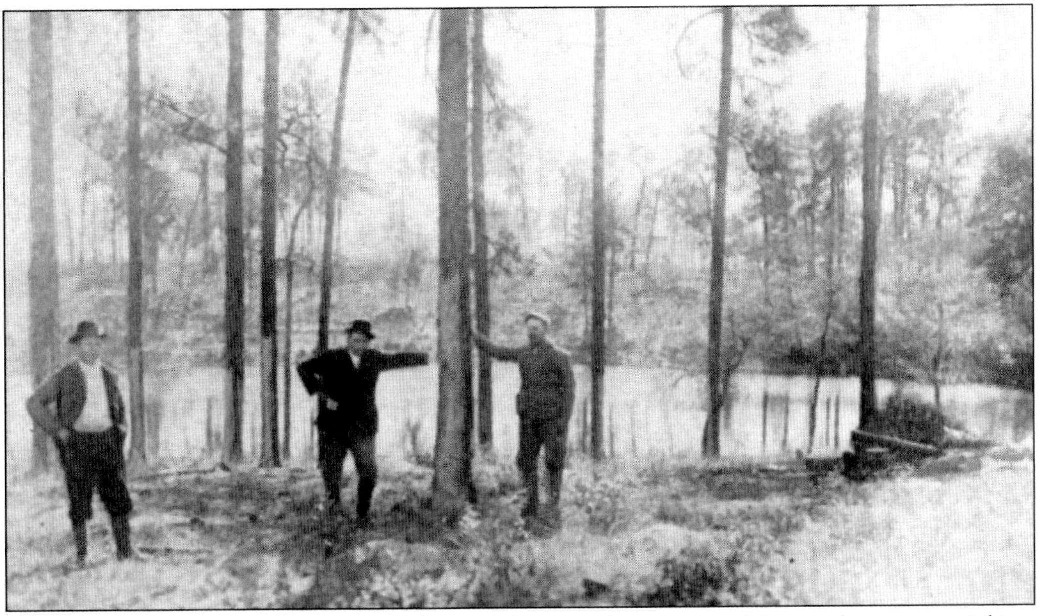

When E.D. Tison arrived on Howey's forested footstep, he gave careful consideration to picking his slice of heaven. Eight years later, in 1919, his 10-acre orchard, one of Howey's first projects, delivered a check for $10,097.97. Groves were planted half orange and half grapefruit, with an ironclad guarantee that the first five crops would return an entire investment or the company would repurchase the property, paying six-percent interest on the investment. (LCHM.)

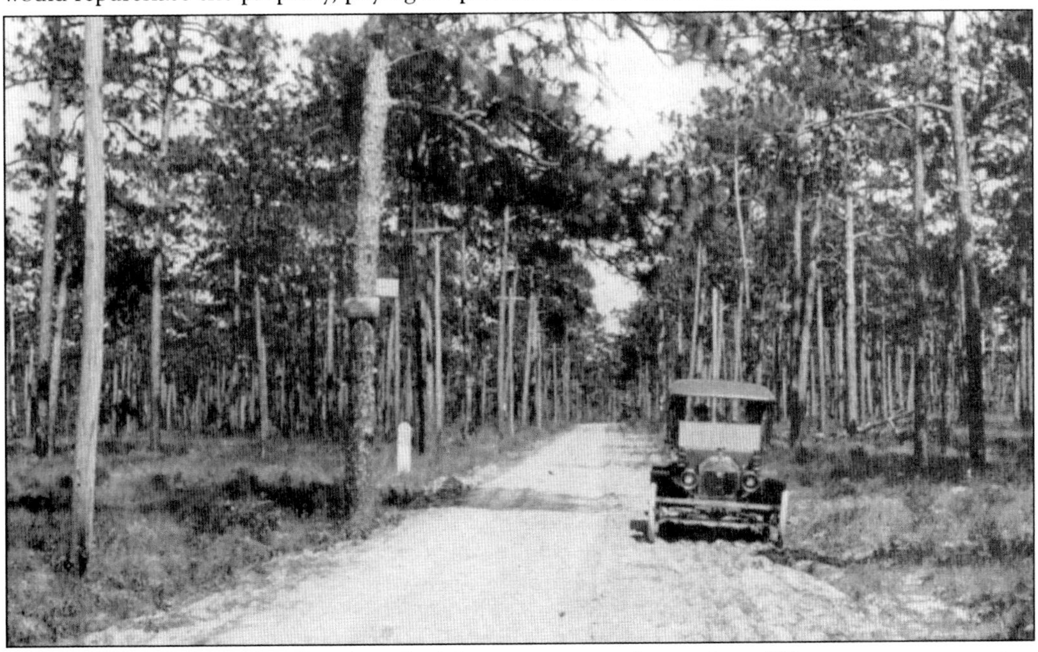

In 1920, this sandy road and undisturbed forest represented a portion of Howey grove properties. Howey lands ranged in price from $525 to $600 per acre, depending on location as related to towns, lakes, public roads, and so forth, and carried a development fund of approximately $140 per acre. To bring a grove to eight years of age, the combined cost on the $525 per acre land came to $665, with a money-back guarantee. (LCHM.)

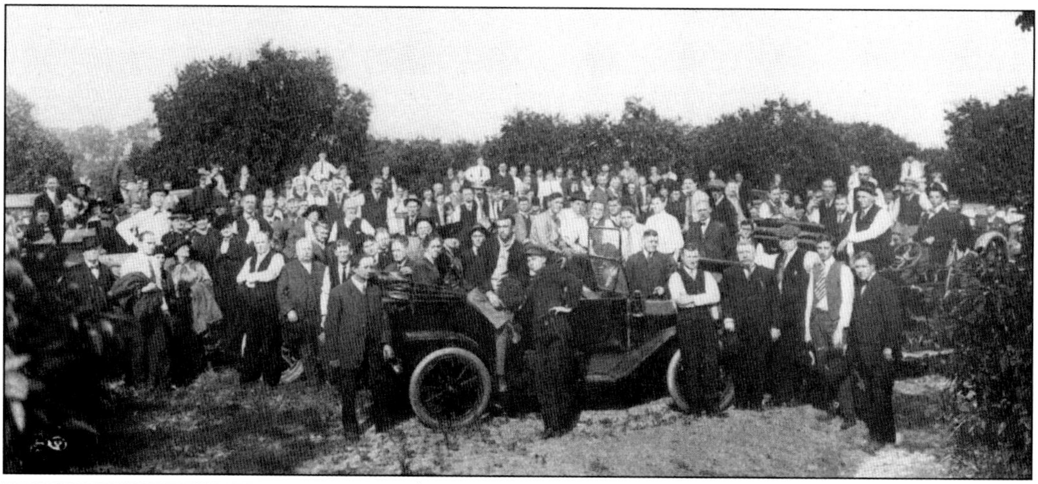

These investors listened carefully to the tips worth knowing when inspecting Florida land, or looking at the pictures thereof, and always noted if there was any palmetto thereon. If so, an investor was to add $50 to $100 per acre to the cost for clearing and was advised to ask authorities if the land was not sour. Other operations had sold palmetto or flat land for citrus fruit growing, but Howey never did. (LCHM.)

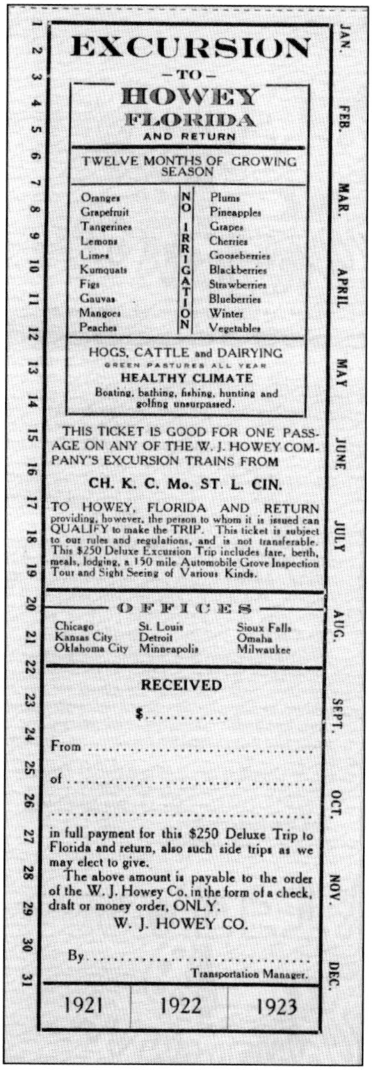

1 2 3 4 5 6 7 8 9 10 11 12 13 14 15 16 17 18 19 20 21 22 23 24 25 26 27 28 29 30 31

EXCURSION
– TO –
HOWEY
FLORIDA
AND RETURN

TWELVE MONTHS OF GROWING SEASON

Oranges	N	Plums
Grapefruit	O	Pineapples
Tangerines	I	Grapes
Lemons	R	Cherries
Limes	R	Gooseberries
Kumquats	I	Blackberries
Figs	G	Strawberries
Gauvas	A	Blueberries
Mangoes	T	Winter
Peaches	I O N	Vegetables

HOGS, CATTLE and DAIRYING
GREEN PASTURES ALL YEAR
HEALTHY CLIMATE
Boating, bathing, fishing, hunting and golfing unsurpassed.

THIS TICKET IS GOOD FOR ONE PASSAGE ON ANY OF THE W. J. HOWEY COMPANY'S EXCURSION TRAINS FROM

CH. K. C. Mo. ST. L. CIN.

TO HOWEY, FLORIDA AND RETURN providing, however, the person to whom it is issued can QUALIFY to make the TRIP. This ticket is subject to our rules and regulations, and is not transferable. This $250 Deluxe Excursion Trip includes fare, berth, meals, lodging, a 150 mile Automobile Grove Inspection Tour and Sight Seeing of Various Kinds.

OFFICES

Chicago	St. Louis	Sioux Falls
Kansas City	Detroit	Omaha
Oklahoma City	Minneapolis	Milwaukee

RECEIVED

$............

From ....

of ....

....

in full payment for this $250 Deluxe Trip to Florida and return, also such side trips as we may elect to give.

The above amount is payable to the order of the W. J. Howey Co. in the form of a check, draft or money order, ONLY.

W. J. HOWEY CO.

By..................................
Transportation Manager.

1921	1922	1923

JAN. FEB. MAR. APRIL MAY JUNE JULY AUG. SEPT. OCT. NOV. DEC.

Personally conducted "selected investigators'" excursions left for Howey several times monthly beginning 1921. Prequalified investors were entitled to a "money advanced," round-trip railroad ticket, including sleeping car accommodations, meals, hotel bills, and all other miscellaneous expenses incident to the trip. To correctly judge the merits and value of owning a Howey grove tract by comparison, a 100-mile automobile tour through Florida's choicest orange and grapefruit grove sections was included. (LCHM.)

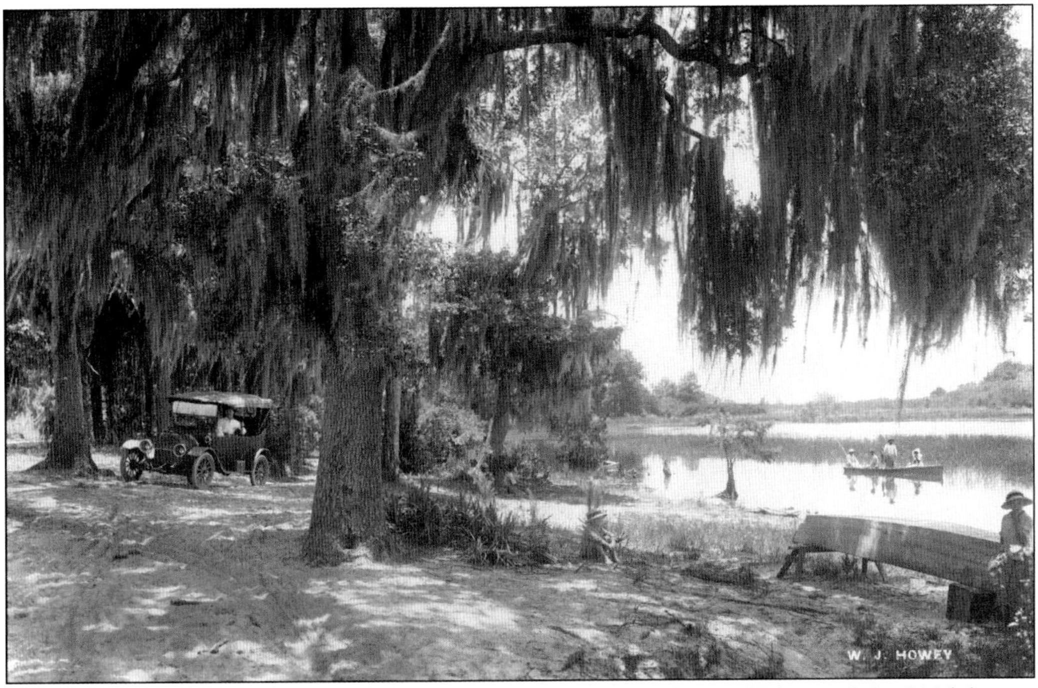

Anglers were hooked on freshwater fishing around the Harris chain of lakes and the 200 lakes on William J. Howey's enormous tract of land. On this lazy day in Howey, fishermen waited for rod and reel or cane pole to bring in black bass, speckled perch, bream, or shell cracker for dinner. Note that everyone wore a hat for shade. (HH.)

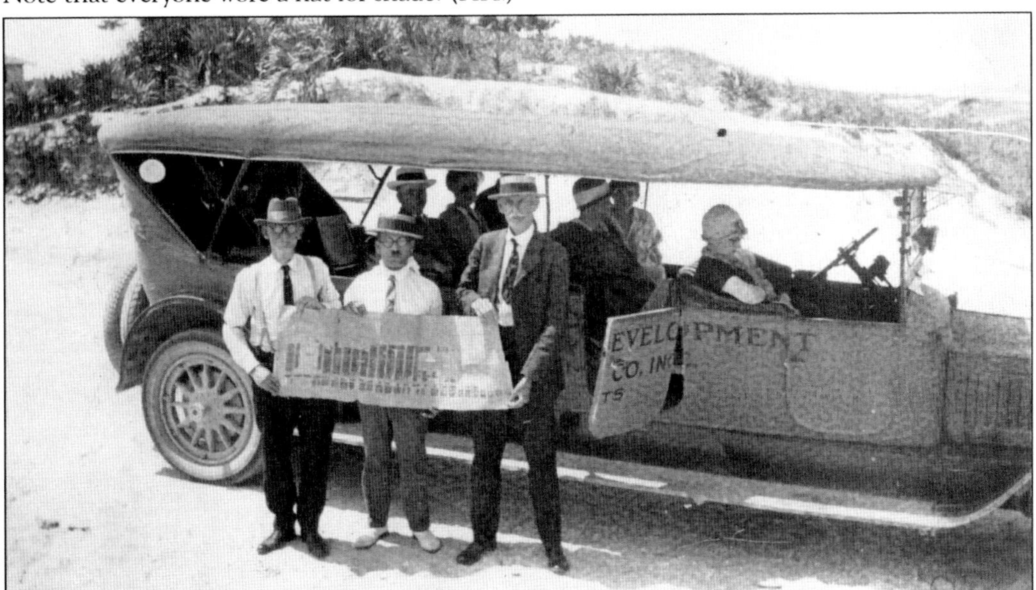

These potential land investors took the 650-mile tour from Miami to Howey and back again, which took a route along Florida's east coast. The tour promotion was arranged by the Howey Company's Miami office to take prospective buyers to investigate the opportunities in Howey. The three men standing on the beach are holding the citrus development plan for Howey. The 12-passenger open-air bus offered leather seating. (OCHC.)

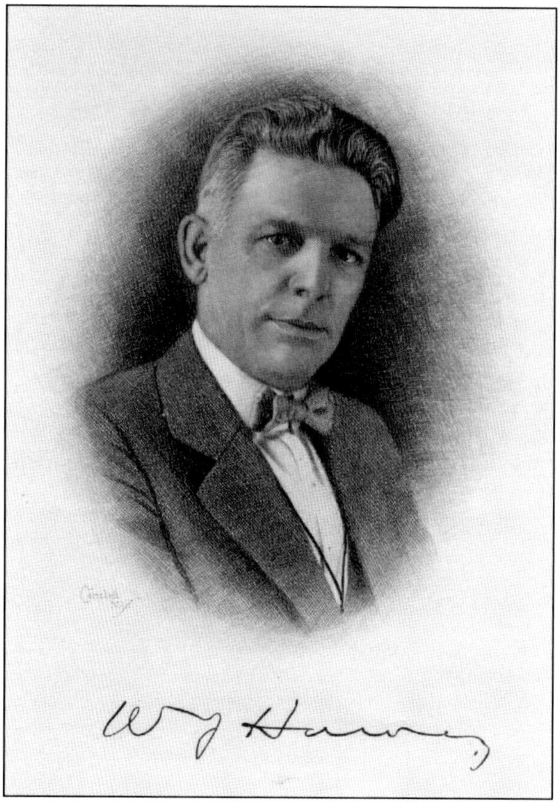

J.K. Campbell of New York was commissioned to engrave this portrait of William J. Howey. The finer points of the etching reveal W.J. Howey's eyeglass around his neck; thick, wavy hair with white around the temples; and his personal signature. (HH.)

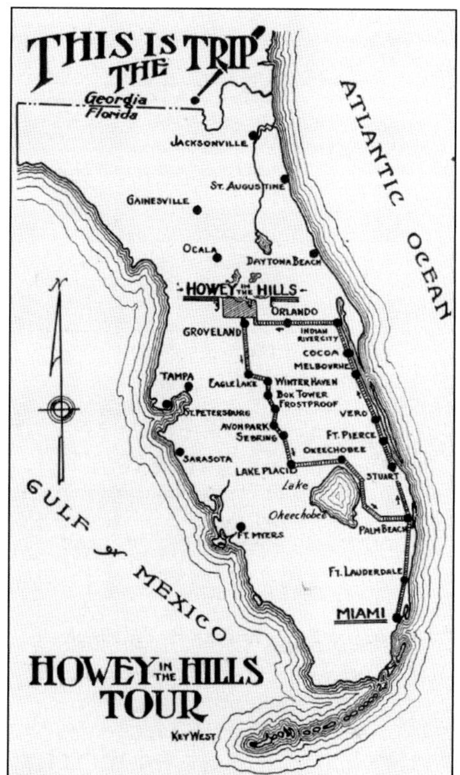

An escorted tour covering 650 miles over four days was promoted as the most wonderful trip in Florida. The Miami office at 100 Biscayne Boulevard, representing the Howey Company, planned the ambitious itinerary at a cost of $25 per person, which included hotels, meals, entertainment, and free transportation aboard luxurious Pullman buses. Points of interest were the Bok Singing Tower, the mysterious Everglades, Indian River, and the famous Howey citrus empire. (LCHM.)

Two

THE NEW CITRUS ERA

Control over all aspects from seedbed to final consumer purchase was W.J. Howey's solution of a problem that had long vexed citrus experts. Management of raw materials and scientific merchandising had shown the way to larger profits in the nation's greatest industries. With a citrus empire of 60,000 acres in the heart of Florida's most productive area, as well as ample capital and more than 20 years of success in Florida's citrus culture and development, Howey had been in a singularly advantageous position to apply this simple business principle successfully to his extensive agricultural operations.

Howey-in-the-Hills became one of the most scientific and business-like agricultural enterprises in America. It was the largest single citrus unit in the world and the only complete citrus development conceived. Half a million orange and grapefruit trees were growing. A total of three million trees, with potential annual revenue of $30 million when fully matured, was the ultimate objective—in addition to quality fruit, properly packaged and merchandised, and undreamed-of profits in the by-products!

All this was made possible by the guarantee on Howey groves that virtually precluded the loss of a penny of principal or interest, a guarantee that was backed by land valuations founded solely on productive capacity. The opportunity to share in the Howey success depended on how ambitious the individual's desire was to achieve personal wealth. Howey invited all to witness the advent of the new citrus era from first-hand observation and to capitalize on the physical advantages and never-failing promise of nature.

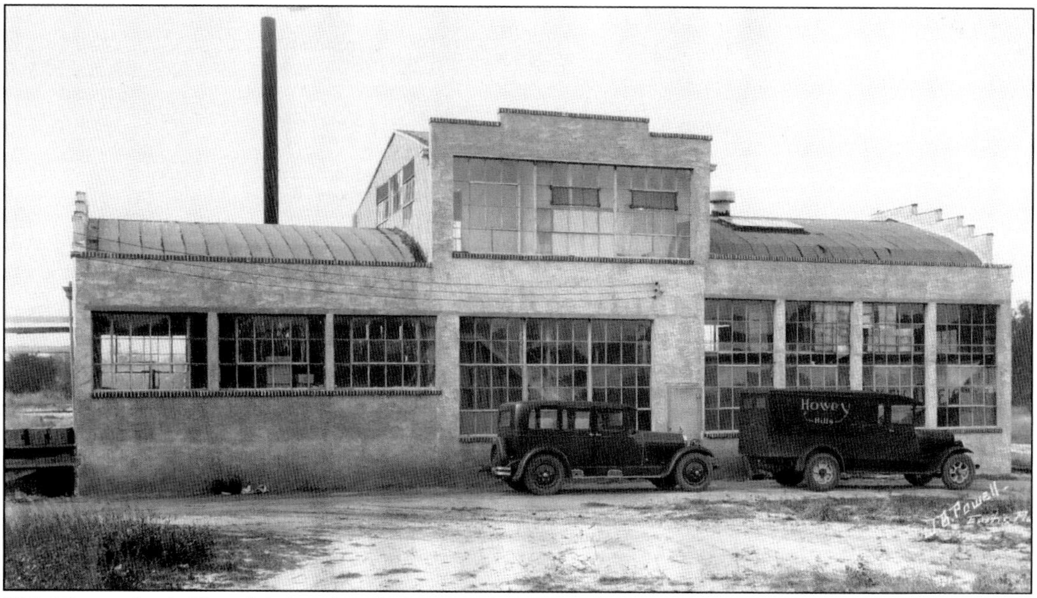

W.J. Howey built Florida's first bottled juice plant to utilize undersized and discolored fruit from Howey-in-the-Hills groves under his label Life Guard. Two primary goals of the prolific Howey operation were to produce only the highest quality fruit and to discover every possible orange and grapefruit by-product. Even after extracting juice, the skins were ground for fertilizer and other valuable by-products. (HH.)

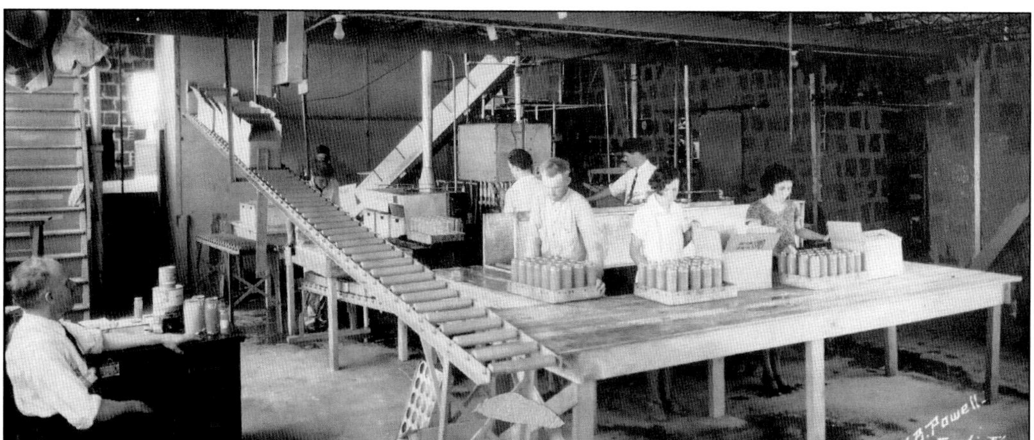

In 1927, W.J. Howey's entire citrus organization numbered more than 500 men and women, who, through the summer months, engaged collectively to perfect the great and revolutionizing glass distribution system. In October, plans were announced to erect this well-supervised juice bottling plant. The bottled juice of oranges and grapefruit, direct from the groves of Howey-in-the-Hills, was distributed to every market center in the country from Maine to Denver. (LCHM.)

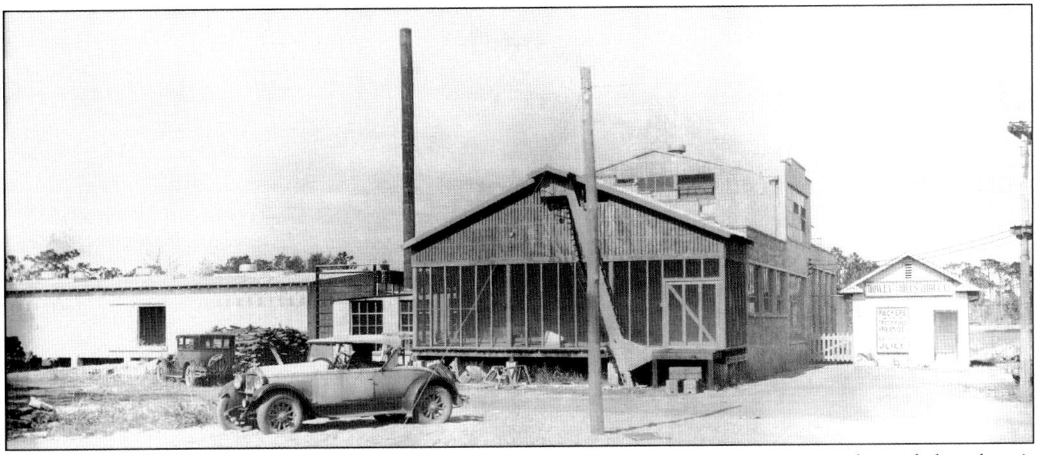

When the Howey Company perfected the juice canning process, W.J. Howey enlarged the plant's size and capacity to quench the thirst of growing demands. Operating 24 hours a day in season, shifts of 60 people turned out up to 5,000 gallons or one train carload with 8-, 18-, and 96-ounce cans daily. The updated cold process equipment preserved the juice for longer shelf life and tripled the output. This improvement, with the new office building and warehouse enlargement to 36 feet by 96 feet, represented an investment of $75,000. (OCHC.)

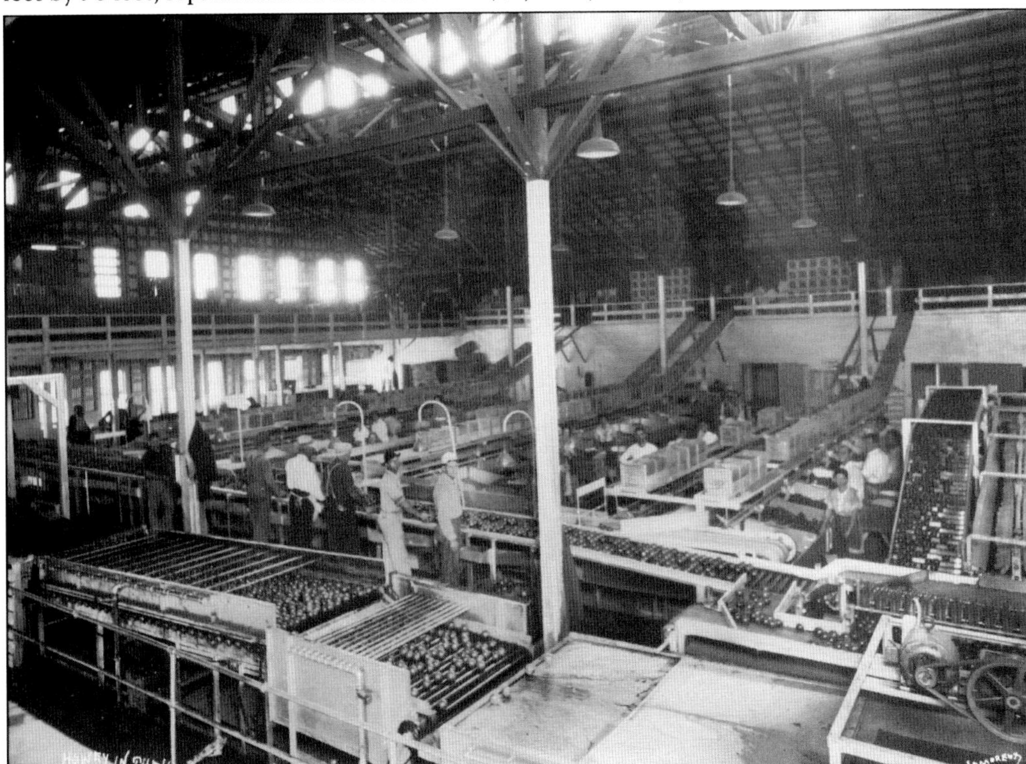

In December 1936, the packing plant was in full swing, but land sales slowed. Following the 1929 stock market crash, sales still held at $500,000 in 1930 but dwindled to $250,000 in 1931. Between the mid-1920s and 1931, company payroll dropped from $1 million to $101,000. Sales for the citrus giant plummeted from its peak of 180 units in 1926 to averaging 23 annually between 1921 and 1938. (LCHM.)

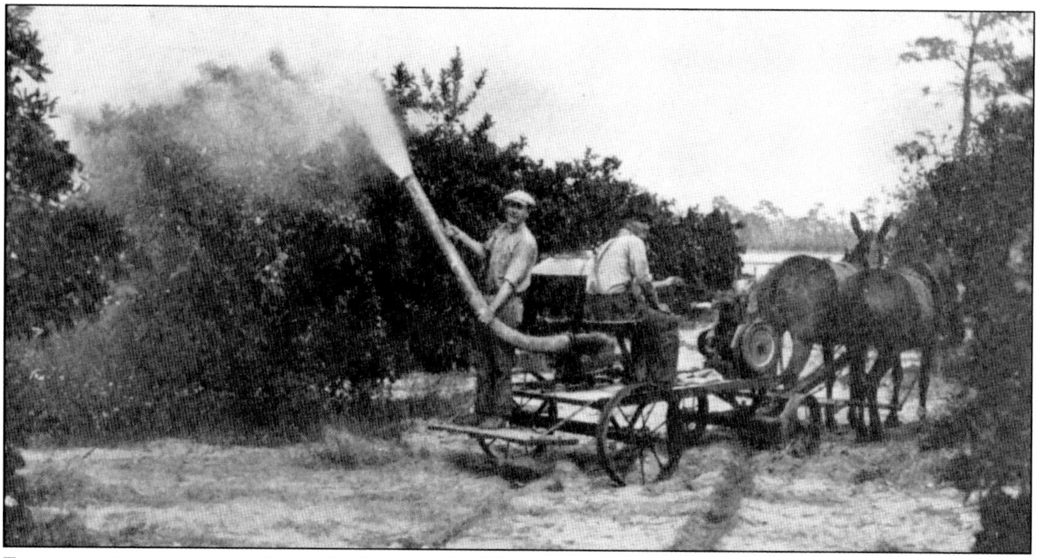

From sunrise to sunset, the early days in the Howey groves were filled with long hours and hard work. Grove hands appreciated the stable of 50 mules that showed up for work daily and pulled their own weight. The original irrigation system of essentially hand watering was similar to how chemicals and fertilizers were applied over thousands of acres throughout the Howey-managed and -owned groves. (MIR.)

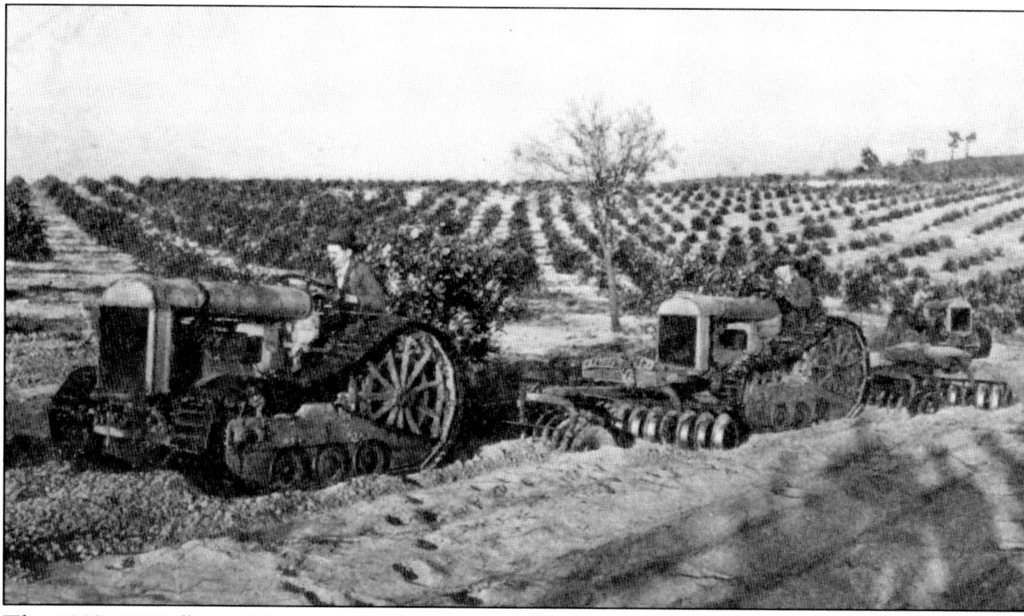

The 1927–1928 fleet of International passenger buses was fit companion to the 16 mammoth McCormick-Deering tractors that plowed their way through sand and soil to create the greatest citrus development in the world in Howey-in-the-Hills. These exceptional workhorses and tireless grove keepers planted thousands of Howey acres in late Valencia orange and Marsh seedless grapefruit. (MIR.)

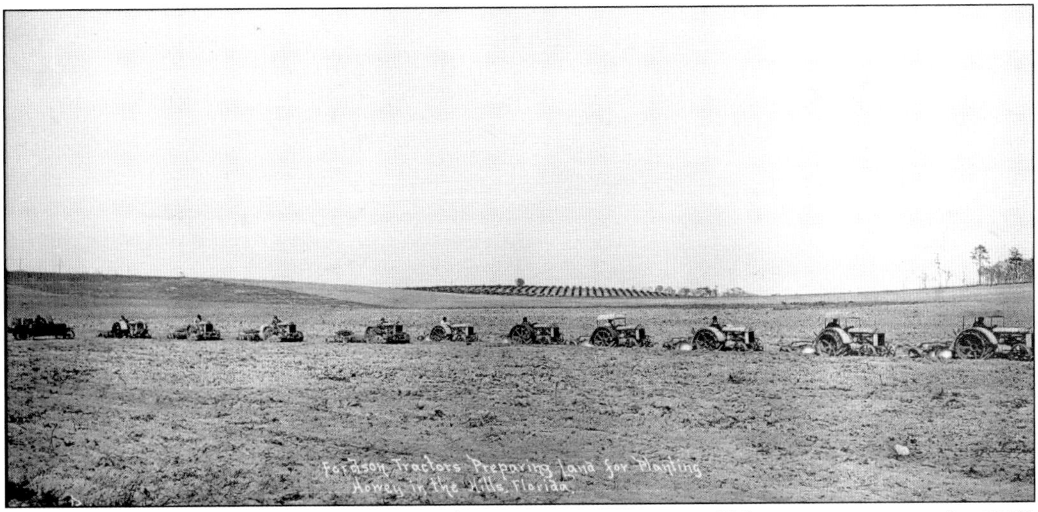

This army of new Fordson tractors marches across open acres of Howey grove tract. In 1927, when the company prepared to plant an additional 6,000 acres, a contract was signed with the International Harvester Company for the largest single order for tractors ever placed in Florida. From the Chicago factory, the regular McCormick-Deering tractors were shipped in four carloads with banners saying they were Florida-bound. (OCHC.)

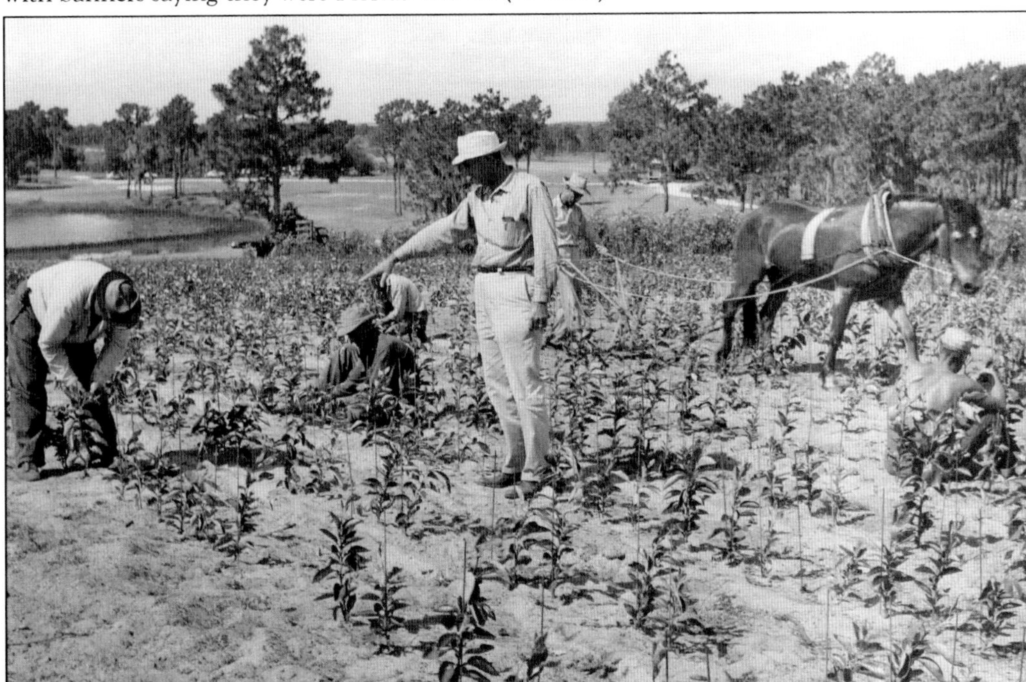

Throughout the Howey tract, clearing and grove-planting operations were carried on in a wholesale fashion in April, assisted by Old Bill the horse. In the mid-1920s, during a 30-day period, 920 acres of land were set to be transformed into a grove, and a considerably larger acreage was cleared, grubbed, plowed, and harrowed. Simultaneously, grove forces carried on their regular spring work: cultivating, applying fertilizer, and sowing cover crops. In June 1938, lime trees were set by hand. (LCHM.)

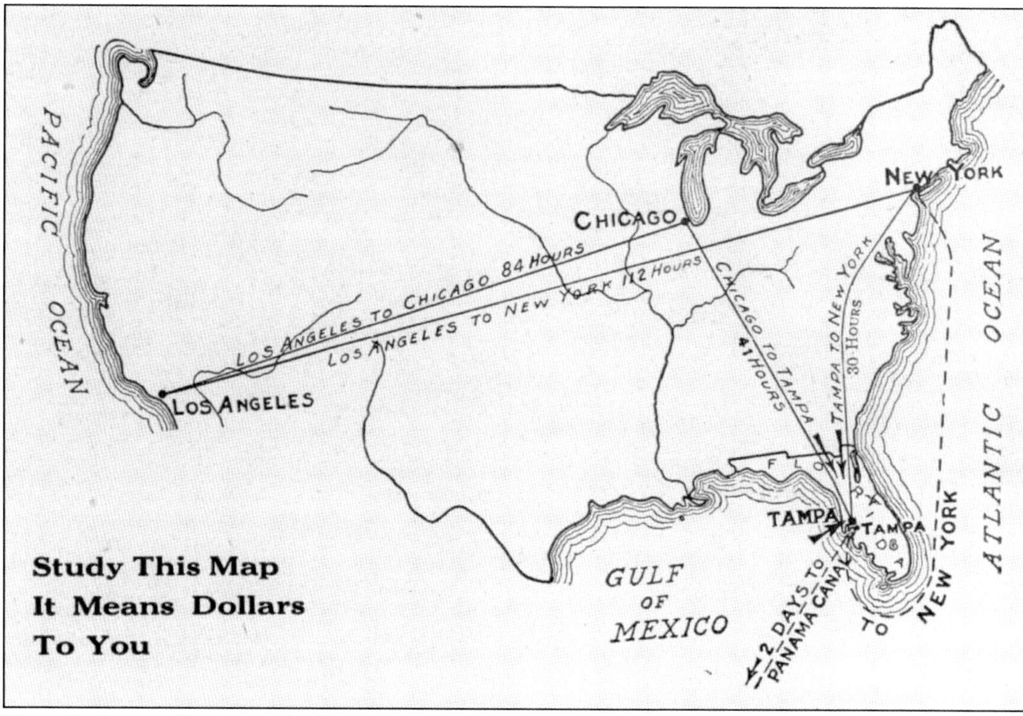

This 1920 map illustrates the big advantage Lake County had over the California shipper. Note how long it took the California grower to reach Midwest and East Coast markets and the time grove and vegetable products were in transit. Spoilage and lost income were disadvantages the Howey growers did not face due to the short haul time to markets, which resulted in higher prices. (LCHM.)

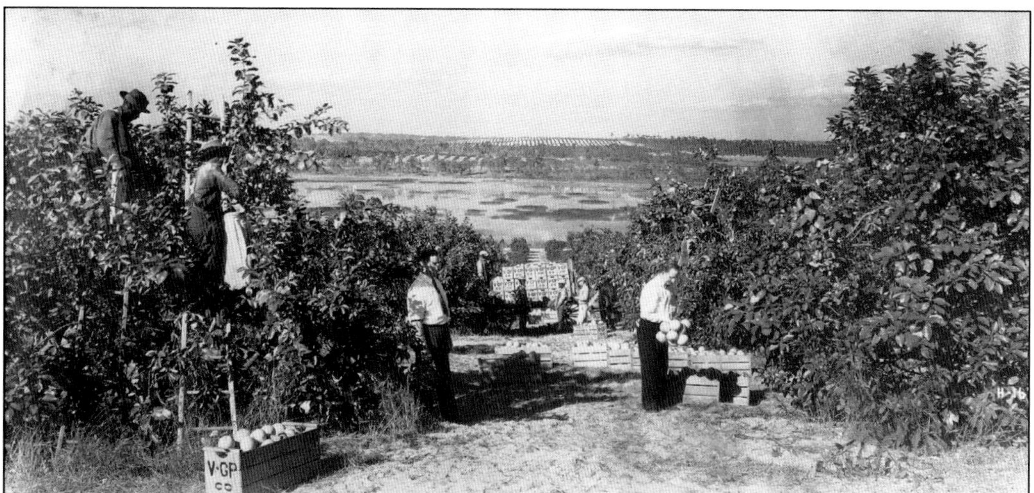

In this early Howey grove-harvesting image, the mule-drawn wagon is loaded and readied to haul thousands of pounds of boxed tree-ripened fruit to the plant. Laborers climbed ladders to pick the mature fruit from treetops, which were as high as 20 feet tall. Vaughn-Griffin Packing handled the shipment of all Howey fruit by this time. (LCHM.)

William J. Howey may have modestly referred to himself as an "Illinois farmer," but his fertile green acres had him squeezing every imaginable idea from his groves. The Howey Plan handled every aspect from seed to delivery, which protected the trademark and eliminated the middleman. By 1928, Howey opened retail stores at the rate of eight per week, with this one being located in Orlando at the Florida Arcade. (HH.)

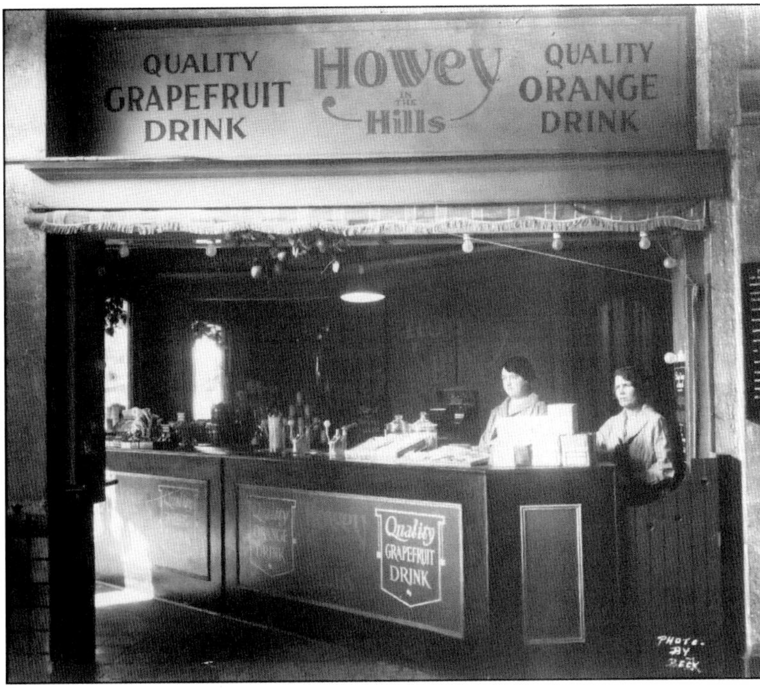

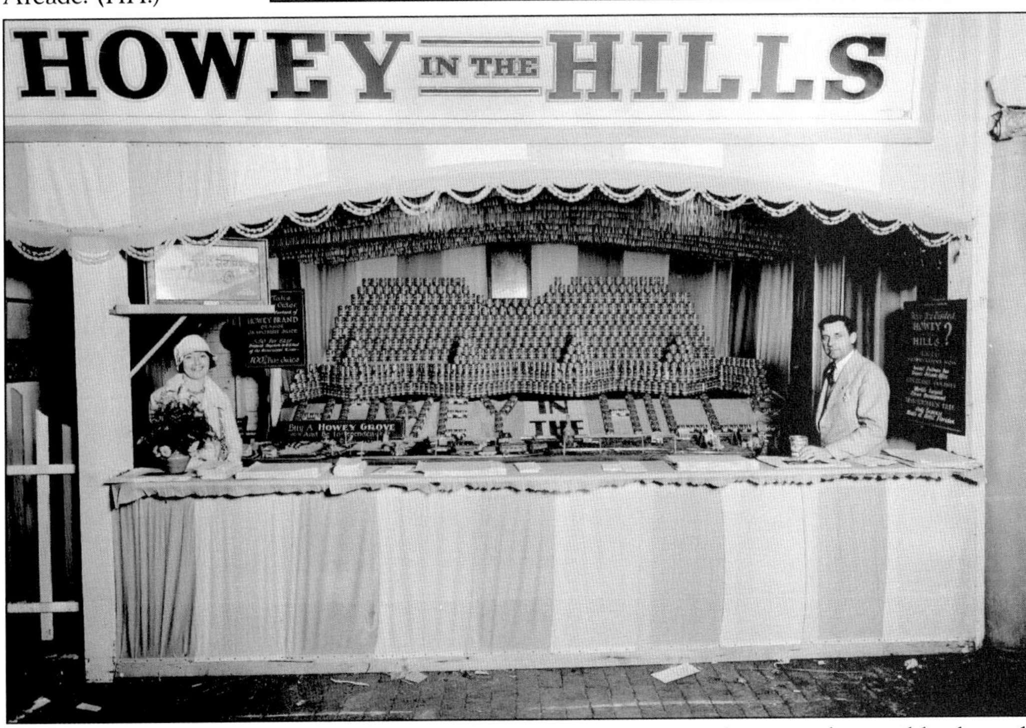

Getting the word out about the Howey groves was a priority and was made possible through company-owned retail outlets, grocery chains, and citrus fairs. Juice cans were stacked to create a hilly landscape and to spell out Howey-in-the-Hills at this booth. A full model of the groves, plant, hotel, and access transportation was displayed behind the counter, where investment brochures and Howey Tribunes were distributed freely. (OCHC.)

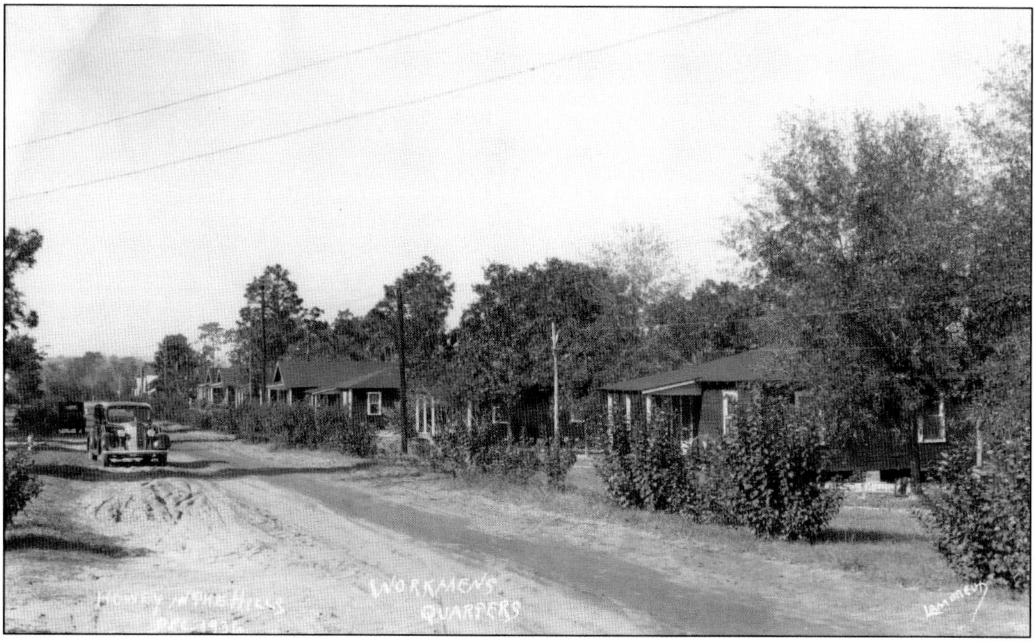

In December 1936, Orange Blossom, a suburb of Howey-in-the-Hills, was the dynamo generating the energy and activities of this great citrus empire. This group of orderly cottages on either side of the hibiscus-lined highway, with green lawns and a profusion of flowers, provided housing for foremen and grove managers. A neat settlement known as Nicksville provided housing, churches, and school facilities for the army of entry-level grove workers. (LCHM.)

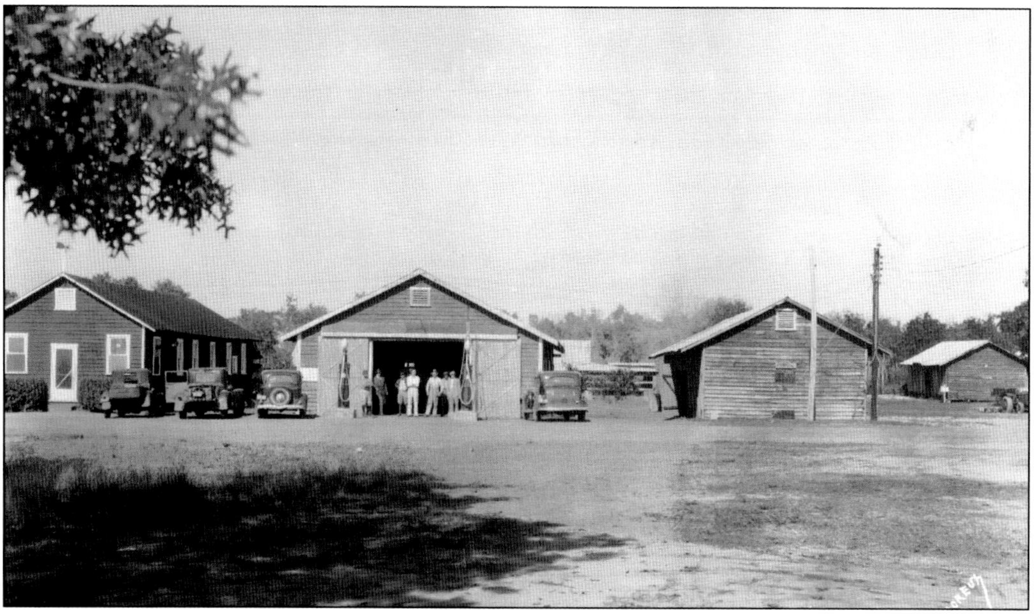

The company's grove maintenance headquarters for its mass of modern machinery was located on Orange Blossom Road at the southernmost border of town. There was a smokehouse, large shop, bus garage, gas pumps, and 50-mule barn. At Howey Heights along the Seaboard Air Line railway and within the shadow of Sugar Loaf Mountain (the highest point in Florida), a warehouse had a capacity of 200 tons of fertilizer. (HH.)

In the competitive citrus industry, labels for crates and cans became an art form that distinguished brands from those of competitors, driving sales through greater visibility. Printed in color at the St. Louis printing company of Woodward & Tiernan, this citrus label was a standout that combined beautiful graphics with easy-to-read lettering. In 1930, the lithographed Howey label touted the metabolic medicinal value of its grapefruit juice. (LCHM.)

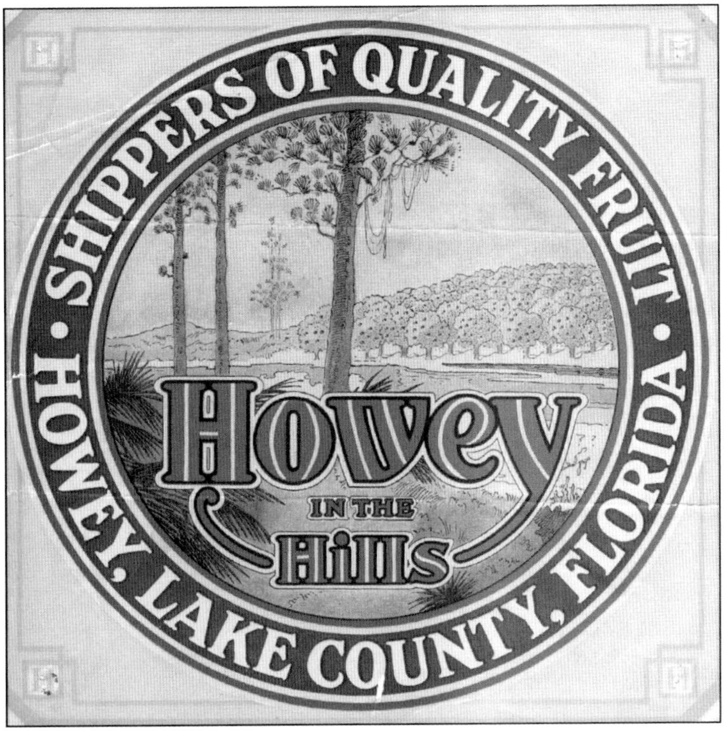

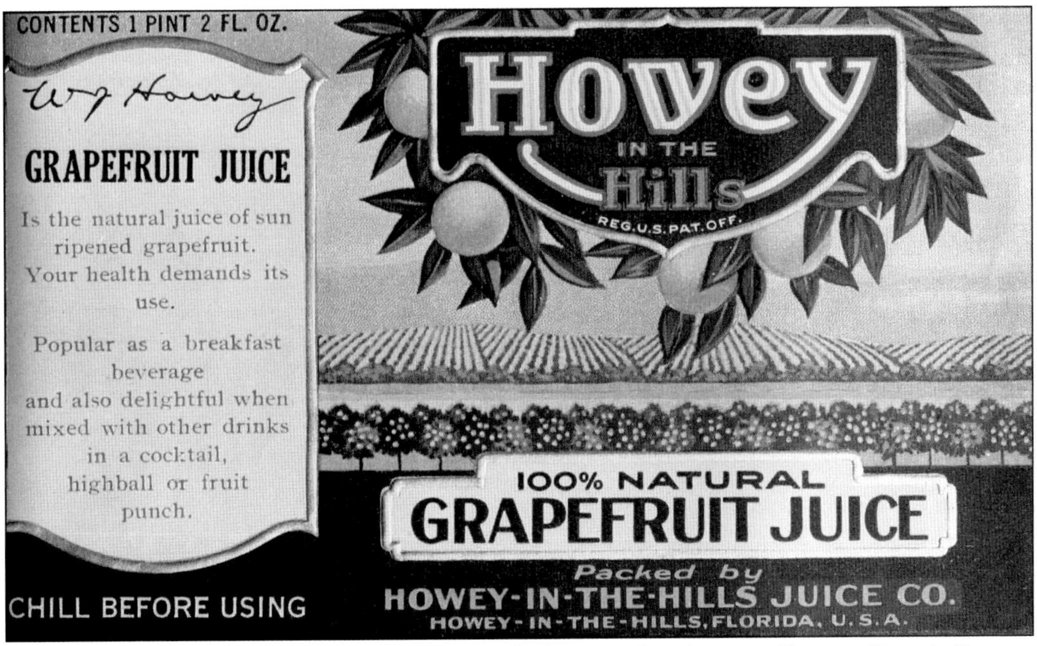

In 1930, Howey Company sales representatives called on merchandisers in Chicago, Detroit, Boston, New York, Philadelphia, and Washington, resulting in record-breaking fruit sales. Aggressive advertising messages were printed, heard over the radio waves, and seen in numerous newspapers, popularizing the Howey fruit juice brand. Early orders put the squeeze on workers to keep juices flowing into labeled cans and packed for quick shipping to various in-state and out-of-state destinations. (OCHC.)

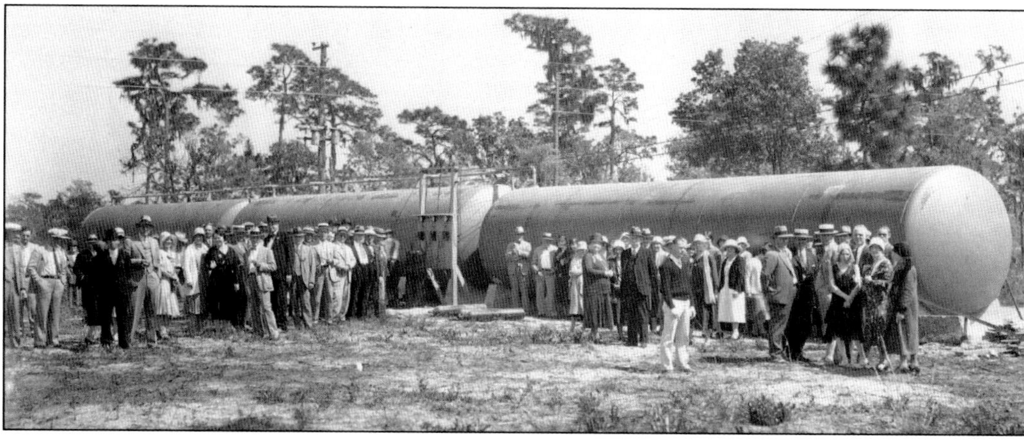

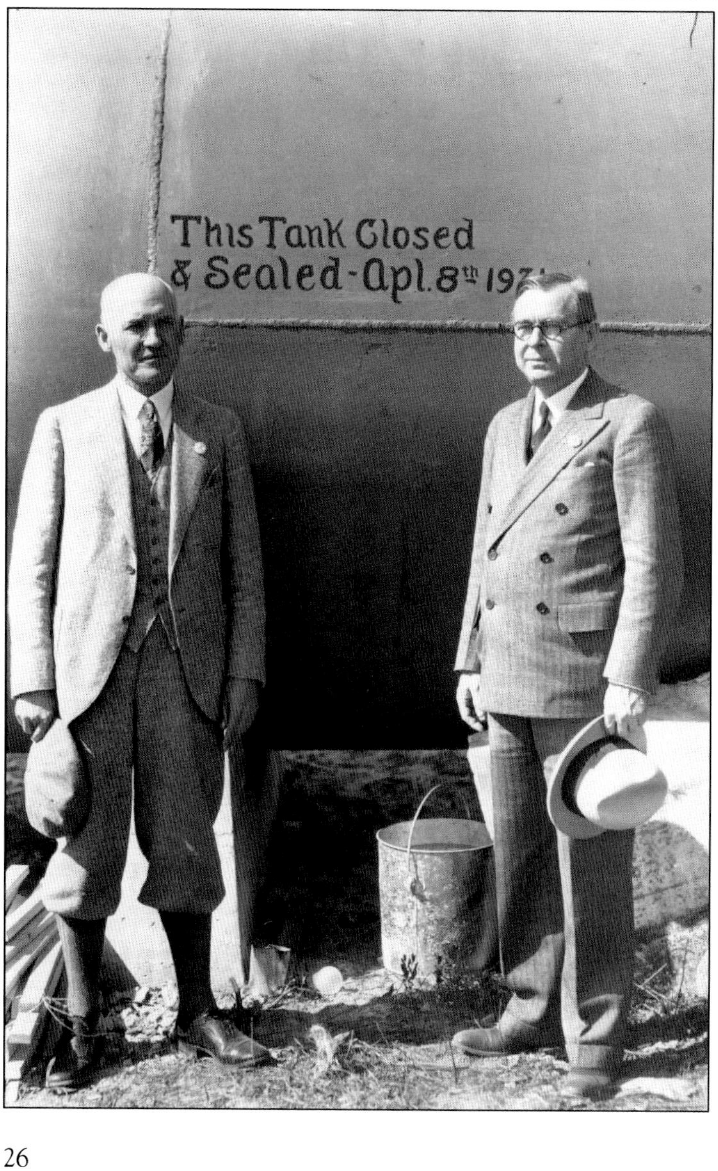

Oranges, grapefruit, and tangerines, 1,800 boxes in all, were placed in three 40-foot-long steel tanks to demonstrate a new anti-oxidation, non-refrigerated storage process, the success of which would revolutionize the citrus industry. Certain the one-year experiment would succeed, Howey first obtained exclusive US rights to "Karbokept." Without compromising patents, W.J. Howey announced from atop his fruit truck platform that the procedure created a vacuum and used inert gas to sustain the absence of oxygen. Scientists, citrus exchange officials, growers, railroad men, shippers, capitalists, and others gathered for the ceremony. On April 8, 1931, John F. Rudd (left) and Dr. Floyd W. Robison (right), the inventors of the process, arrived from their New York City headquarters and sealed the tanks. The test failed, but the theory was validated when technology later improved. (Both, HH.)

Three

WHEN CITRUS WAS KING

Howey-in-the-Hills would probably not exist today without its main squeeze, citrus. The minute William J. Howey amassed his 60,000th acre in 1920, the proverbial "orange" was already rolling for what he described "City Inevitable." By researching growing practices, Howey determined Central Florida's ridge was the best place to produce citrus due to the hilly countryside and abundant lakes.

Howey originally purchased land for an average $9 per acre and sold it for 100 to 200 times more after it was cleared and planted with four dozen citrus trees per acre. Compounding this juicy industry was the Florida Land Boom, which tripled Howey's enterprises and prompted the town's incorporation on May 8, 1925. The state's first orange juice canning plant was then joined in town by another top-notch citrus facility.

In 1928, Howey offered the 25-year old C.V. Griffin Sr. a citrus-packing contract with the stipulation Griffin would build a plant in town. In 1930, the new $75,000 packing plant handled up to nine railroad cars a day. Within five years, Griffin had become the second largest shipper of fresh fruit in Florida.

The town still shows its roots in the horticultural and agricultural industries; however, citrus groves suffered several hard-hitting freezes in the 1960s and 1980s and gave way to sprouting home developments and commercial facilities.

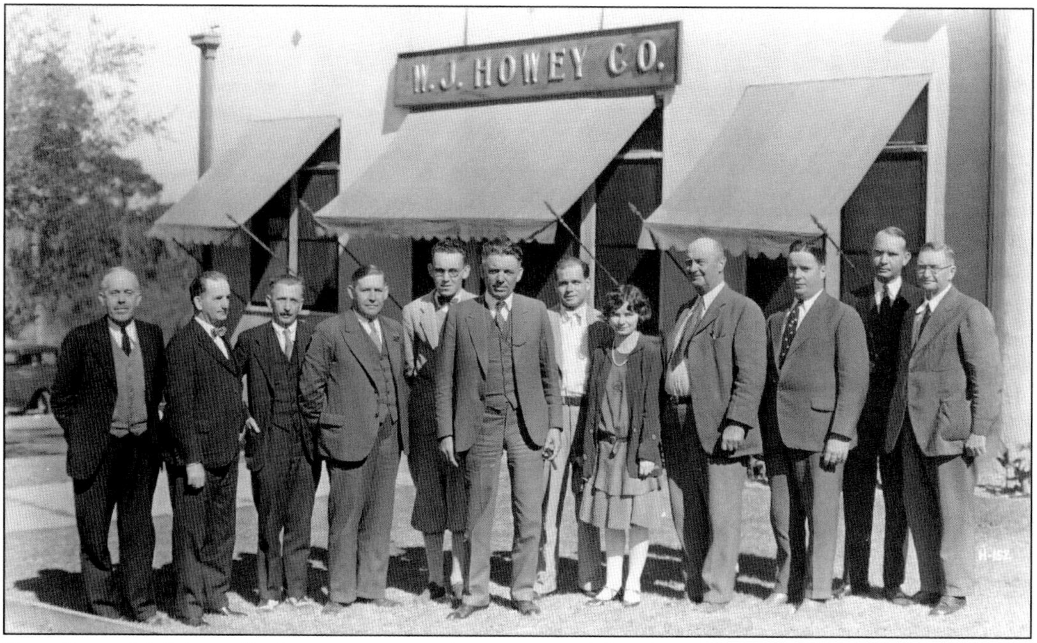

Standing with his staff of executives at the company's headquarters in the north wing of the Floridan Hotel is William J. Howey with his familiar cigar and eyeglass (center). A young Dodge Taylor is seen beside Howey on the right. By 1927, the company had offices in Chicago, Boston, Indianapolis, Philadelphia, Ocean City, and Atlantic City and seven more throughout Florida from coast to coast. (OCHC.)

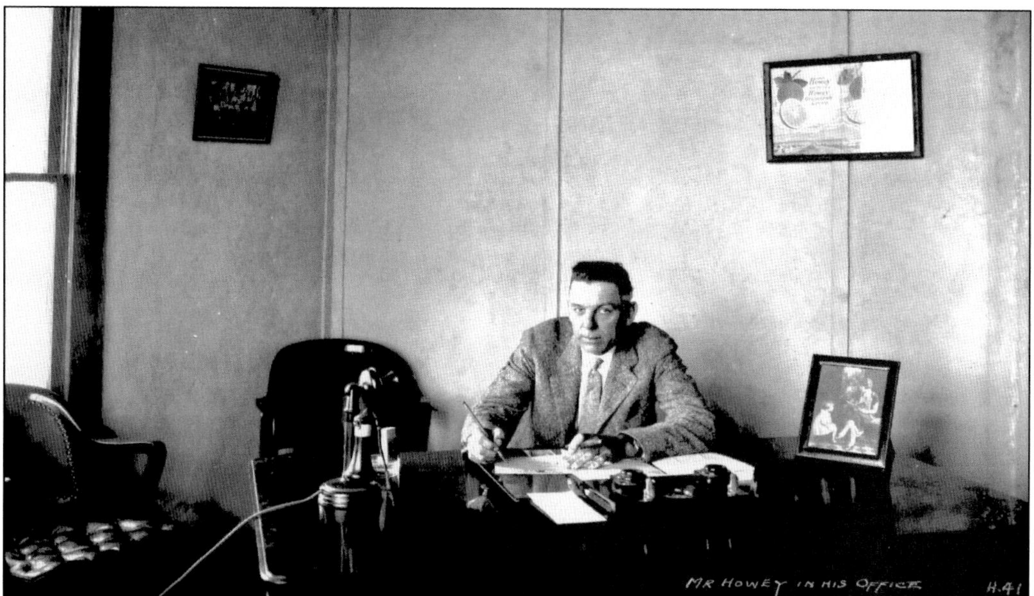

Sitting behind his large wood desk, the site of millions of dollars worth of transactions, is citrus genius William J. Howey, pen and lit cigar in hand, with a single-line phone. It was here that Howey started such companies as Howey-in-the-Hills Juice, Ridge Holding, and Orange Belt Securities and created the Howey Plan to be all-encompassing and controlling of the citrus industry from purchase to first seed and maintenance to final delivery. (OCHC.)

In 1926, the Lake County Board of Commissioners granted permission to the W.J. Howey Company to erect large concrete and stucco monuments on various county roads at entrance points to the vast Howey development. This line-art sketch graced the cover of the Howey Company's 32-page marketing brochure in 1927, which, in thorough detail, revealed every aspect of the investment opportunity cycle from purchase to planting and production to profit. (HH.)

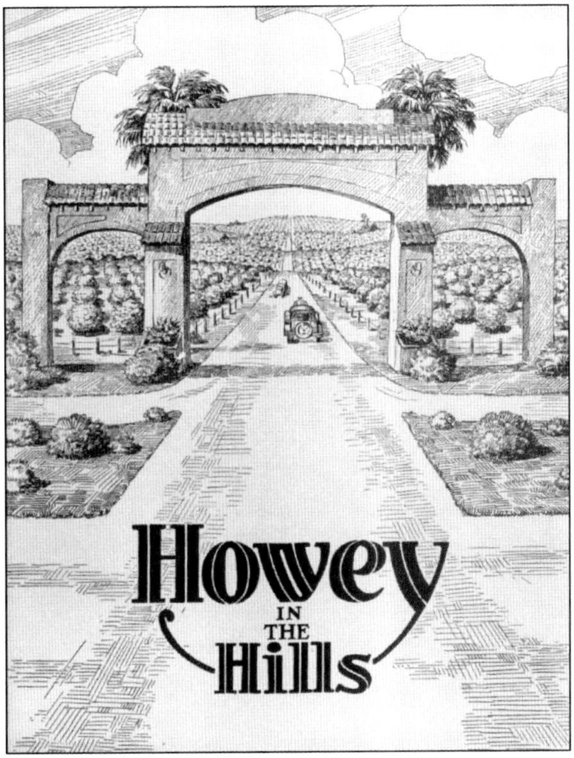

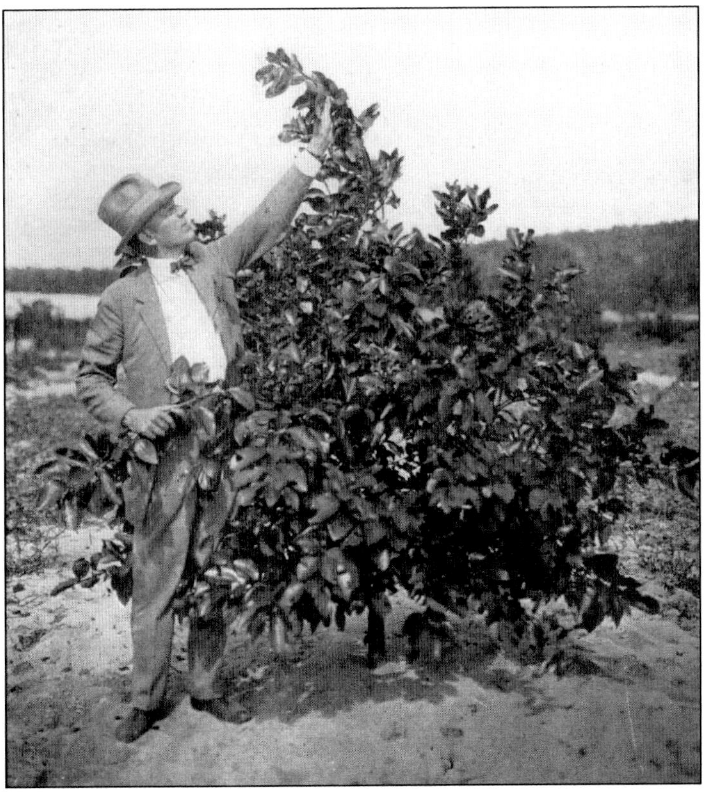

Prominent research scientists Dr. Frederick W. Inman and Dr. Ross were W.J. Howey's mentors and greatly influenced his citrus growing practices and the final selection of Central Florida's ridge as the best site to produce quality citrus. Inman was known for developing a highly successful method of growing root systems from lemon seeds and for grafting orange tree buds to seedlings that ultimately produced fruit four years later. Howey was photographed inspecting his younger grove. (HH.)

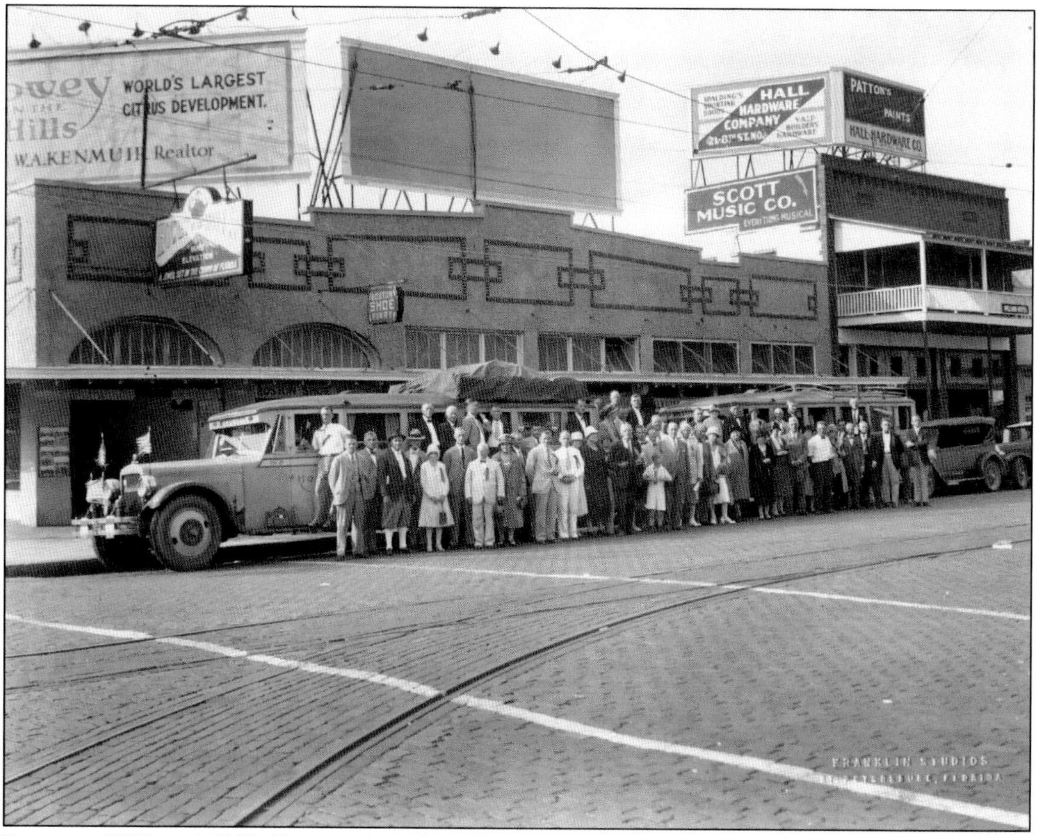

Between 1928 and 1929, Kenmuir's realty office transported 2,317 prospective buyers to Howey and generated a staggering $1 million worth of grove sales, labeling his staff the most successful. These 70 members of the St. Petersburg organization, led by manager W.A. "Bill" Kenmuir, lined up outside the Sunshine City's Howey office before boarding a fleet of International buses bound for the November 1928 conference, which had over 200 people in attendance. (HH.)

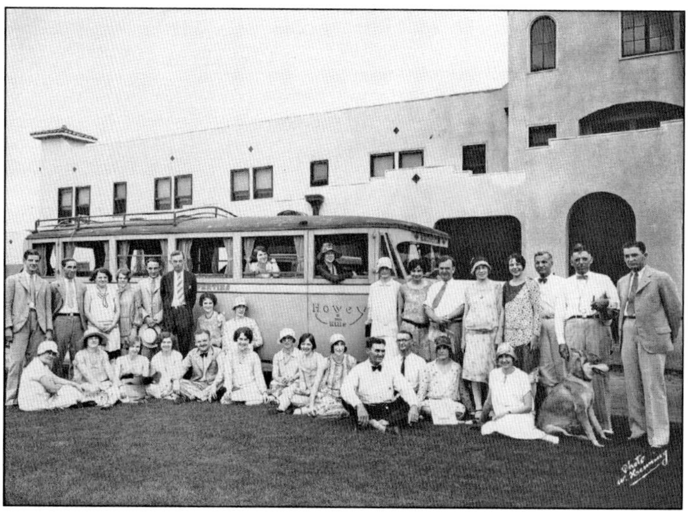

In 1925, this Lake County advertising bus toured 17 states with the slogan "the Alps of Florida" on its side, which made pedestrians on New York's Fifth Avenue and other large cities' main thoroughfares wonder, "How come?" The driver carried proof, an album of photographs of Lake County's hills, to skeptical northerners. The bus and marketers returned to pose with William J. Howey and his faithful four-legged friend Big Boy at his side. (HH.)

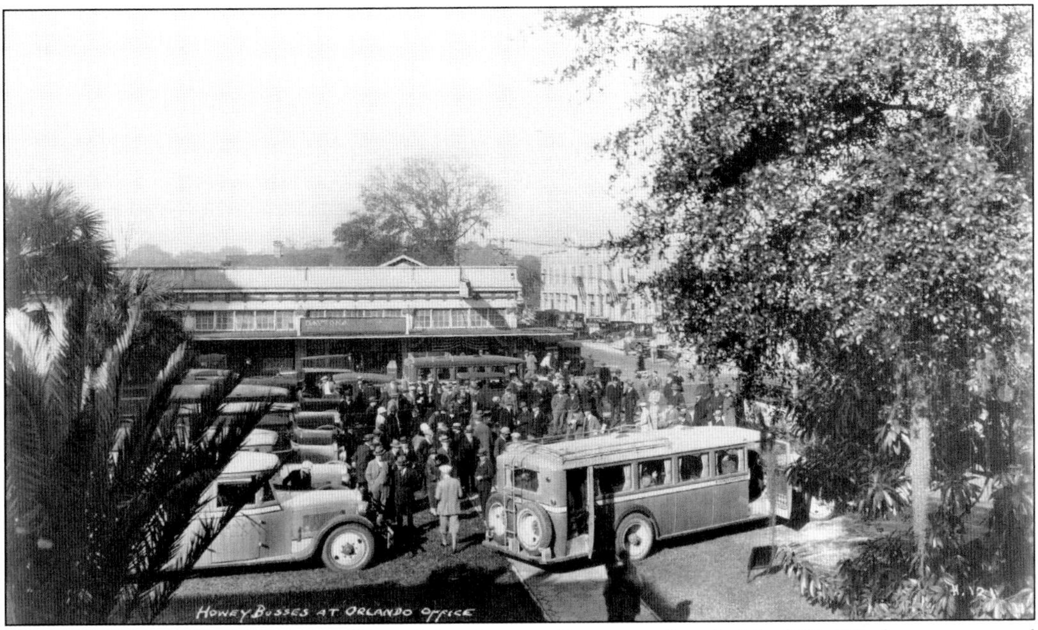

In January 1930, the Orlando office of the Howey Company, headed by F.C. Workman, created a show-stopper window display stunt that halted thousands at 122 North Orange Avenue. The comparison between wintry northern scenes and idyllic Howey grove lands in the nearby rolling Lake County countryside got the right attention. The sales office booked hundreds of prospective investors into company motor coaches to tour Howey groves. (HH.)

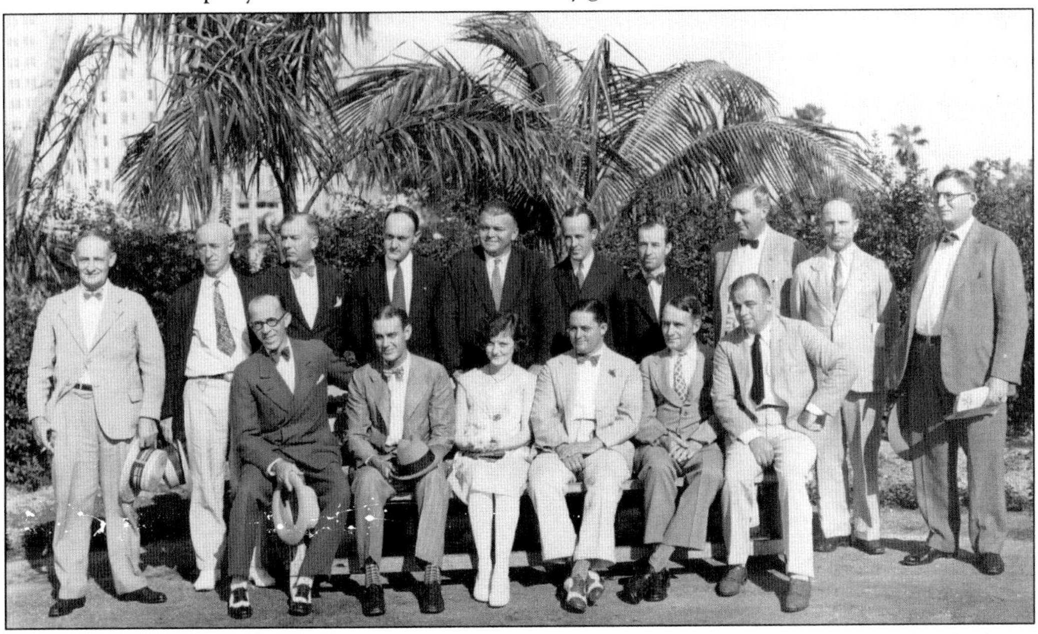

The 1929 Howey-Miami office was so optimistic over the season's prospects that two-day sky hops from Miami to Howey-in-the-Hills were offered to prospective investors. Cabin planes carrying seven passengers and two pilots left Bay Biscayne and landed on Lake Harris. The airliner soared over the same route used by Miami-to-Howey buses, up the east coast and back via Bok Tower, Avon Park, and Okeechobee City. (HH.)

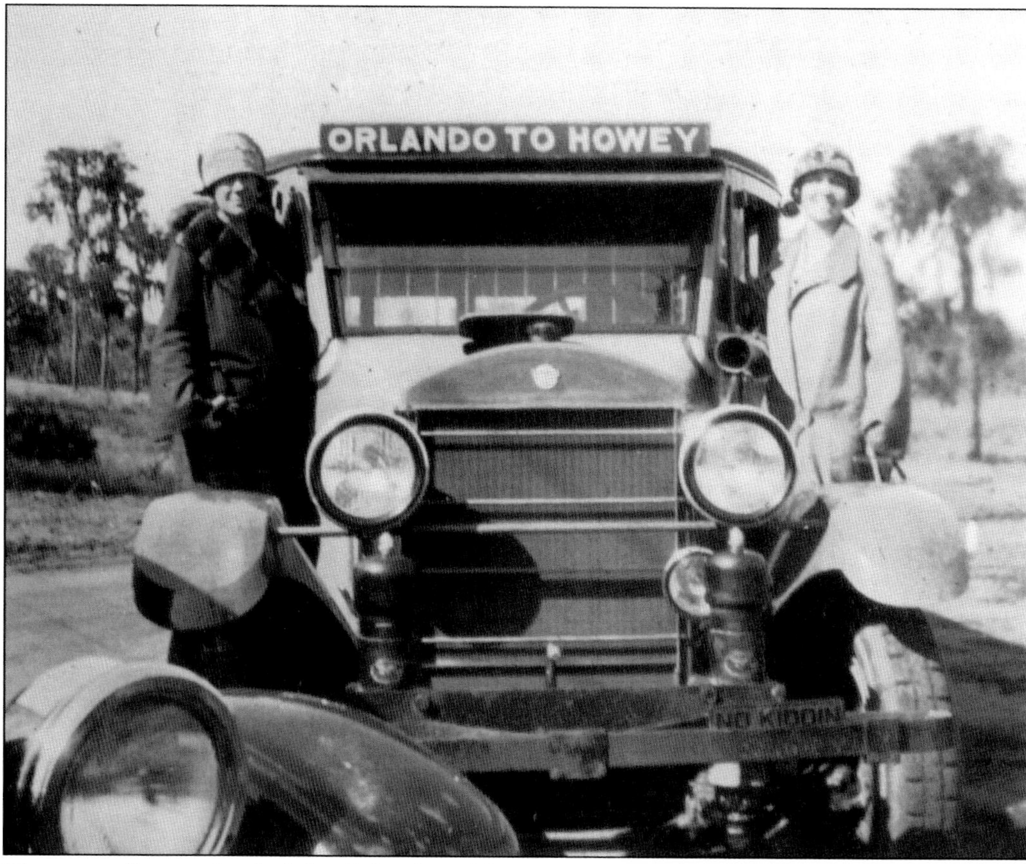

These two flappers booked the Orlando-to-Howey winter motor tour to inspect the citrus tract first hand. After the gals posed by a fruit-bearing tree, they checked into the Floridan Hotel to be further entertained and educated by salesmen about available lands. (OCHC).

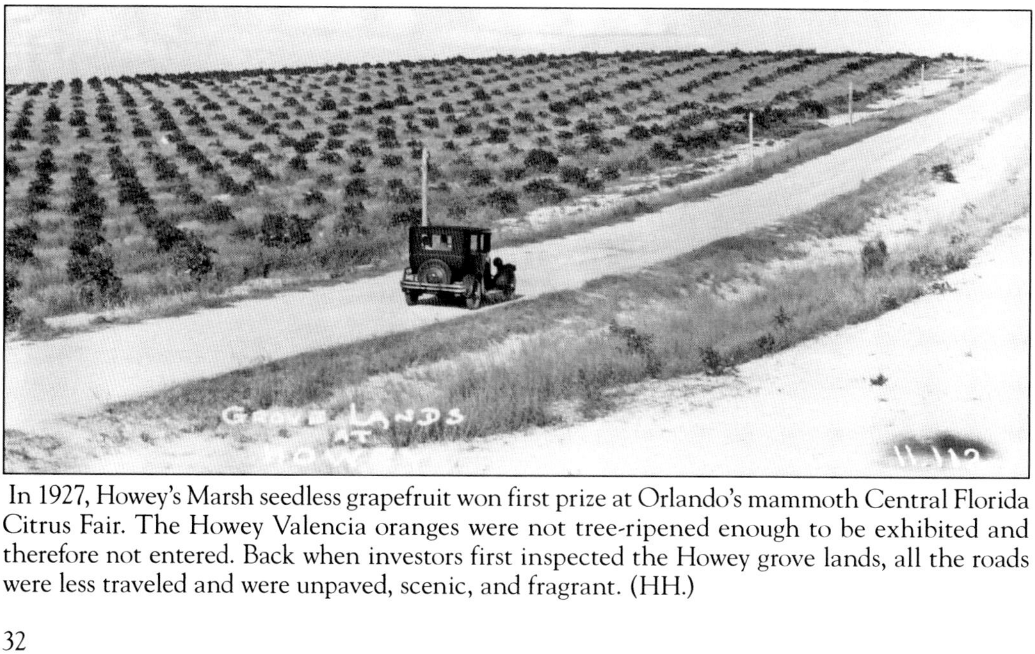

In 1927, Howey's Marsh seedless grapefruit won first prize at Orlando's mammoth Central Florida Citrus Fair. The Howey Valencia oranges were not tree-ripened enough to be exhibited and therefore not entered. Back when investors first inspected the Howey grove lands, all the roads were less traveled and were unpaved, scenic, and fragrant. (HH.)

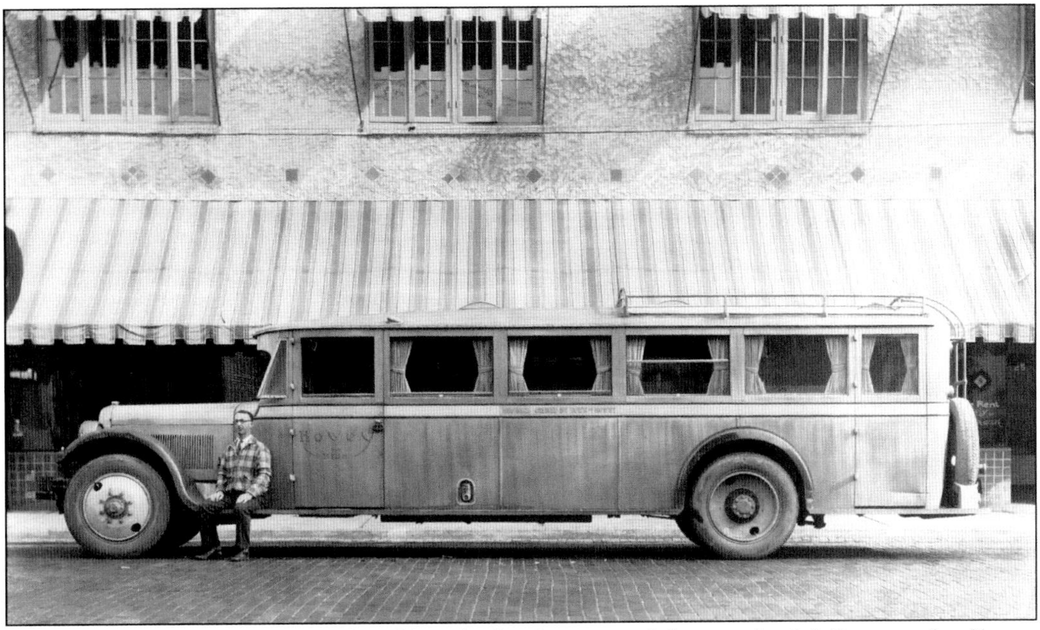

The W.J. Howey Company employed hundreds of men, used thousands of dollars worth of buses and tractors, and never spent a penny on upkeep cost. A fleet of International buses hauled prospective grove purchasers on trips from points as far as 1,000 miles from Howey. They were not spared but rather purchased to get the people to Howey in comfort. These two trusty beauties hauled thousands of satisfied customers to Howey-in-the-Hills, racking up 50,000 miles each without any upkeep or repair cost. This was a record, according to Thomas Hardin, a veteran bus driver of the Howey organization, who added, "Do not think that these or any other busses will perform in this manner unless they are handled by drivers who know their onions." Thomas Hardin (above) and son Vernon (below) are ready to go the extra mile during the 1927–1928 season. (Both, HH.)

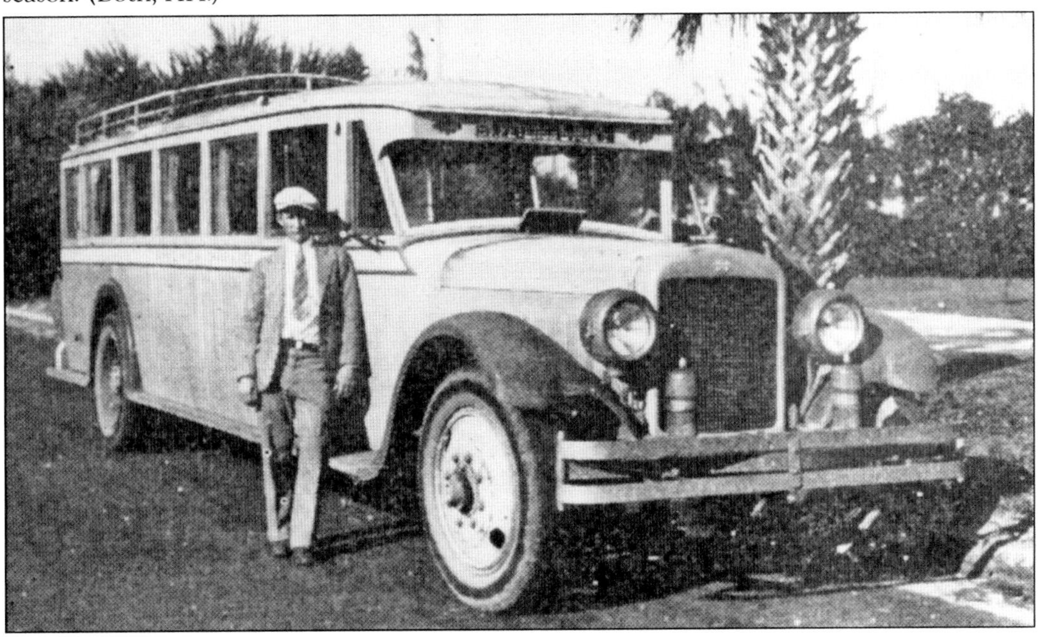

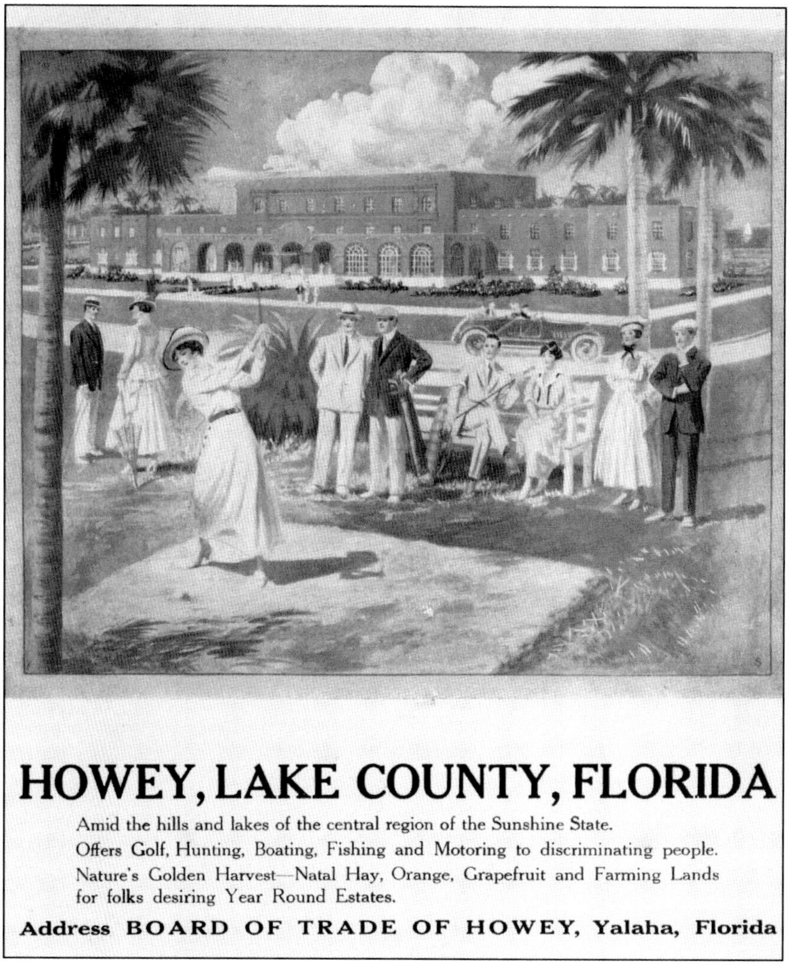

When Dr. Edwin C. Taylor retired from medicine in 1925, he followed his son Dodge Taylor to Howey-in-the-Hills. Instead of relaxation, he headed W.J. Howey's new Howey Sanitarium to study the therapeutic values of hill-grown grapefruit. Hundreds of doctors and patients participated in the study here. Tree-ripened grapefruit and canned juice were used to treat diabetes and hypertension. (HH.)

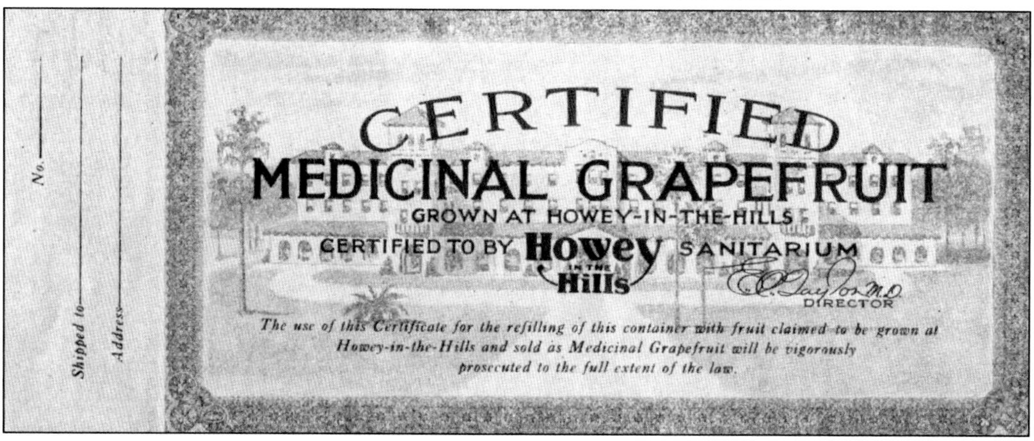

This label made the distinction that the Howey-in-the-Hills tree-ripened grapefruit was certified "Medicinal Grapefruit" by Howey Sanitarium director Dr. E.C. Taylor. During the winter of 1929, more than 300 doctors visited to observe laboratory work and methods of treatment. Of 100 patients treated, only three, according to the report, required insulin after following the prescribed Howey grapefruit plan. (LCHM.)

Four

The Howey Time Capsule

There was a short period of time in Howey-in-the-Hills when nothing could stand in its way of progress or celebration. During the Roaring Twenties, Howey-in-the-Hills was the only place to be.

The 15-story city hall was designed to overlook the town's commercial center, but when sales dropped and the steel was held up by a shipping embargo, those plans were put aside, never to be built. The arched Mediterranean gateways to the city were, however, erected at entry points on various roadways, giving a sense of having arrived at a place worthy of an astonishing journey.

The wooden bridge that spanned Little Lake Harris, connecting Howey to the west and Astatula to the east, was an economic boom to the town, as traffic between Jacksonville and Tampa saved 52 miles by crossing the new bridge, which opened in 1927.

When the New York Civic Opera performed at the Howey Mansion "Park," the divas arrived in horse-drawn carriages along Palm Avenue, sure to make an entrance before the crowd of thousands. An event that also raised a few eyebrows was the first passenger transport plane landing at the new municipal airport at Orlando, a charter by the Howey Company's St. Petersburg office, causing excitement to soar throughout aviation circles.

In 1930, when the 54-piece *Orlando Star Reporter* newsboy band started to march and play, Opie Read's official "Home Welcoming" festivities commenced. A favorite winter resident and friend to all, Read was always a welcome sight to Howey-in-the-Hills.

Howey campaigned vigorously as a Florida gubernatorial candidate in the 1928 and 1932 elections. He visited all 67 counties, frequently making as many as six speeches in a day. While he did not win, he garnered 39 percent of the vote, qualifying Republicans to hold their own primary election. Howey appeared to be the leader of a new progressive Republican party in Florida.

By example, Howey never stopped dreaming, inventing, marketing, or perfecting, and the same can be said of C.V. Griffin and Nick Beucher, who followed in his footsteps.

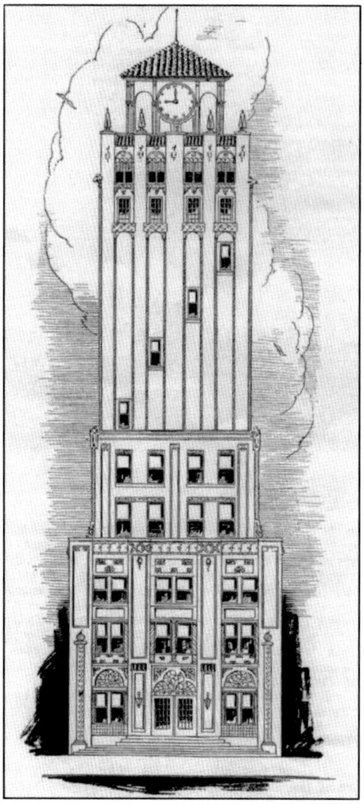

Rising 165 feet above a landscaped city park on Lake Illinois on Central Avenue, the City Inevitable landmark was to rise higher than any other building between Jacksonville and Tampa. The Spanish-style 15-story city hall provided lower-level offices and a top-floor pressure tank for additional water system and fire protection support. Due to the land boom collapse, this 1926 Howey project never got off the ground. (HH.)

These entrance portals were conceived by W.J. Howey, and once, the golden gates to Florida's "Ultimate City" stood on No. 2 Road, now the crossroads of 455 and 561, near Astatula and Montverde at the southern end of the Howey grove development. Built on a road paved in the gold of publicity, these welcoming gates no longer exist, but the town that is rich with history does. (HH.)

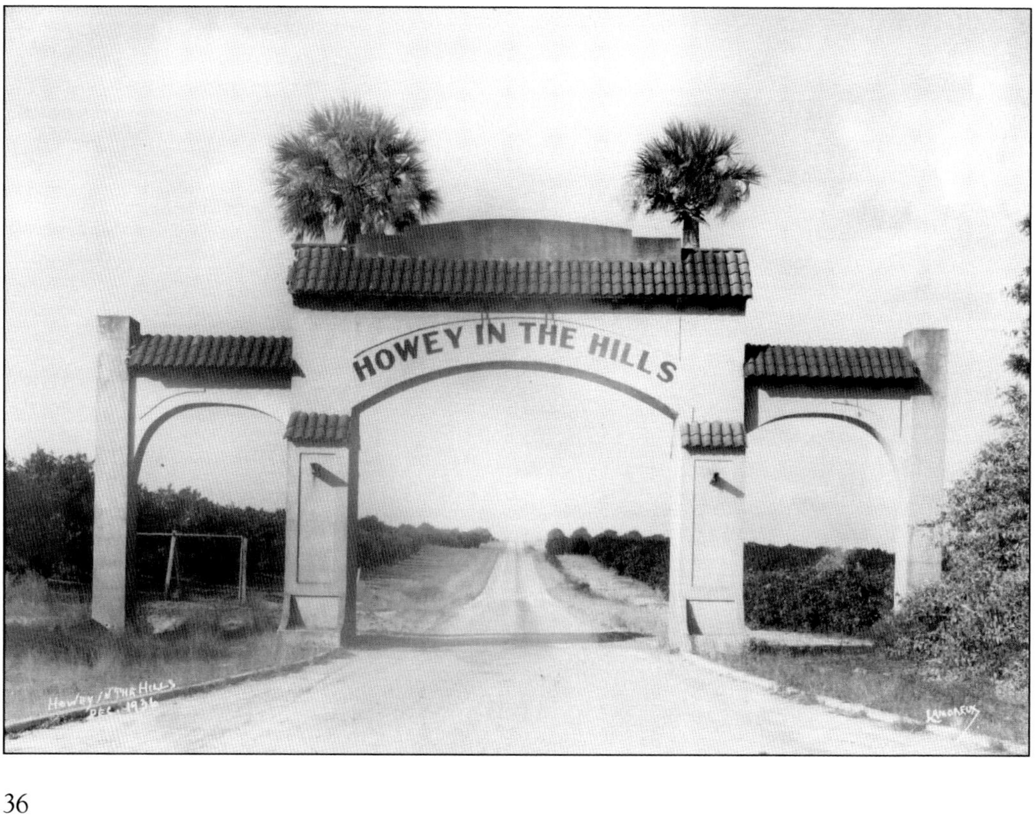

In January 1926, work began on the 7,890-foot wooden Howey-Astatula Bridge, the pivotal link in the cross-state highway between Jacksonville and Tampa, when pile driving rigs and other engineering machinery arrived. Simultaneously, construction commenced in Howey, where the bridgehead was located, and in Astatula, on the eastern side, and met in the middle. By mid-February, 60 carloads of piles, at a rate of two cars per day, shipped from Georgia over the Seaboard and Tavares and Gulf Railways to Astatula. When the Horace Williams Company of New Orleans completed the short route across Little Lake Harris, the span was the longest free bridge in Florida, cutting off two hours and 52 miles. The new stream of traffic routed down Central Avenue through the business district of Howey, and travelers frequently patronized the Howey Lakeside Service for gas, groceries, and liquor. (Both, HH.)

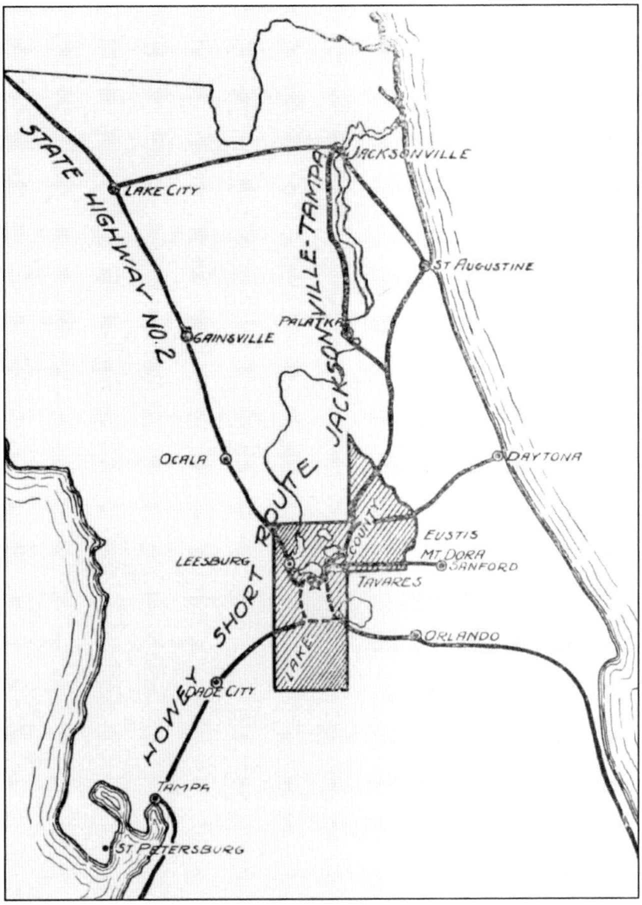

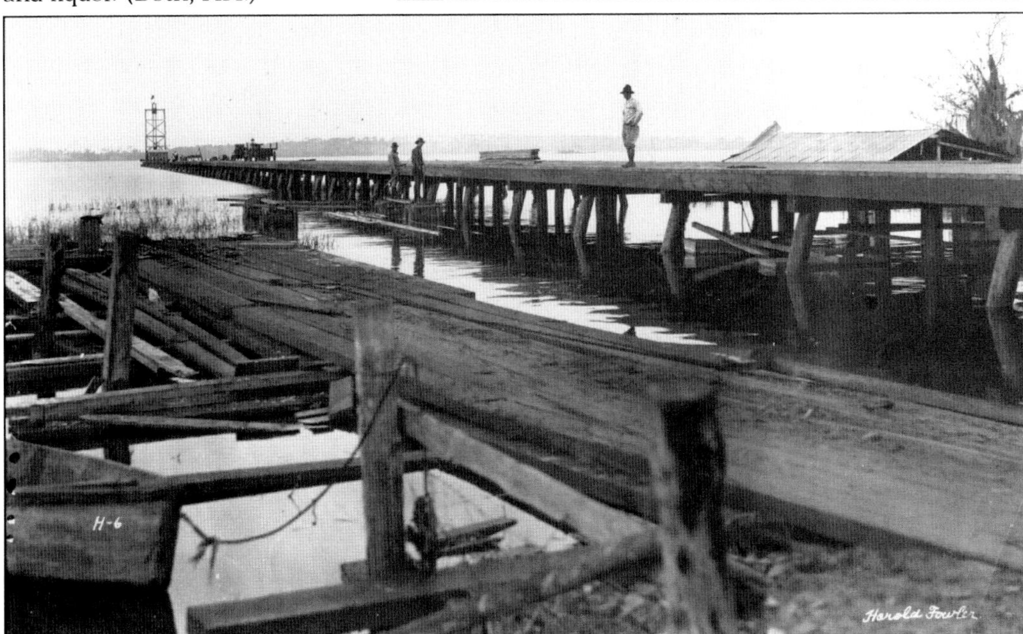

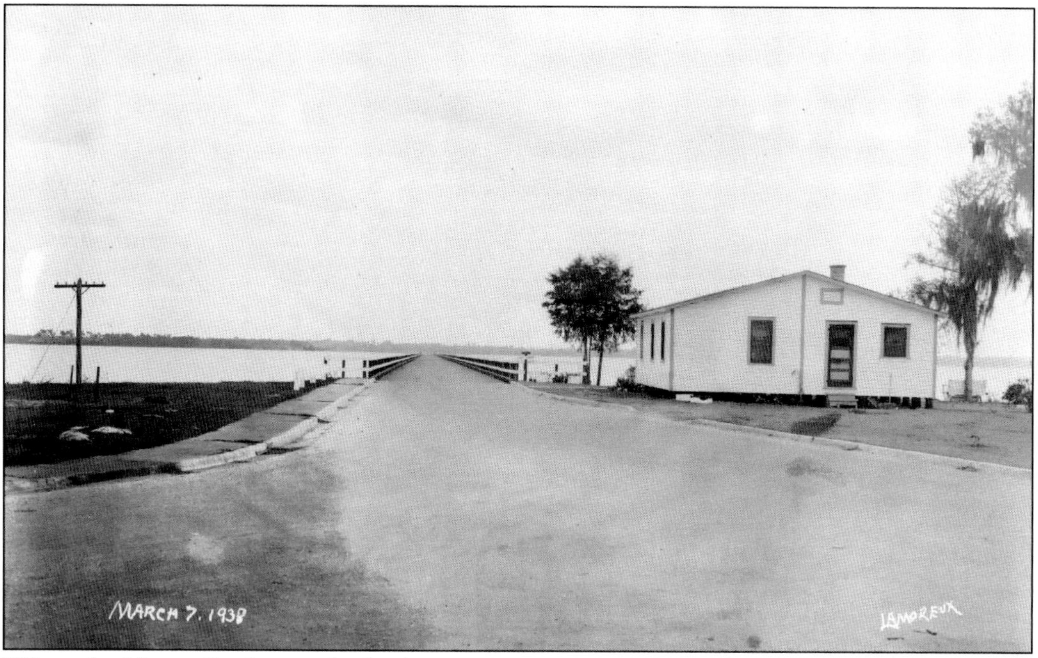

When the Howey Bridge was built, direct motor access to Astatula, Tavares, and beyond was available, without having to take the longer unpaved route around the south end of Little Lake Harris. Given the signal, bridge operator Charlie Ard would leave his gatekeeper's house, walk to the middle of the 18-foot-wide roadway with two 26-foot turnout spaces, and hand crank the bridge open for larger boats. (HH.)

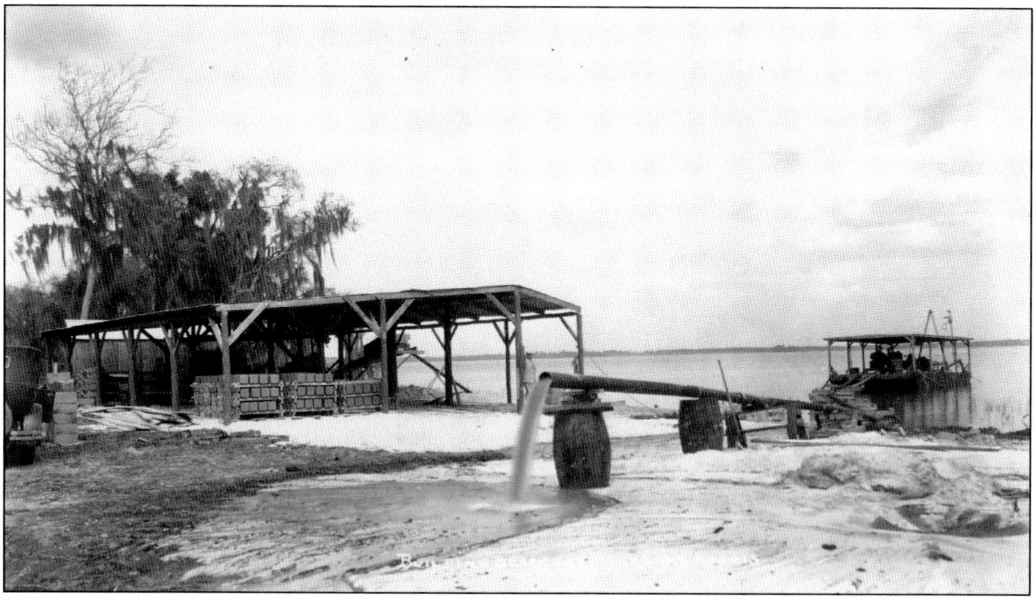

In May 1926, the US War Department's Army Engineers approved town plans for extensive lakefront improvements along Little Lake Harris, including a mile of smooth white sand beach, the construction of two municipal Mediterranean-style pavilions, and a general landscaping beautification program. Sand was dredged from the lake bottom for cement blocks, but the planned 200-foot-wide beach along Lakeshore Boulevard was never completed. (LCHM.)

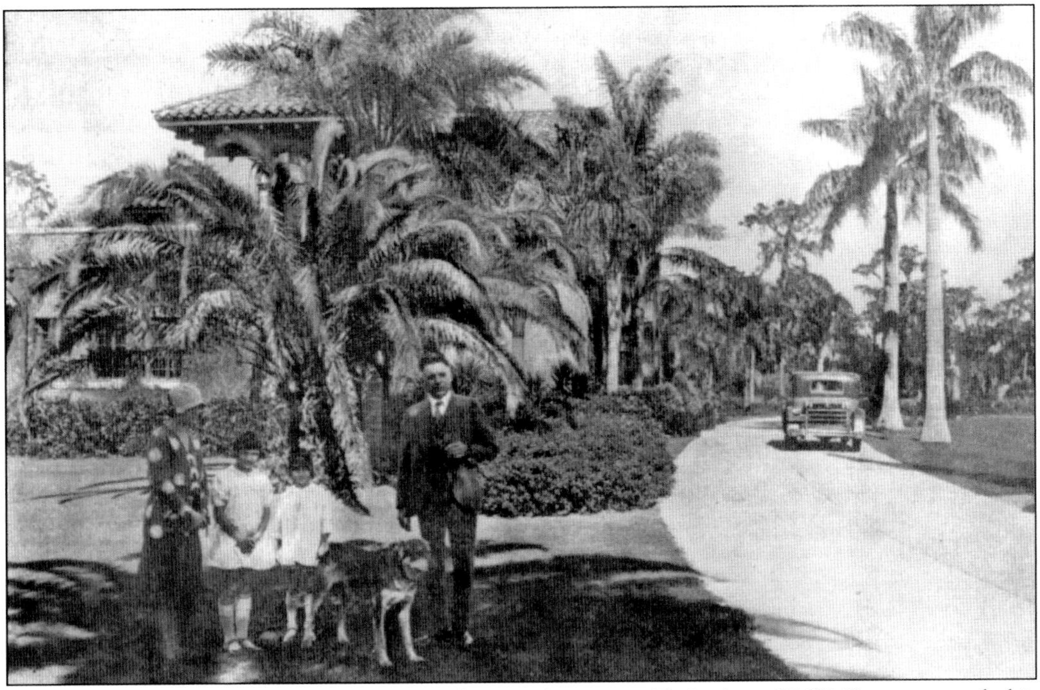

Few photographs of Howey's mansion and grounds were published, as "Bill" Howey regarded it as a home and not an institution. Howey repeatedly refused permission for photographs, despite numerous requests, including some from *House Beautiful* magazine. From left to right, second wife Grace, adopted daughters Mary and Lois, the family's faithful police dog Big Boy, and William J. Howey pose for this informal snapshot on the mansion's south lawn. (HH.)

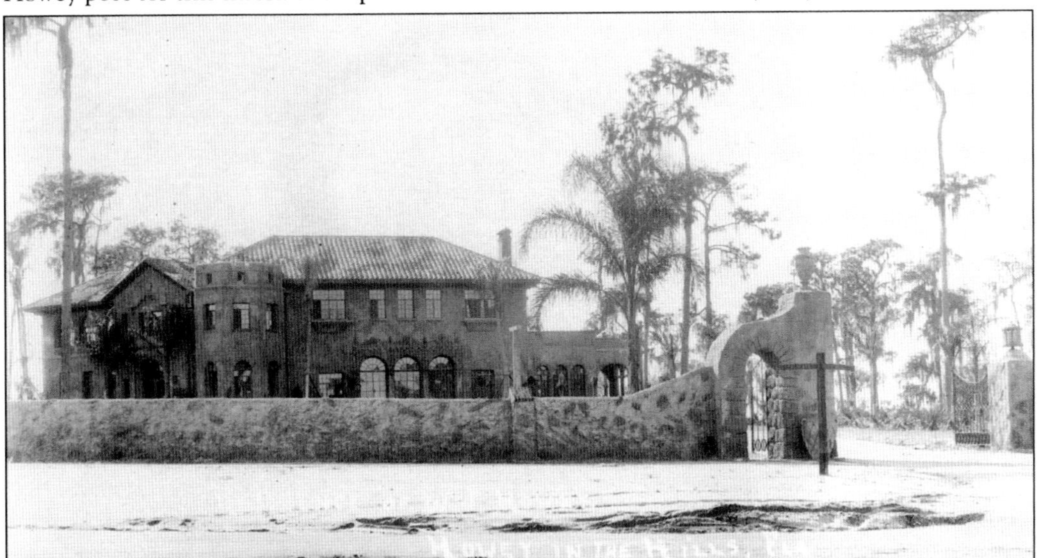

This photograph captured the Mediterranean-style Howey Mansion when it was first completed in 1927, prior to "the Park" or the 15-acre estate grounds being fully landscaped. Eventually, Grace Howey donated the original wrought iron mansion gates to the war effort to be melted and used for scrap metal. The street marker (right) reads "Palm Avenue," as the main street ran in front of the mansion. (HH.)

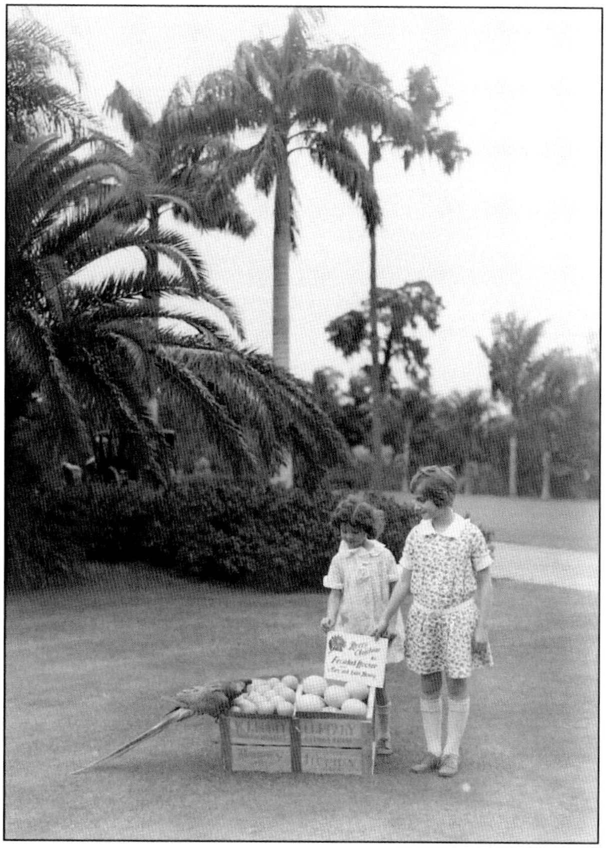

On the breezy south lawn of the Howey Mansion, Lois (left) and Mary Howey eagerly await the arrival of US president Herbert Hoover. The girls' pet parrot closely guarded their greeting card and gift crates of tree-ripened, fresh Howey citrus. (OCHC.)

The ballroom-sized drawing room of the 20-room, 7,200-square-foot Howey Mansion was designed to accommodate large dances and social gatherings. Architectural features included a massive beamed ceiling, a gorgeous fireplace, and inner walls over one foot thick were textured and painted by a European artisan who worked alone behind closed doors to ensure his coveted signature painting formulas and techniques remained his trade secrets. Concealed behind shelved library books was an unlocking device for a false entry hall door that revealed a hidden stairwell to a cellar. (HH.)

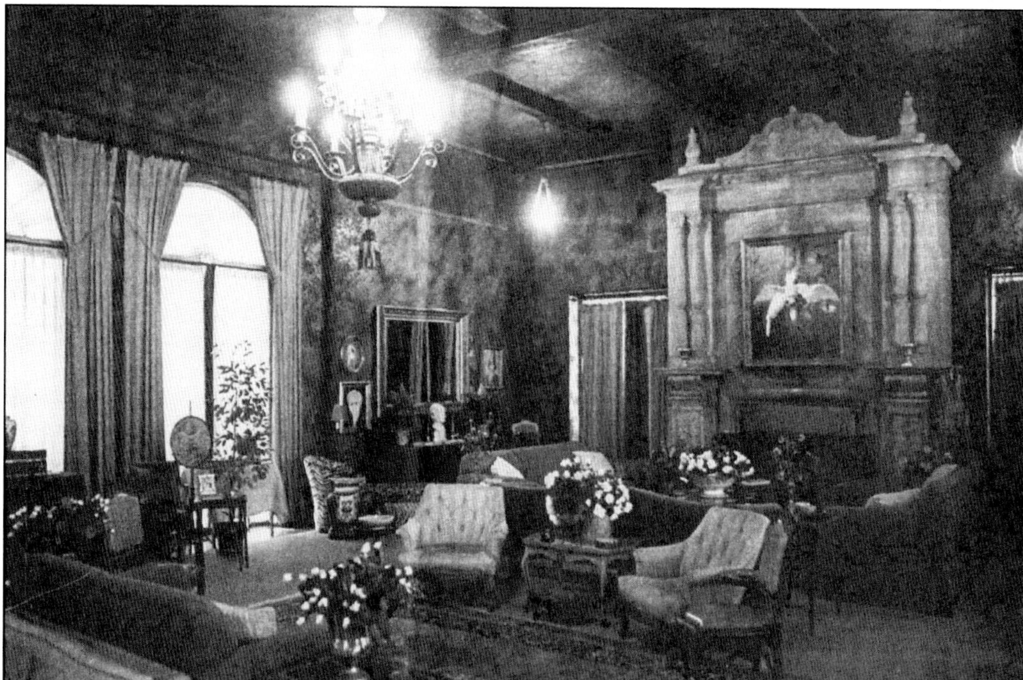

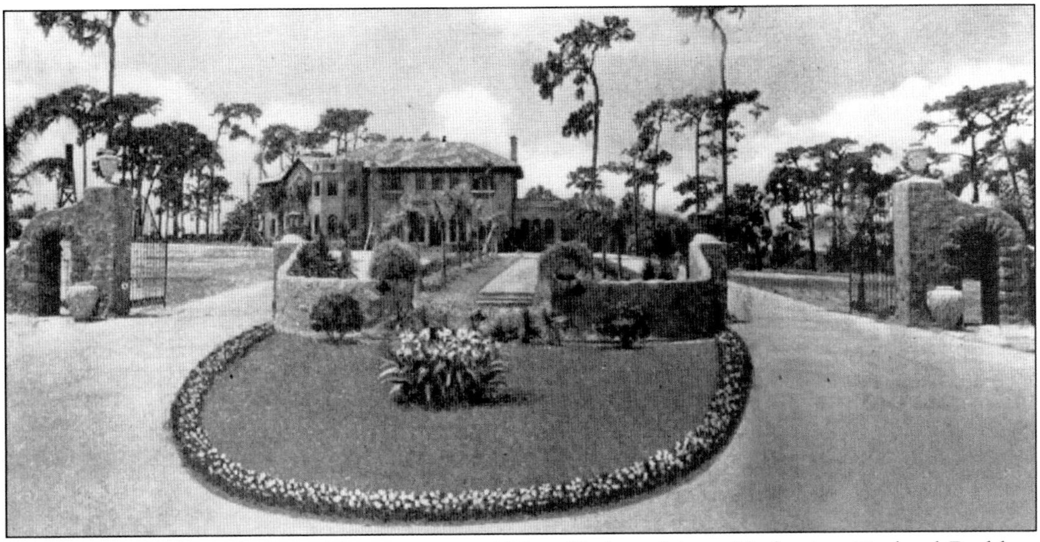

In 1924, William and Grace Howey retained New York architect Katherine Cotheal Budd to design their palatial home. Built by W.E. Boyce, it was completed in 1927 at a cost of $250,000 and reflected the Mediterranean influence of Spanish and Italian architecture, which was popular in the 1920s, with a spectacular landscape design. The concrete and stucco home was placed in the National Register of Historic Places on January 27, 1983. (HH.)

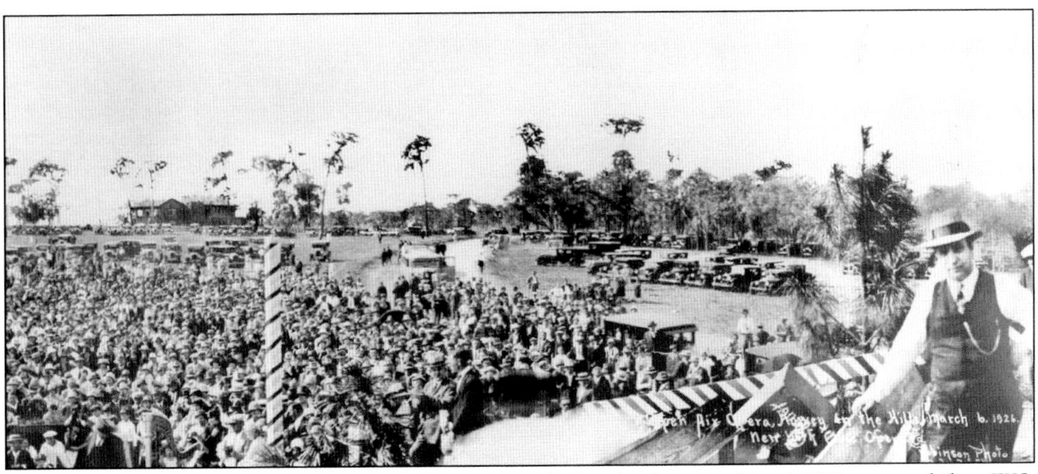

On March 6, 1927, before a crowd of about 16,000 that had arrived in 4,000 automobiles, W.J. Howey hosted the New York Civic Opera Company's 100 artists for a free outdoor performance on the Park at his newly completed mansion. *Cavalleria Rusticana* and *Pagliacci* were performed on a stage erected for the occasion, while the audience sat in an amphitheater of hundreds of rows of camp seats that reached down to Little Lake Harris. Note the golden harp (center). (HH.)

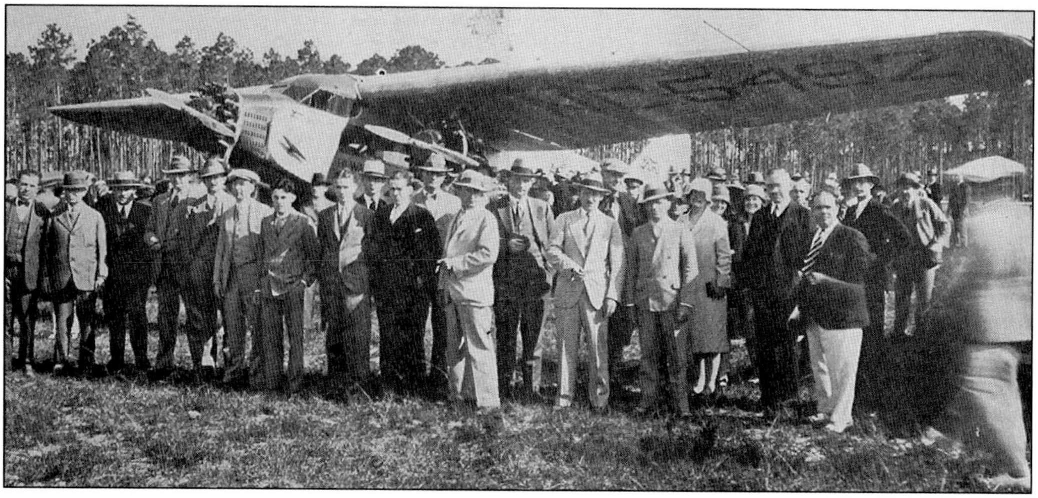

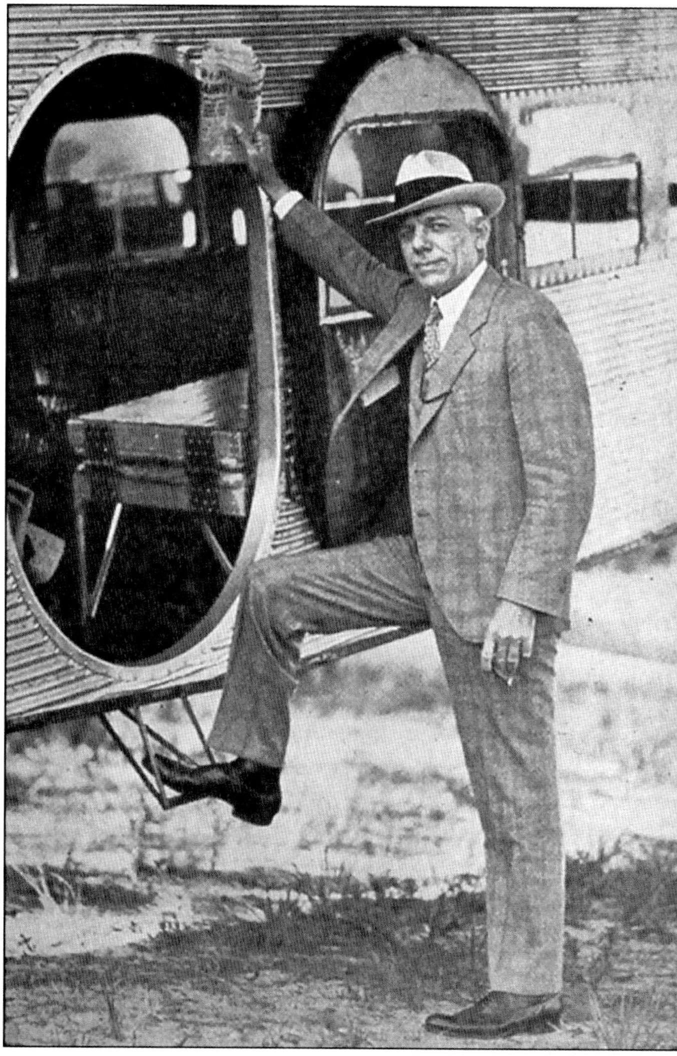

Inaugurating a regular passenger transport service between Howey-in-the-Hills and St. Petersburg, the first air cruise of the Ford Tri-Motor monoplane "Hi-Way" was sponsored by the Howey Company's St. Petersburg office and completed in December 1928. Owing to the size of the plane, W.J. Howey announced prior to take off that longer runways for larger planes would soon replace the existing field at Howey-in-the-Hills and predicted scheduled tours from Florida and northern points to the world's largest citrus development. Pilot Perry Hutton flew prominent businessmen over coastal and inland towns and circled Howey-in-the-Hills. Hundreds thronged the field to witness the historic landing. Greeted by Mayor Latta M. Autrey, the huge 14-place, three-ton hunk of steel was the first passenger ship to land at the new municipal airport at Orlando and caused quite a sensation throughout Florida aviation circles. (Both, HH.)

In 1928, William J. Howey was free from political entanglements and defined his platform by leaving no one in doubt as to where he stood on issues. Although he lost in 1928 and 1932, gubernatorial candidate Howey garnered more than the required 30 percent of total votes cast, which gave credence to a two-party, statewide system and the new Florida Republican party. Howey remained the titular party head for eight years, until 1936. (HH.)

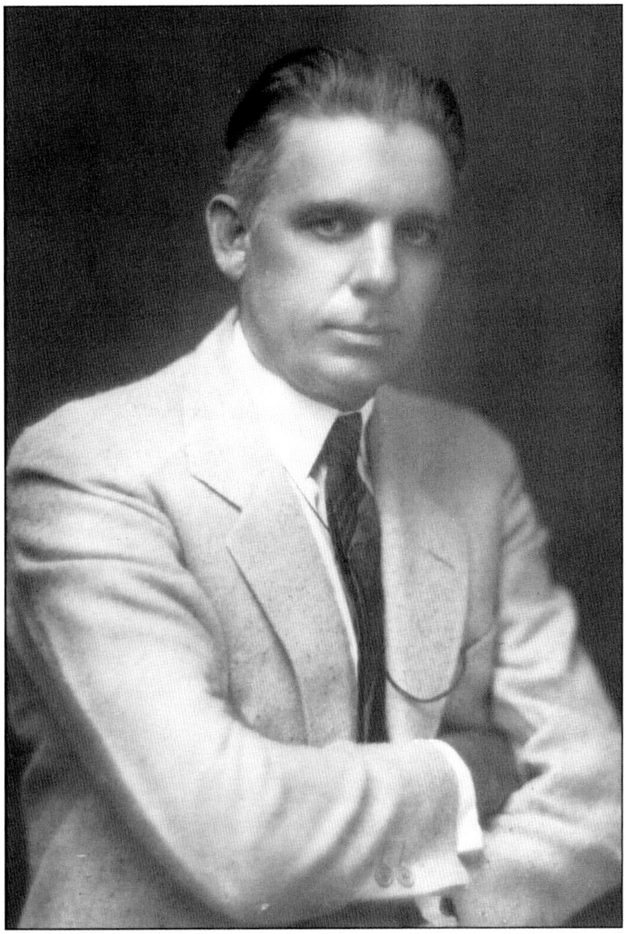

In the 1928 campaign, Florida's Republican candidate for governor, William J. Howey, received 95,018 votes to 148,455 for Democratic opponent Doyle Carlton and received his highest number in Pinellas County, which was 9,338 as compared to Carlton's 4,671. Howey's total vote far exceeded any previous total for a Republican candidate. "Hoover, Howey and Happiness" was the election slogan, and the calling card and buttons are mementos of the vigorous campaign of 1928. (PBC.)

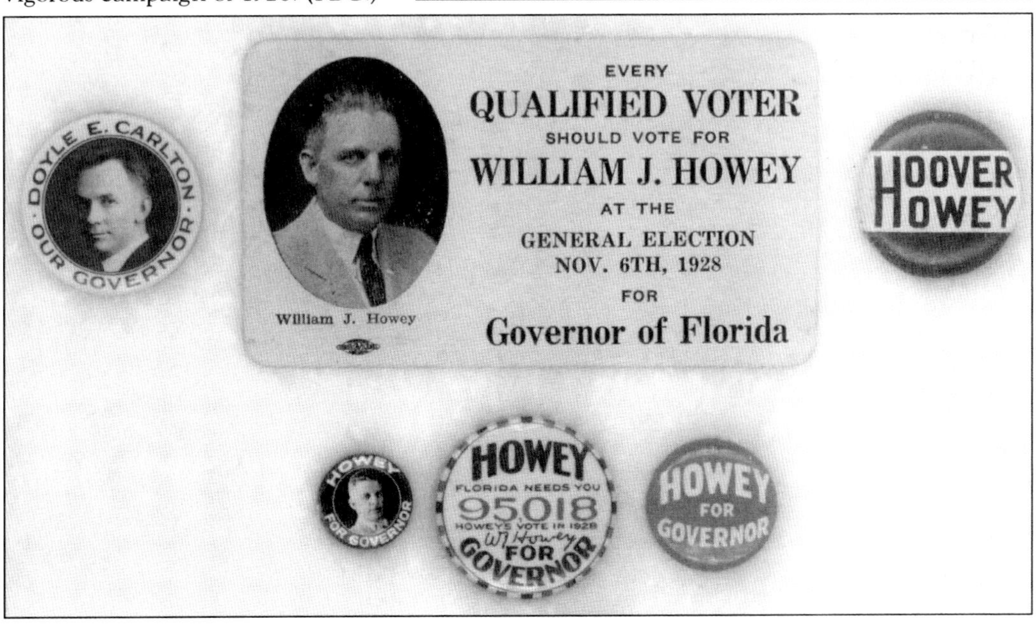

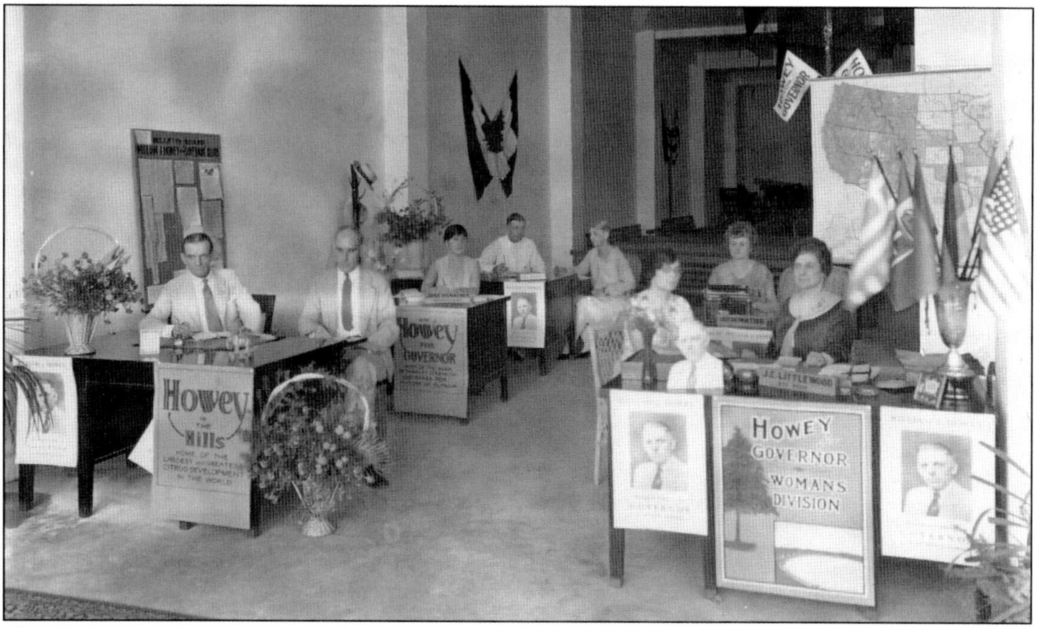

The Ta-Miami Campaign Headquarters of gubernatorial candidate William J. Howey in 1928 notably included a Woman's Division. The desk sign, "Howey-in-the-Hills—Home of the largest and greatest citrus development in the world," indicated Howey was qualified to successfully run an enormous business and, therefore, a state. He was the man of the hour with the ability, strength, and power for Florida's future. (FSA.)

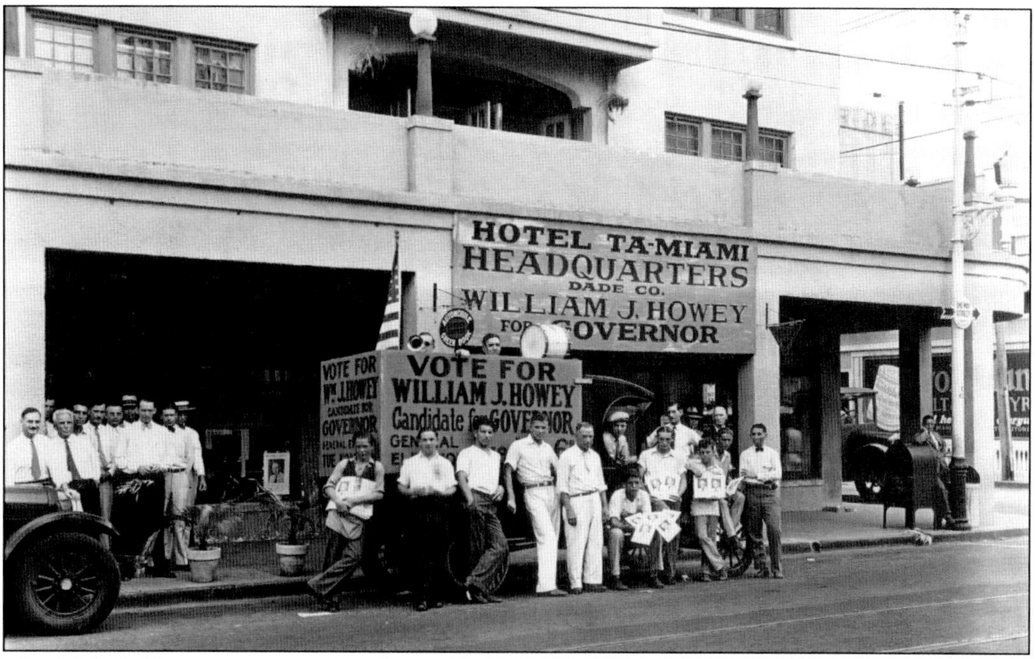

The 1928 Ta-Miami Campaign Headquarters of Florida gubernatorial Republican hopeful William J. Howey included the use of a drum, loudspeaker, and American flag to help get Howey posters into the hands of Miami voters and spread the word about Howey's plan for a fiscally responsible government. (FSA.)

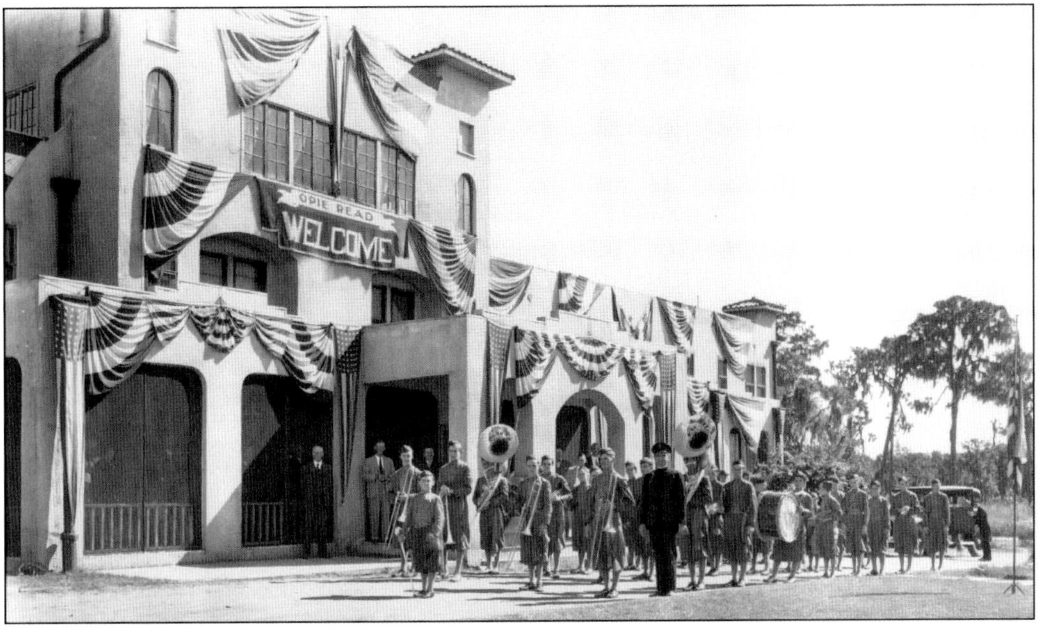

In December 1930, hundreds celebrated Opie Read's literary achievements and gave him a proper "Home Welcoming." The *Orlando Star-Reporter* newsboy band led the procession to the festivities at the Floridan Hotel. Between guest speakers, the newsboys continued their musical scores from the platform. A prolific American journalist and humorist, Read was credited with 60 published books. (HH.)

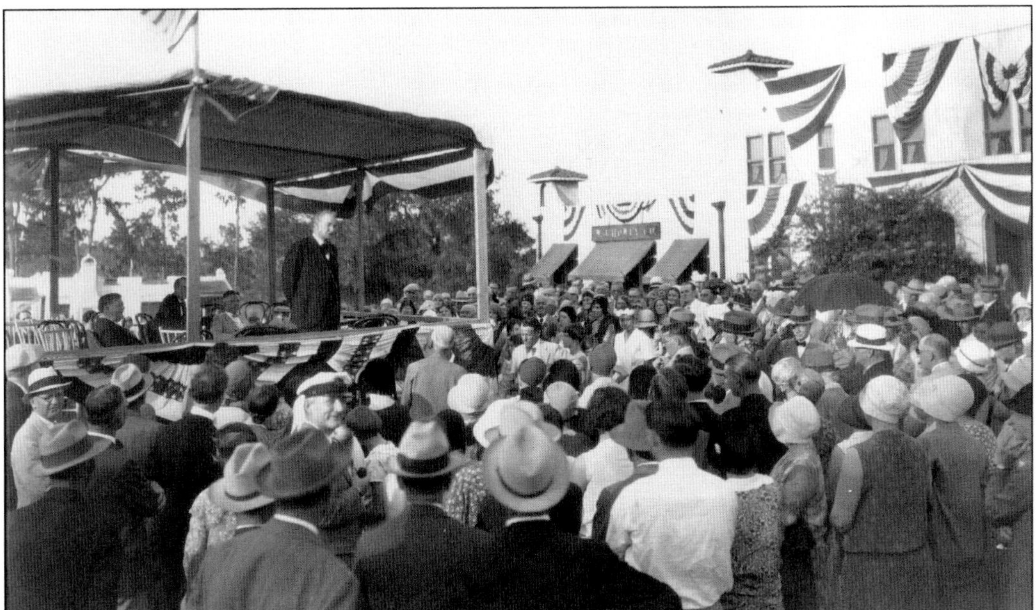

"There he comes," was the cry of banquet guests, who arose en masse, waving napkins and applauding vigorously. The band played "Hail to the Chief" when Opie Read, the robust six-foot, three-inch author with tousled hair, approached the throne-like chair of friendship at the speakers' table. Music, flowers, and good cheer dominated the luncheon portion of Read's Home Welcoming. Outside, an even larger throng gathered, entranced by Read's speech. (HH.)

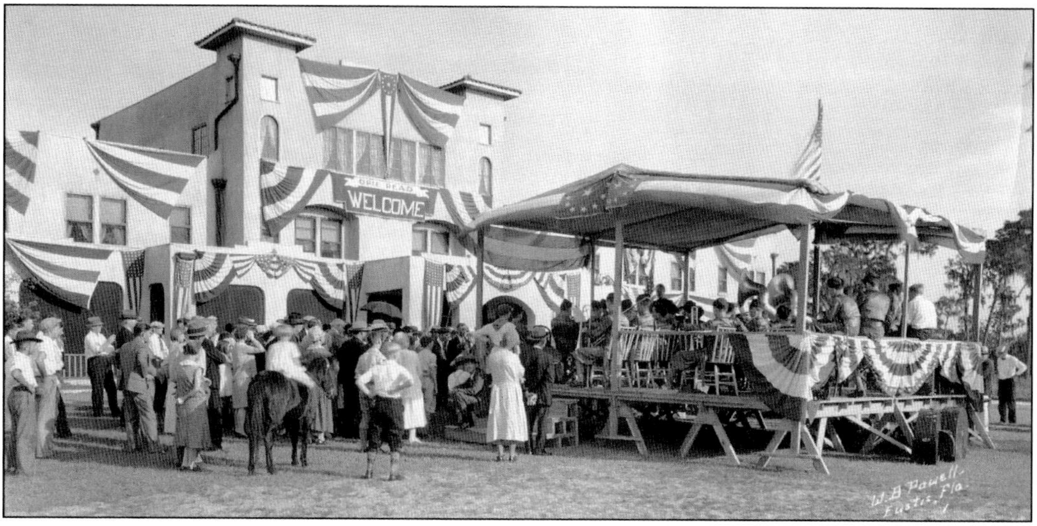

Jean Hewitt freely rode her little black pony, Everyone's Friend, all over town, including at the 1930 Home Welcoming festivities celebrating Opie Read's return for the winter. Jean's family lived in the hotel, where her father, Bill, was manager during the late 1920s and early 1930s. Jean attended Howey Elementary and played daily with her two best friends Lois and Mary Howey. (HH.)

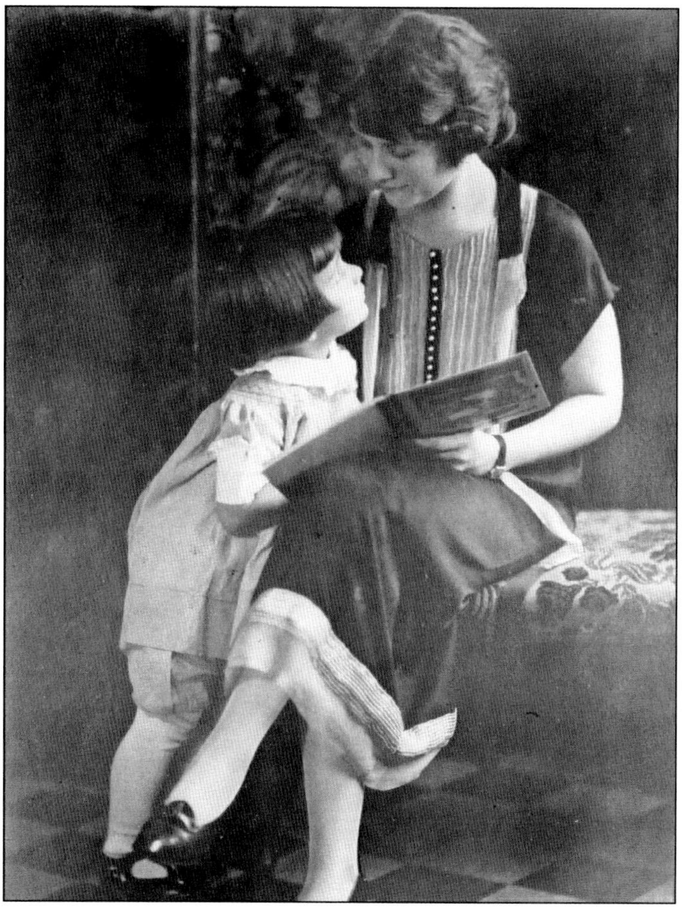

In the prime of her life, Mary Grace Hastings Howey was the quintessential southern hostess, extending hospitality to neighbors, customers, dignitaries, and US presidents. Born on September 11, 1889, in Ohio, by 1890, Grace lived in Kansas, where Bill Howey produced seven cars with his short-lived Howey Automobile Company from 1907 to 1908. Thirteen years younger than her husband, Grace lived in the mansion until her death on December 18, 1981. (HH.)

Five

The City Inevitable

In 1910, young William J. Howey saw an opportunity to build a vast commercial enterprise in the heart of Florida with the citrus industry as the means to an end—not merely the raising of oranges and grapefruit but their cultivation on a large scale. By 1920, Howey turned opportunity into reality and brought untold thousands of first-time visitors to Howey-in-the-Hills. Through the years, construction of infrastructure fueled the town's identity.

To replace the first Tent City, which housed visiting land prospectors and citrus buyers, a two-story boardinghouse was constructed in 1917. Located near the future Howey Mansion site, the Bougainvillea lasted three years before succumbing to fire.

In the 1930s, Howey's downtown corridor along Lakeshore Boulevard began to sprout commercial enterprises and small residential cottages. Town-founder William J. Howey named the thoroughfare after the famed street in Chicago. The Cory Home, located at the corner of Lakeshore Boulevard and Central Avenue, was a good indicator of the growing community. The mixed-use building featured two apartments upstairs and a filling station and storefronts on the street level.

In addition to an academy, hotel, and citrus-packing facilities, the most important construction project for Howey was, perhaps, the Howey-Astatula Bridge. The 7,890-foot-long wood plank bridge saved two hours and 52 miles and established a short route between Jacksonville and Tampa. Traffic between the two cities crossed the bridge and passed through Howey-in-the-Hills.

The fashionable Floridan Hotel and town businesses bustled, new homes were started, and the town, feeling its growing pains, was in need of a cure. That cure came in the form of town officials passing a $300,000 municipal bond to fund the expense of city improvements: water works, 30 miles of hard-surfaced streets, a fire department, and a 165-foot-high town hall. Howey's City Inevitable was taking shape and preparing for the future.

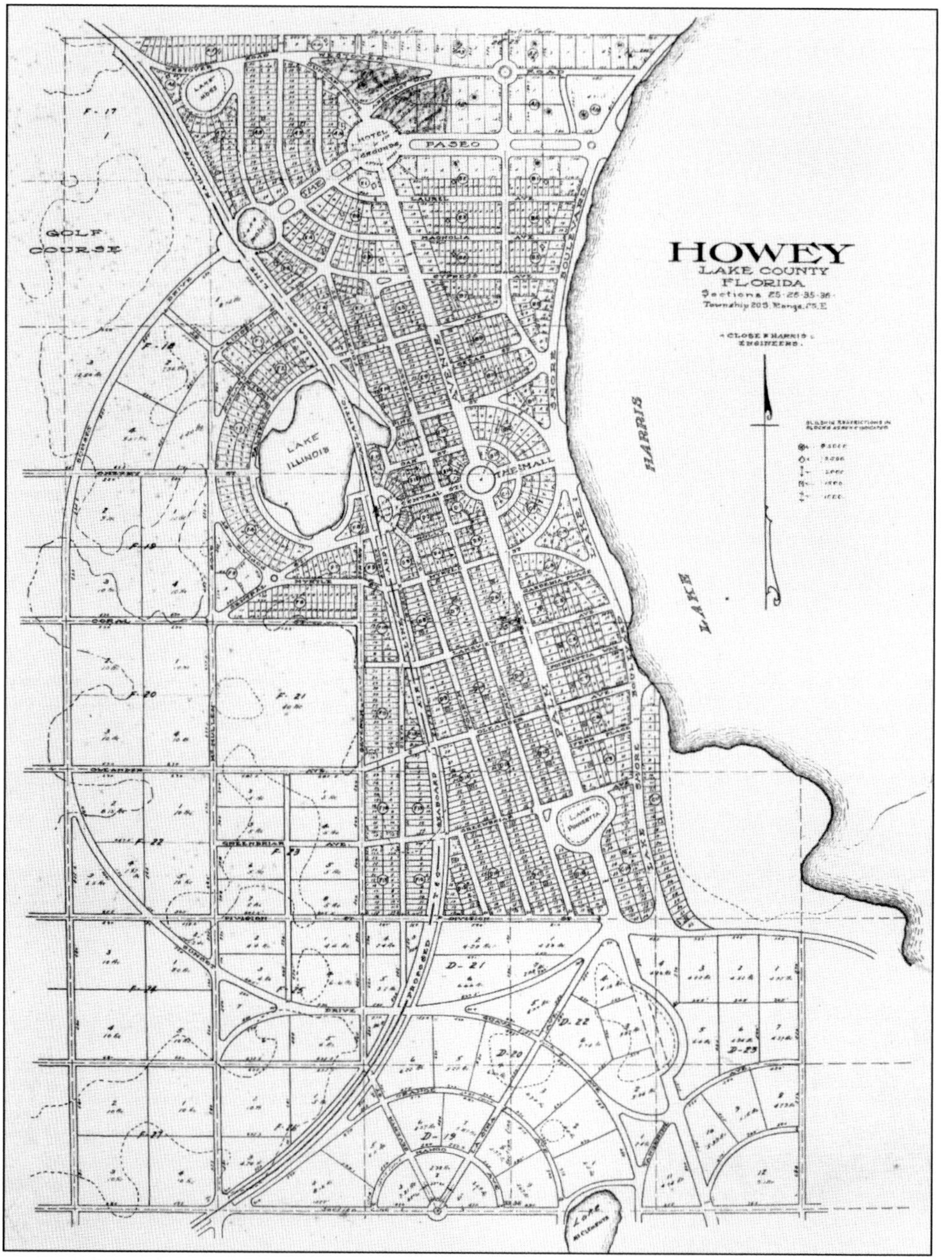

Engineering firm Close & Harris was clearly influenced by the finest cities abroad when it planned the dream city of Howey in the early 1920s. Spanning the city's length, Lakeshore Boulevard captured a stretch of waterfront for all to stroll or take leisurely drives. The Mall defined the city's center with Little Lake Harris to the east and the proposed Tavares & Gulf (T&G) Seaboard Air Line and Atlantic Coast Line Railways depot just west of Palm Avenue. Even a landscaped roundabout was designed to handle the highly anticipated stream of traffic. Sunset Drive flowed to the west of town and was to be a hub for leisurely evenings, a place to converse with neighbors, and the spot to witness the sun set behind the golden groves of Howey. North of the main roundabout, the Paseo flanked the circular future Hotel Grounds with a divided, majestic drive reaching from railroad tracks to waterfront. (HH.)

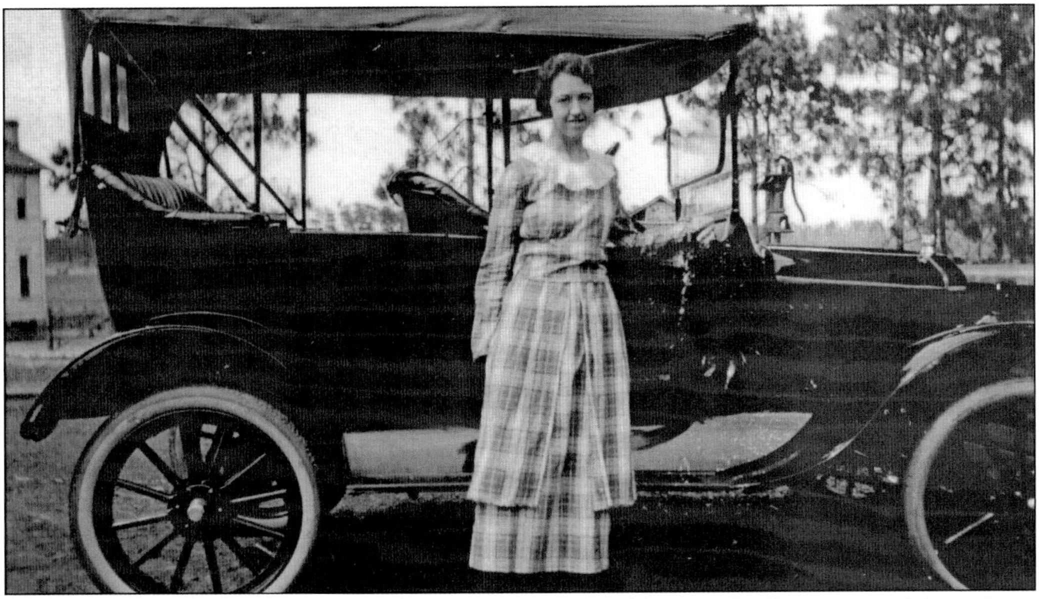

Charles H. Emery's wife enjoyed driving her open-air car featuring leather seats and drop-down windshield. She is dressed in plaid with a ruffled collar. This pioneer's car is parked in front of a hand water pump. (HH.)

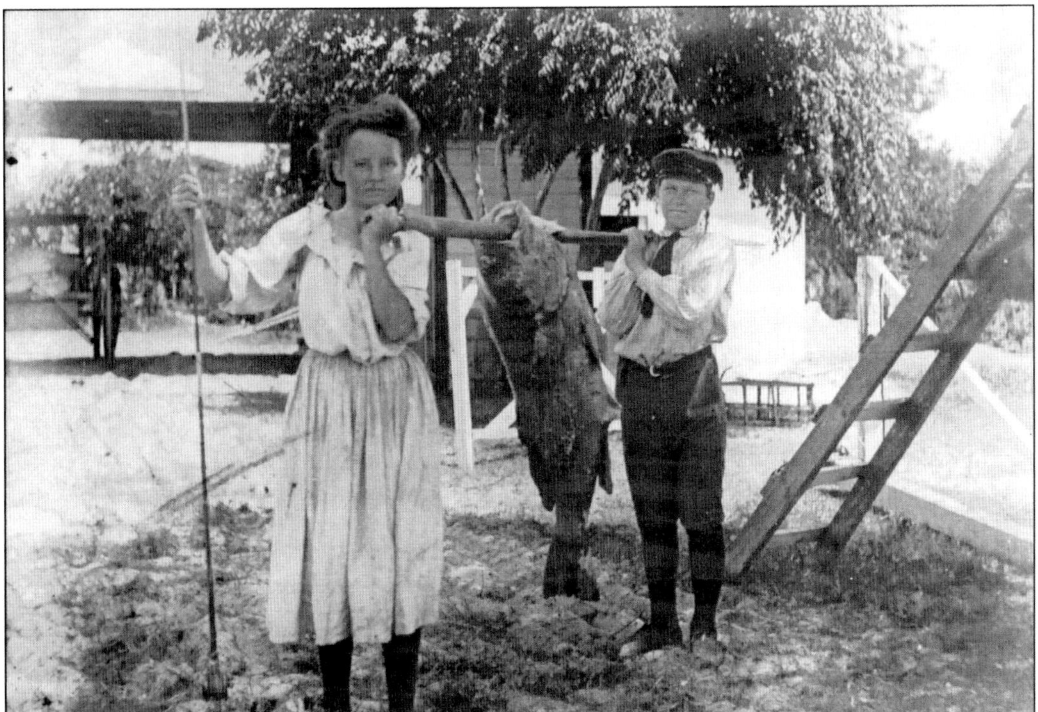

This fish tale was a whopper, one for the record books in the 1920s, and just as big as the youngsters who mounted it on the branch and carried it home shoulder high. They had thought about using the wagon, but it was laden with dry goods. There is no telling how long it took to bring this one to shore, but these looks of sheer determination and exhaustion say forever. (HH.)

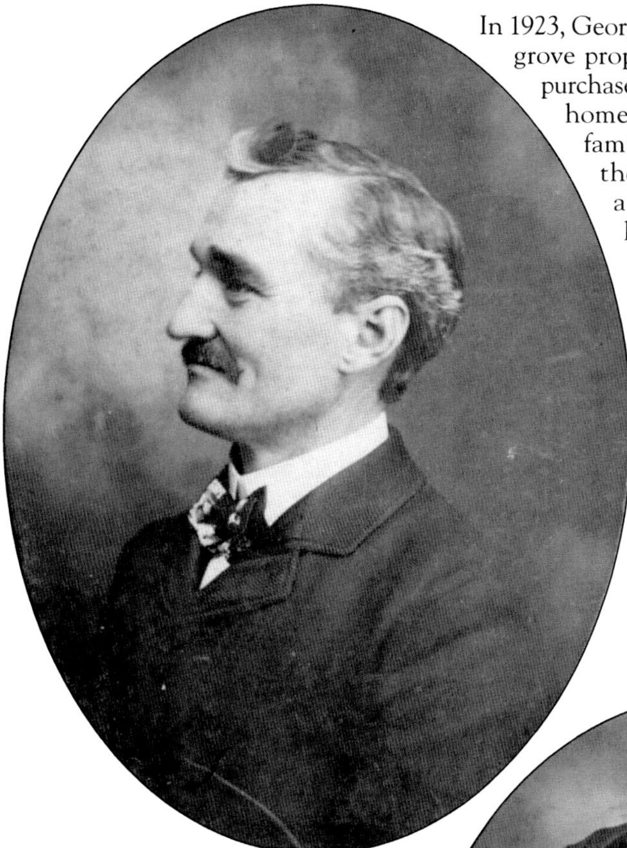

In 1923, George Brooks Buck was invited to inspect grove property and was immediately sold. He purchased 10 acres of property before returning home to move his family. Buck and his family of four arrived from Michigan in their Dodge touring car and pitched a tent in Tent City until they built a house. (HH.)

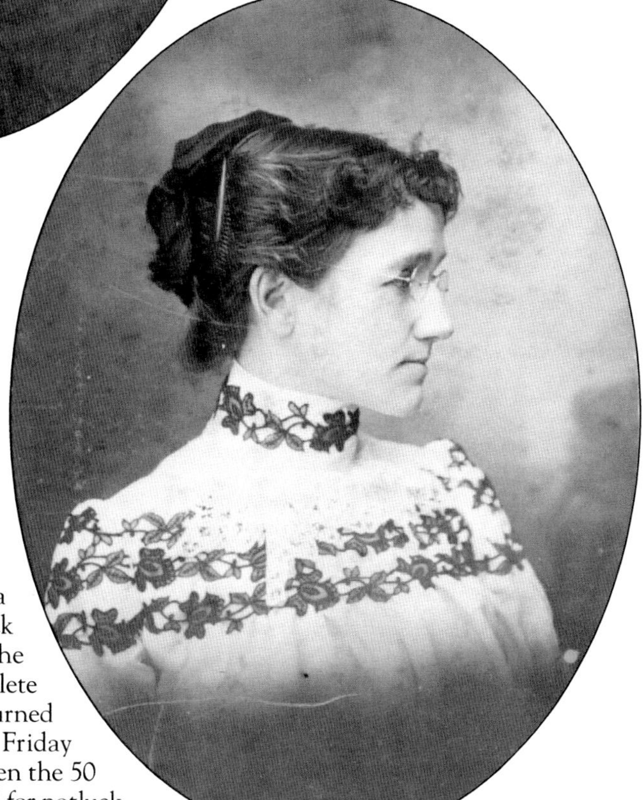

After years spent teaching in a Colorado mountain school, LuLu Buck was an old hand at pioneering. The cabin-like tent became home, complete with a recycled bathtub from the burned ruins of the Bougainvillea Hotel. Friday nights were real social occasions when the 50 or so Tent City inhabitants gathered for potluck dinners and dances. (HH.)

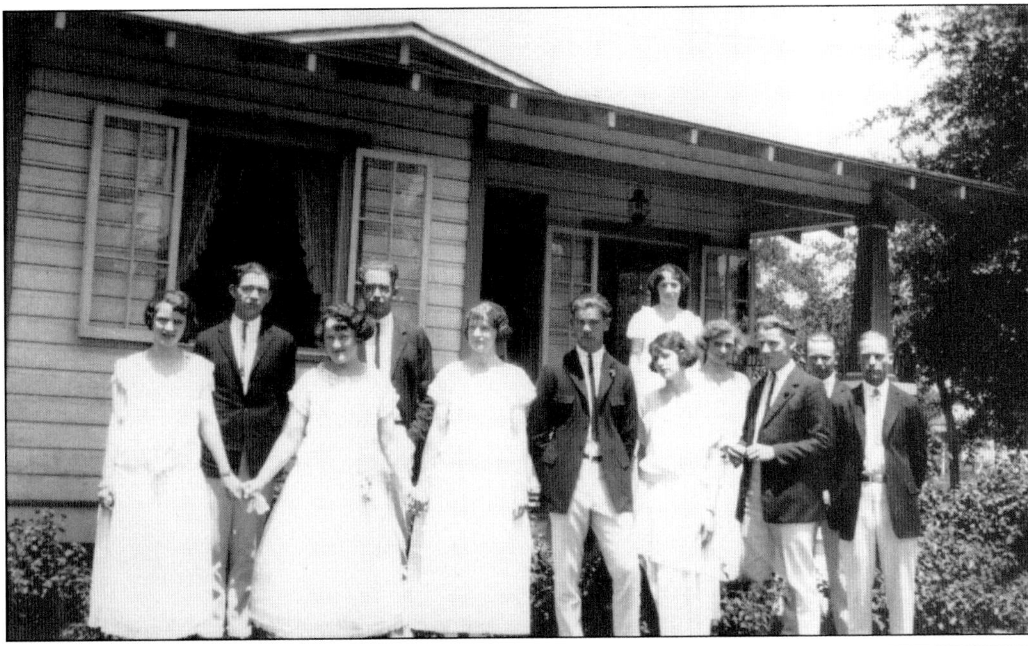

On December 10, 1923, Helen Buck (second from left) and her family rolled into Howey, having spent 10 days in a car en route from their Portland, Michigan, home. Helen was a senior in high school and, once settled into Tent City, returned to school at nearby Montverde. Buck was salutatorian of the senior class of 1924 and gave a splendid graduation speech to gathered classmates, family, and friends. (HH.)

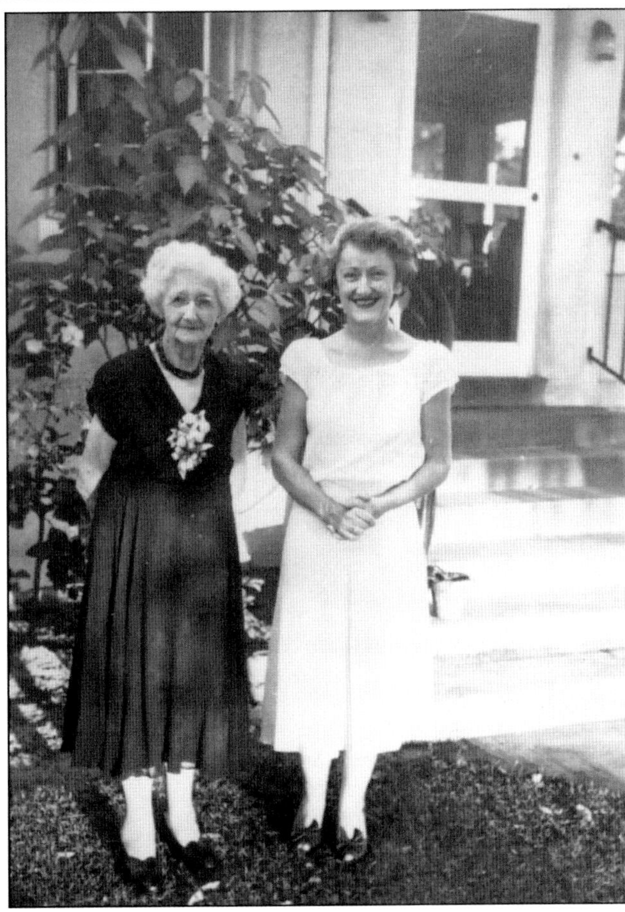

After attending a Jacksonville secretarial school, Helen Buck (right) moved home with her mother, LuLu (left) in 1927 and began working for the Howey Company as secretary to Dodge Taylor. Buck held the position until 1950, when she began her 22-year-long career with the Lake County public school system, serving five school superintendents. Most familiar with Howey-in-the-Hills, tireless Helen Buck went on to get her real estate license in 1972. (HH.)

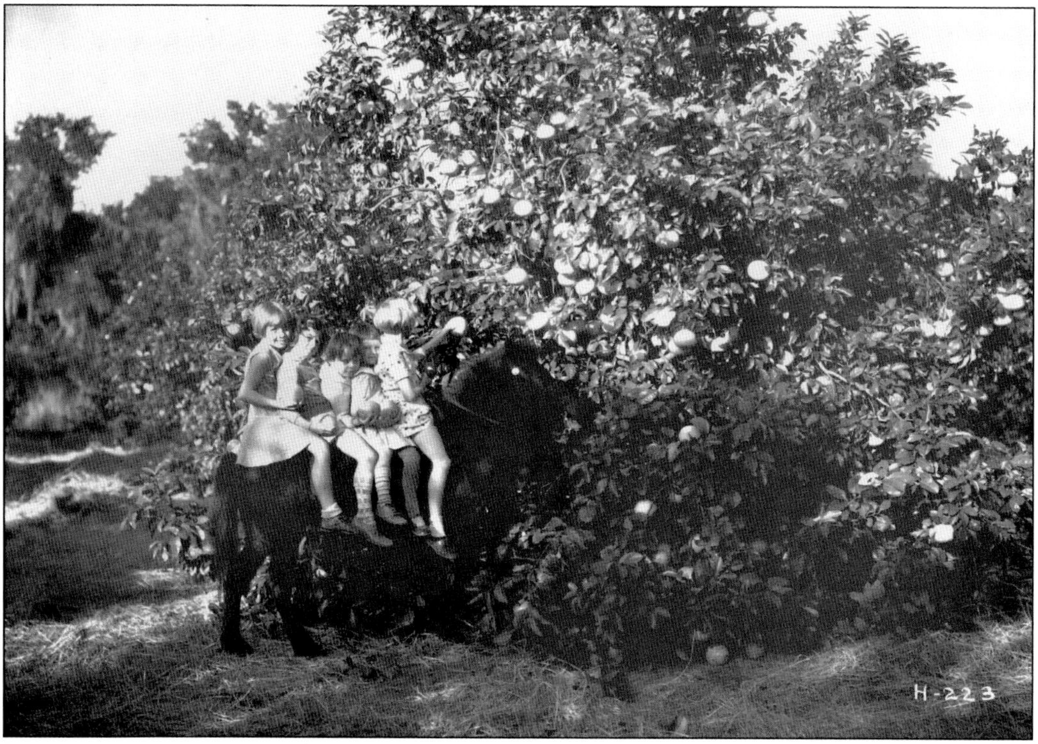

Jean Hewitt was captain of this craft, and her hometown crew of grapefruit grabbers did not care a hoot if the photographer did snap. The day this picture was taken in 1931, it was 11 degrees below zero in Chicago. Those pictured are, from the tail to the head, Elizabeth Weaver, Lois Howey, Virginia Mare, Juanita Roberts, and Jean Hewitt. Jean said there were plenty more girls but she ran out of pony. (OCHC.)

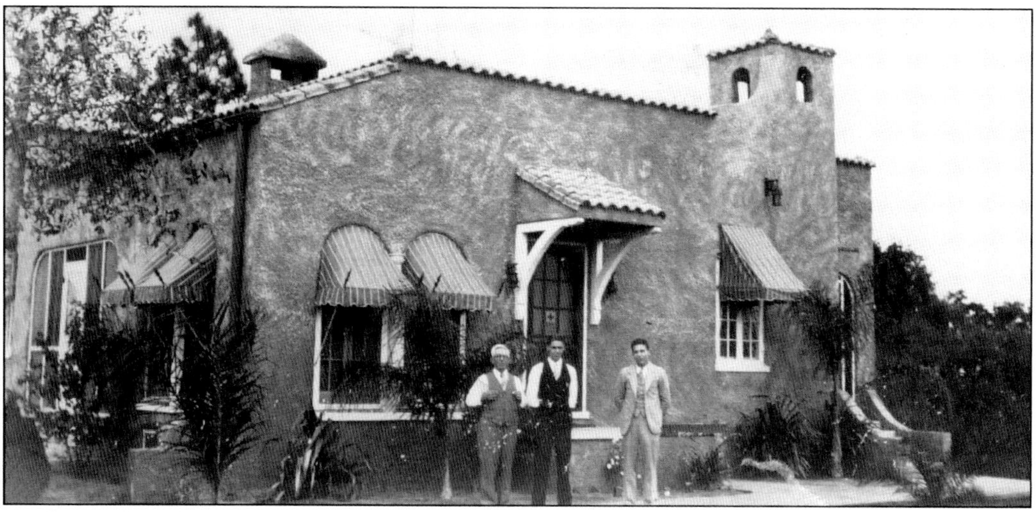

Jacob Joseph Wolfe (left) stands in front of his newly acquired family home in Howey-in-the-Hills with his son, Jasper (center). Lettie Wolfe loved growing flowers, while Jasper enjoyed boating on Little Lake Harris. The Wolfes stored their boat in one of three large wooden boathouses that once stood along Lakeshore Boulevard. The home remained in the Wolfe family from 1930 to 1980. (HH.)

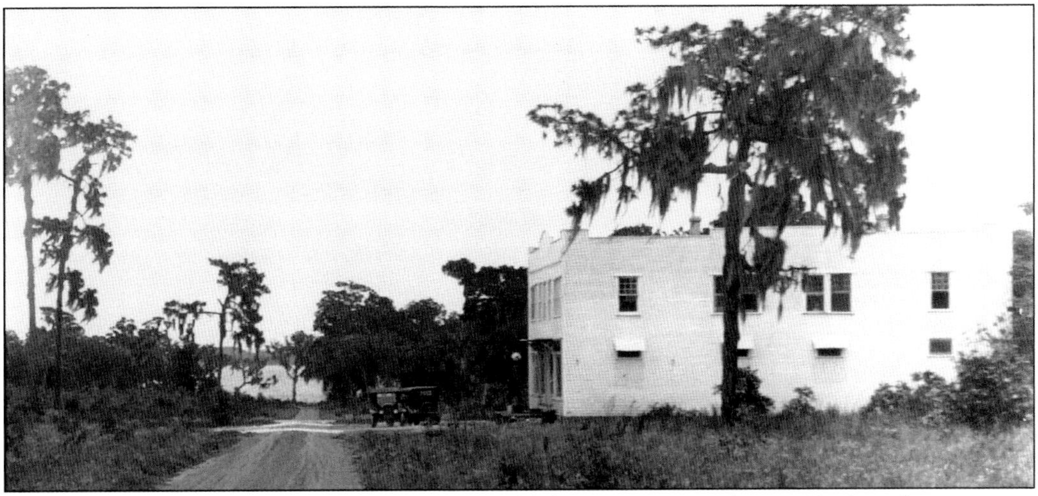

Arthur Roberts and his father, Harvey, left Oklahoma in November 1920 aboard a train car packed with livestock, furniture, and personal belongings. Harvey purchased 20 acres near the liquor store on Howey's Lone Pine Hill and then traded up to 40. The senior Roberts opened the first filling station and commercial building. This building and gas pump are on Central Avenue with Little Lake Harris to the east. (HH.)

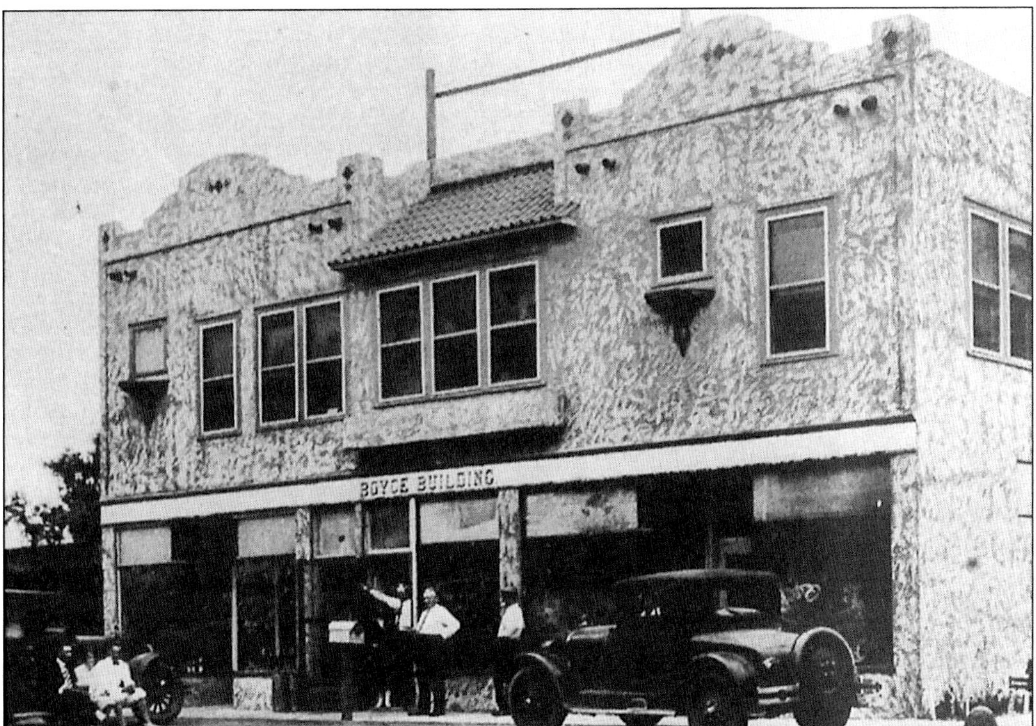

In March 1926, contractor W.E. Boyce completed this Spanish-style, two-story store and apartment building that centered on an interior court. The Central Avenue location contained three lower-level stores and several furnished apartments upstairs. Howey postmaster F.S. Archer relocated the post office here, and Boyce's woodworking mill, which provided building trim to local builders, was to the back. (HH.)

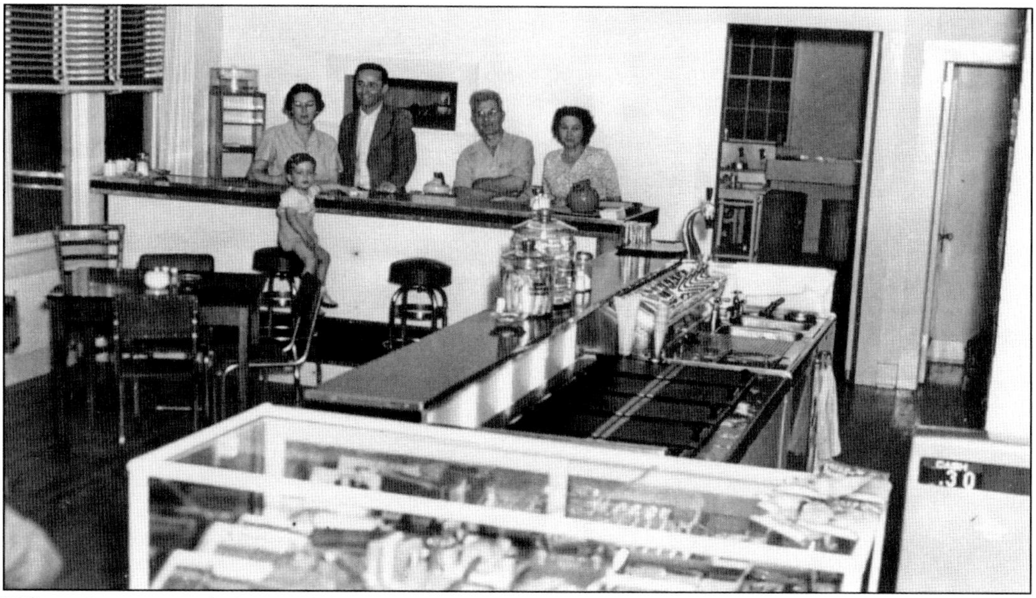

When George Buck (second from left behind the counter) and sister Helen arrived in 1923, George helped his father clear their new acreage in preparation for planting but lacked an interest in tending a farm or grove, and after spending time behind bars as postmaster, he escaped that career as well. Buck opened a sandwich and ice cream parlor in the Boyce Building on Central Avenue and later a sporting goods store across from the hotel. (HH.)

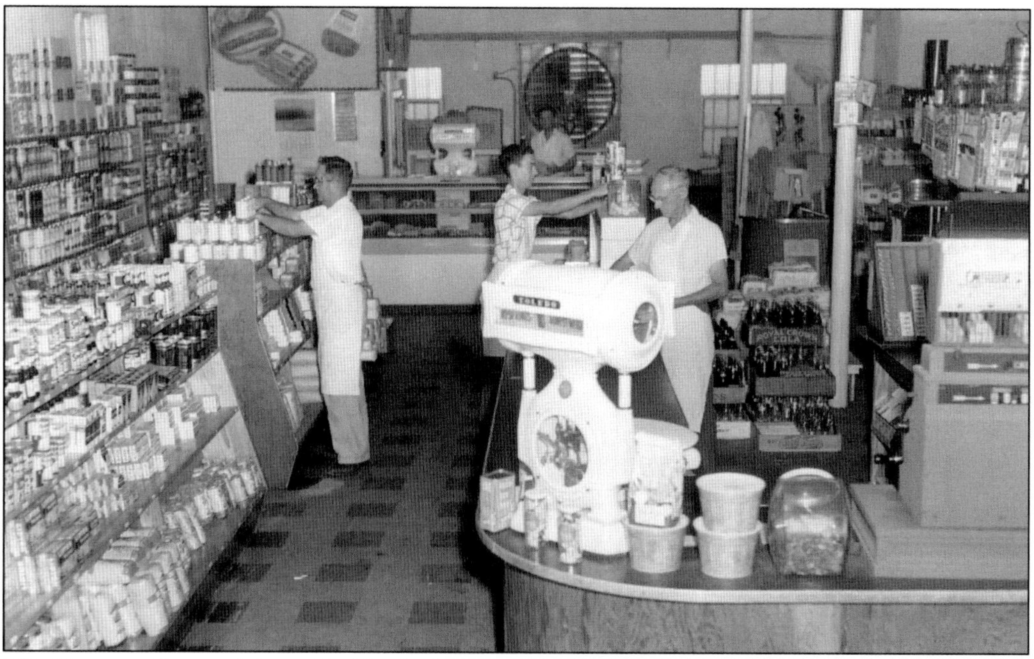

W.J. Howey influenced Peter VanEss (right) to sell his seven Chicago grocery stores and move to Howey-in-the-Hills in 1924. VanEss built a home and purchased a grove. When Howey convinced VanEss to open a grocery store in town, the company channeled all payroll checks through the store for final payment. Assured of getting paid, VanEss extended credit to the laborers and relieved the company of the burden. (HH.)

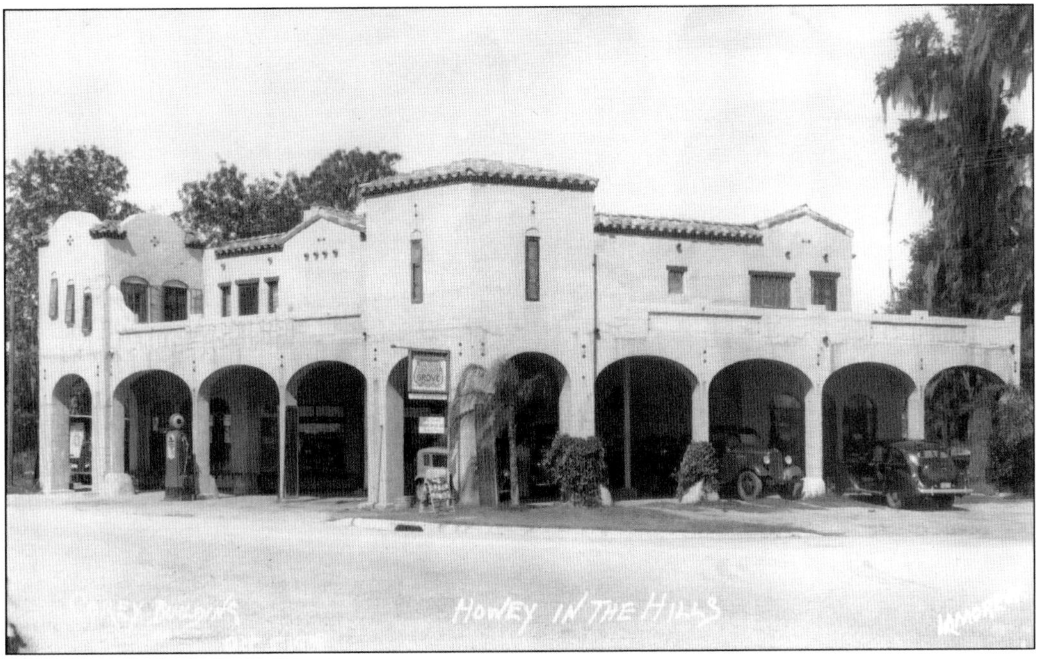

In 1926, following doctor's orders, Russell Cory, with wife Mabel, traveled south from their New Jersey home to Howey-in-the-Hills. Their vacation souvenir was a 48.5-acre parcel from the Howey Company that was immediately planted in citrus. The couple returned annually, spending winters at the Floridan Hotel until 1930, when Cory, a prominent New York architect, designed and built this two-story, mixed-use winter home at Central Avenue and Lakeshore Boulevard. (HH.)

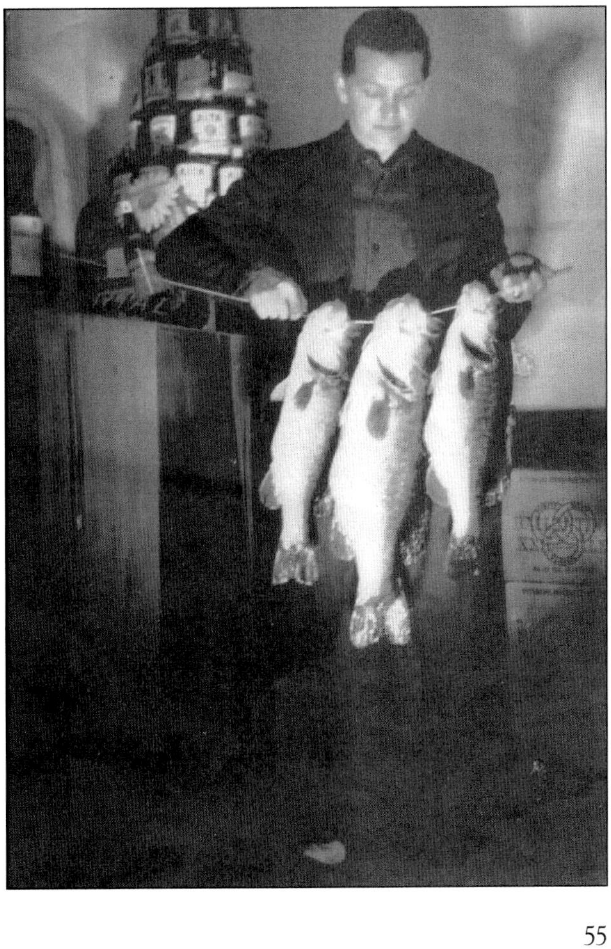

Chester Wrobel (right) was lured away from Pennsylvania coal mining on a Florida fishing trip that resulted in Wrobel relocating his family and going into business with his brother Stanley. They bought the Corey Building and operated Howey Lakeside Service, which included a Gulf Oil station, general store, and liquor store. The county was dry but not the town. The Floridan Hotel and the Wrobel brothers held the only two liquor licenses and remained especially popular on Sundays. (CW.)

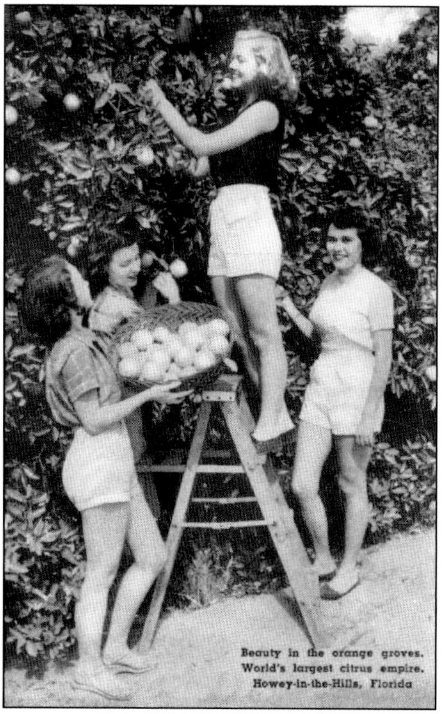

These young ladies participated in a postcard promotion for the W.J. Howey Company. The glamorous photograph advertised their natural beauty enhanced by the sun-kissed groves. Atop the ladder is Dodge Taylor's daughter Mary Jane picking the perfect oranges for the Floridan Hotel's lobby basket. (CB.)

On May 14, 1959, Clay and Blanche Price (holding a mixer at left) opened the doors to Price and Son Hardware, located next to the post office, with a drawing and grand prize awarded. The winner was nurse Mary Salmonsen and husband, Ed (right), who received the modern kitchen mixer. Years later, owner Glen Miller expanded the Palm Avenue store to include antiques. (HH.)

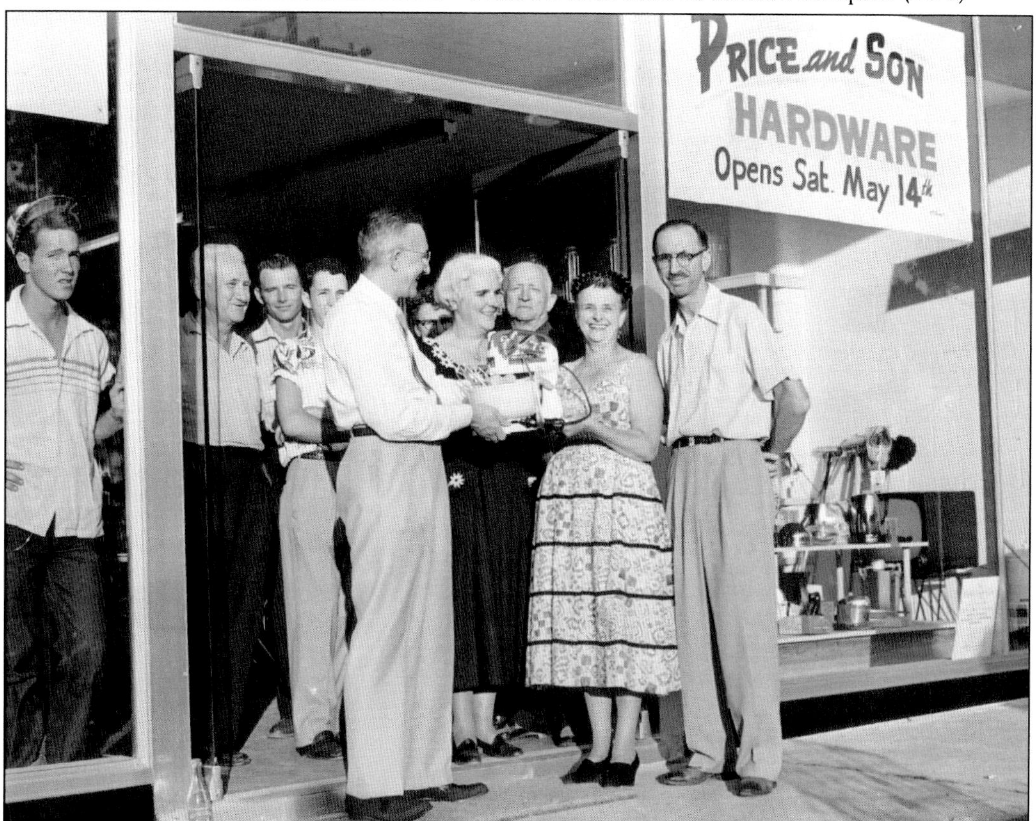

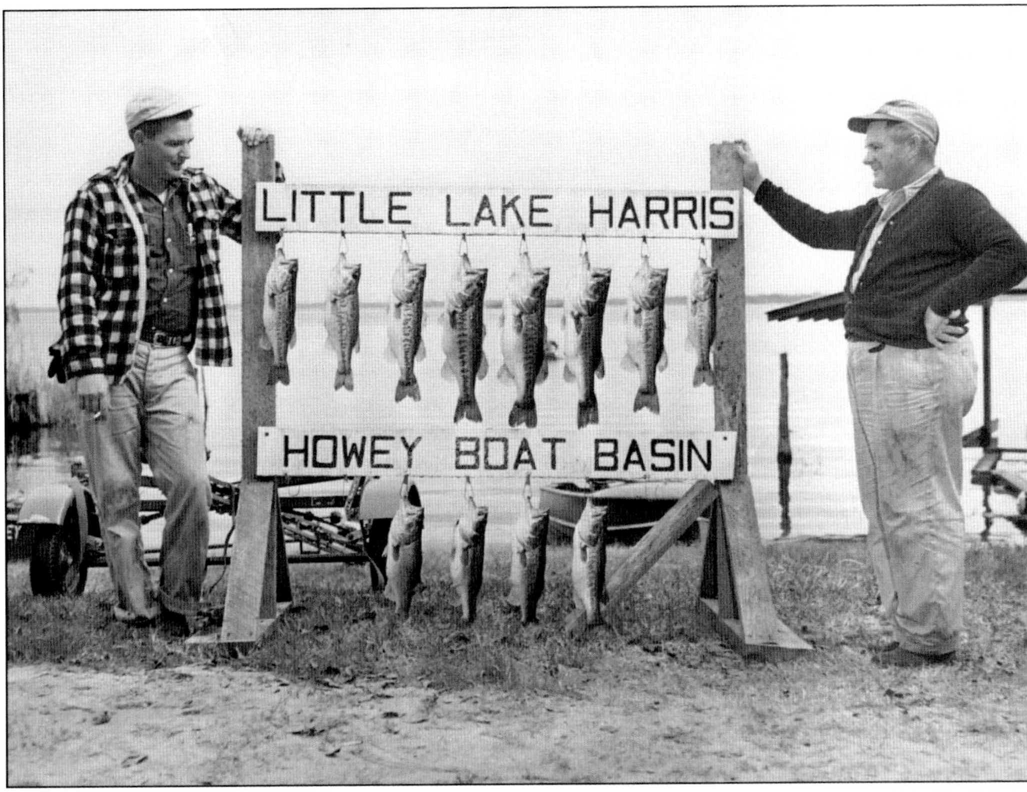

In 1964, after baiting their hooks, these anglers felt nibbles turn to bites and reeled a dozen in. Avid fishermen knew Little Lake Harris was chock full of largemouth bass year round. During the winter months, they turned the State Road 19 Bridge into a lantern-lighted spectacle while night fishing for speckled perch. (HH.)

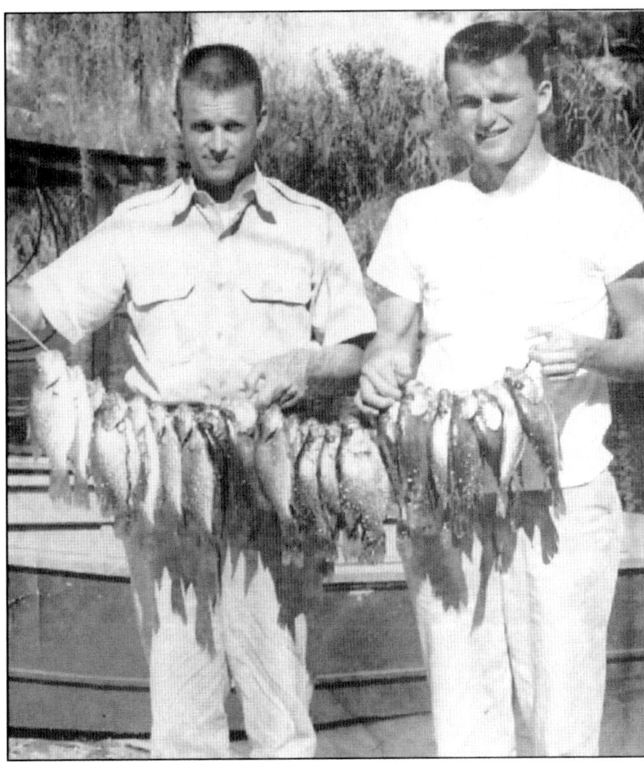

Buddy Purser (left) and Rodney Griffin pose with their fresh catch of the day at the Howey Boat Basin. Buddy, who served in the Air Force, married Mary Jane Taylor, Dodge Taylor's daughter, and resided in Howey-in-the-Hills after being stationed with his family at numerous military bases. Rodney married Ann Linn, whose grandparents were Howey residents. (ARG.)

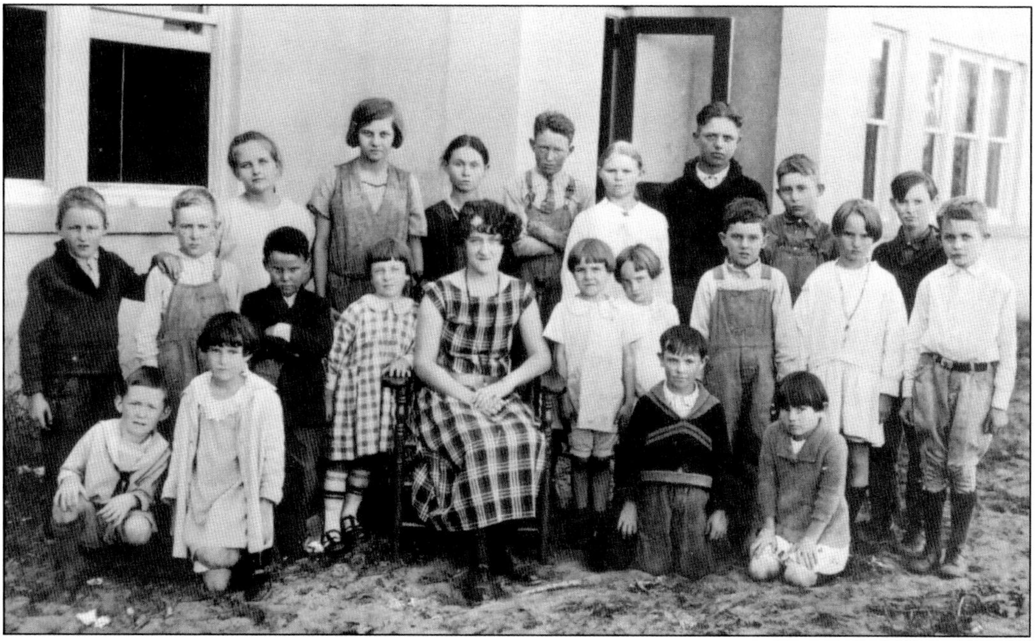

When the stucco building on Palm Avenue, then only a sandy trail, was built in 1923, Howey Elementary School's first teacher was Helen Buck (seated in a plaid dress), who graduated with honors in 1924 from nearby Montverde School. At 16 years old, the young and energetic Helen Buck was the lone instructor and presided over eight grades of little rascals. After one year, she decided to return to school for business and bookkeeping courses. (HH.)

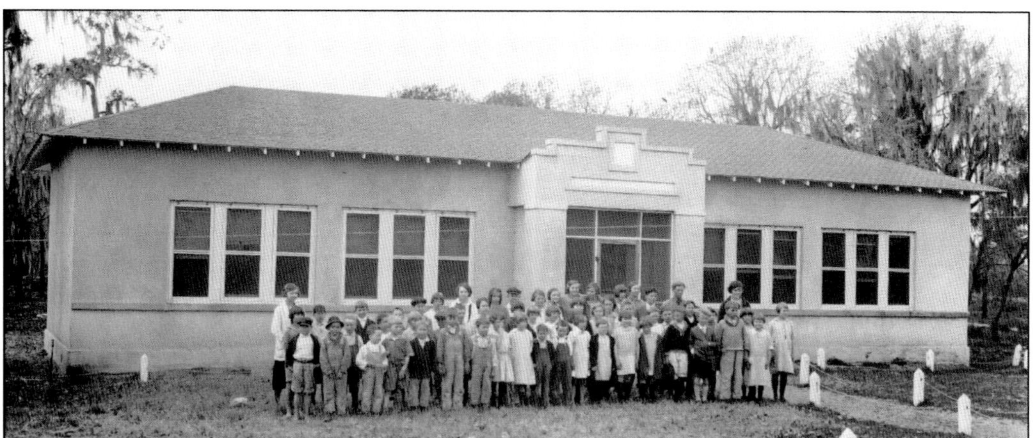

By 1925, the children in Howey attended class in this modern elementary school building, which was built on Palm Avenue across from the Floridan Hotel. Later, school trustees considered building a junior high school in town, reducing the need to transport students to area public schools. In 1956, when the hotel property became Howey Academy, this building was used as a chapel. (HH.)

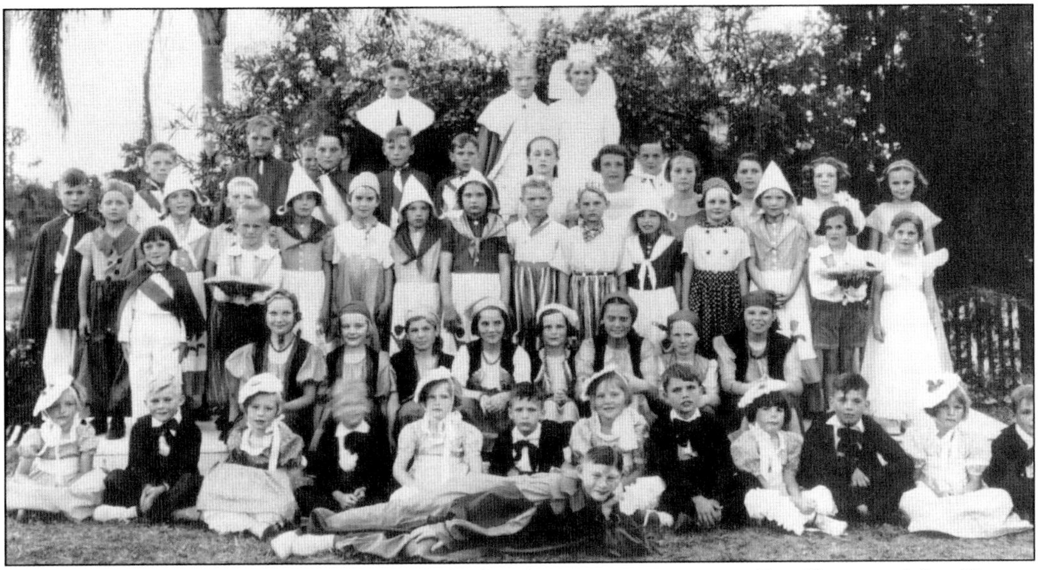

Howey's first Tent City students attended school in a tent near a small golf course lake. Howey later established Lake County's first kindergarten, and Myra Coates Brandon, a graduate of Cincinnati's Kindergarten Training School, was one of the first to officially conduct class. The second school was founded adjacent to the Howey Company offices at the hotel and started on January 4, 1926. (HH.)

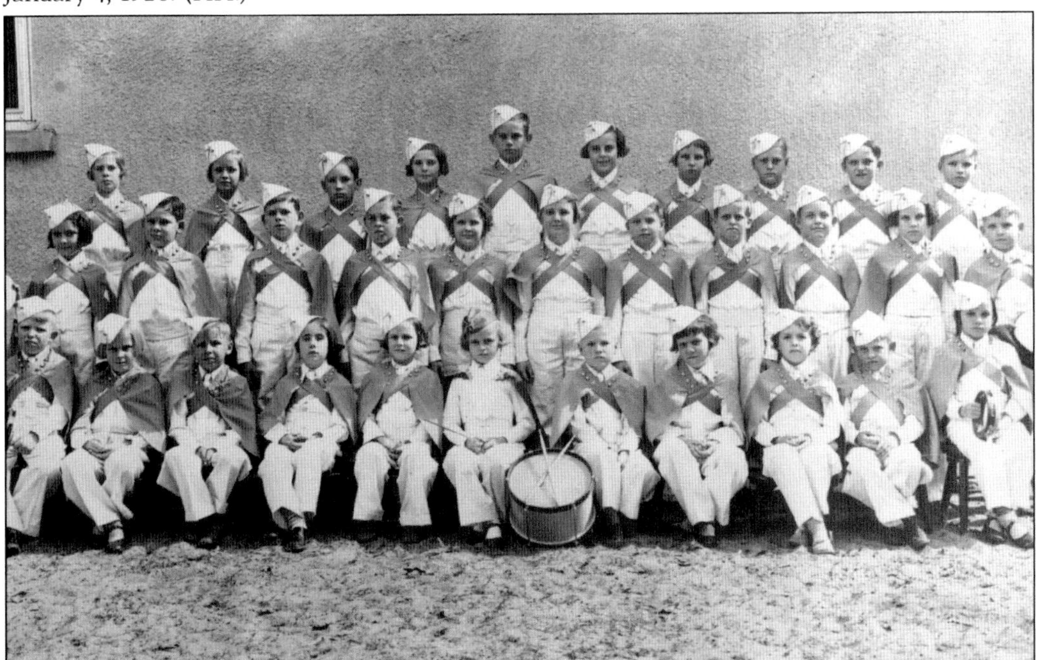

Howey Elementary School students displayed their talents at pageants and plays, where they were often in full costume. This uniformed marching band performed before doting family and friends in front of the new school that William J. Howey built directly across Palm Avenue from his office and hotel. Over time, the town's educational facilities went from a one-room tent to the college-preparatory academy. (HH.)

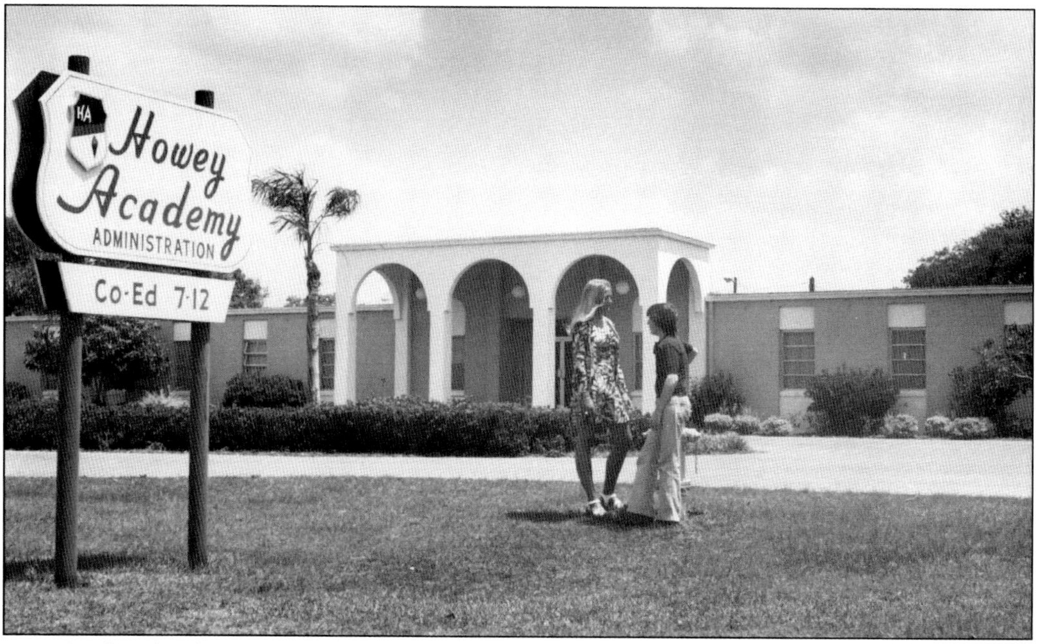

In 1956, the Floridan Hotel was converted to Howey Academy, with a country club campus. Dr. James D. Miller founded the school, but it was C.V. Griffin who led the academy over a 23-year period, graduating thousands of students from around the world. After Dr. Miller's retirement, Dr. C.A. Vaughn Jr. became the Howey Academy headmaster. (HH.)

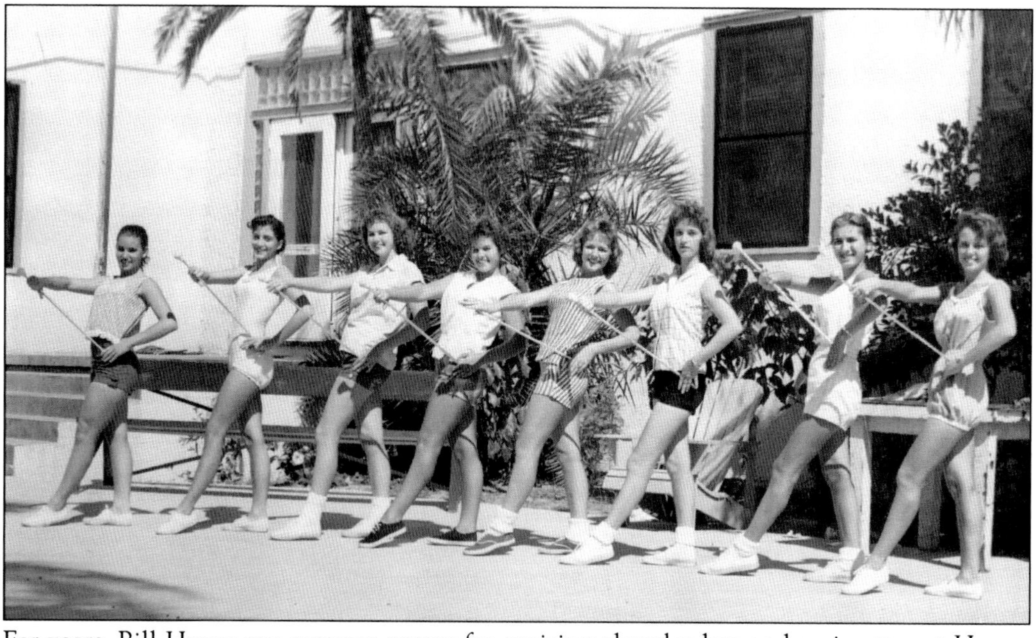

For years, Bill Horan ran summer camps for aspiring cheerleaders and majorettes at Howey Academy. Traditional school months, however, were filled by students attending classes and studying, followed by afternoons and weekends spent horseback riding, golfing, boating, and sunbathing on the school's private beach. (HH.)

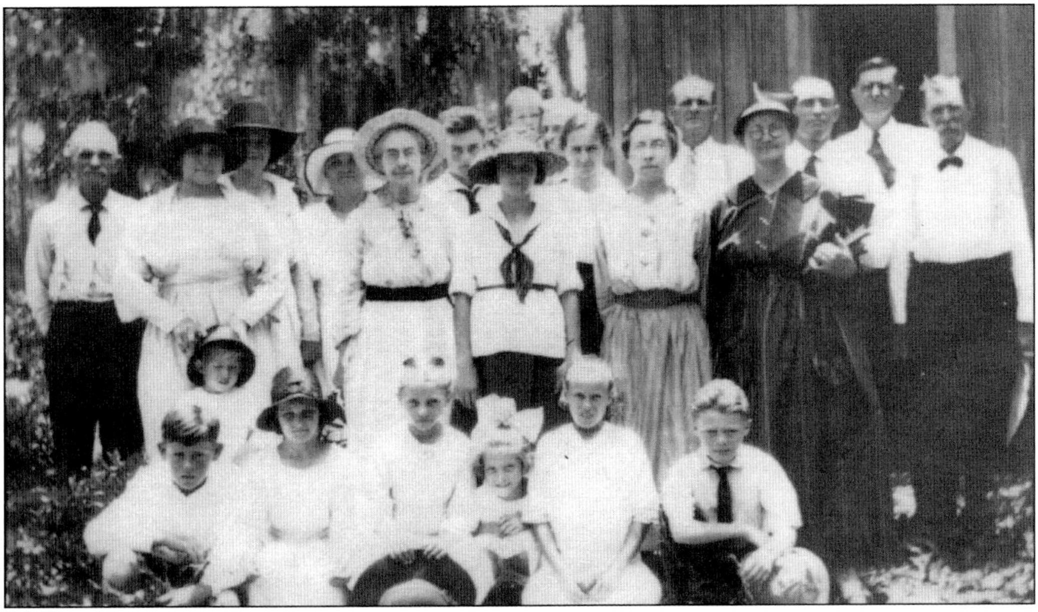

In 1920, when Palm Avenue was the only street in town and just 17 homes existed within a three-mile radius, 10 dedicated souls gathered in the schoolhouse for the first Sunday school. Services moved to Tent City in 1922 and to the new schoolhouse across from the hotel in 1925. On January 1, 1927, a petition was signed to establish a church. Their prayers were answered on February 12, 1928, when the Community Church was approved. Presbyterian "supply pastors" led the faithful for years. In 1942, the W.J. Howey Company donated land for the present sanctuary. The Yoder family of Cleveland contributed so generously to the building fund that the name was changed to Yoder Memorial Community Church. C.V. Griffin donated the opera theater seats, which arrived in Tavares by train and were drayed across Little Lake Harris from Astatula. (Both, HH.)

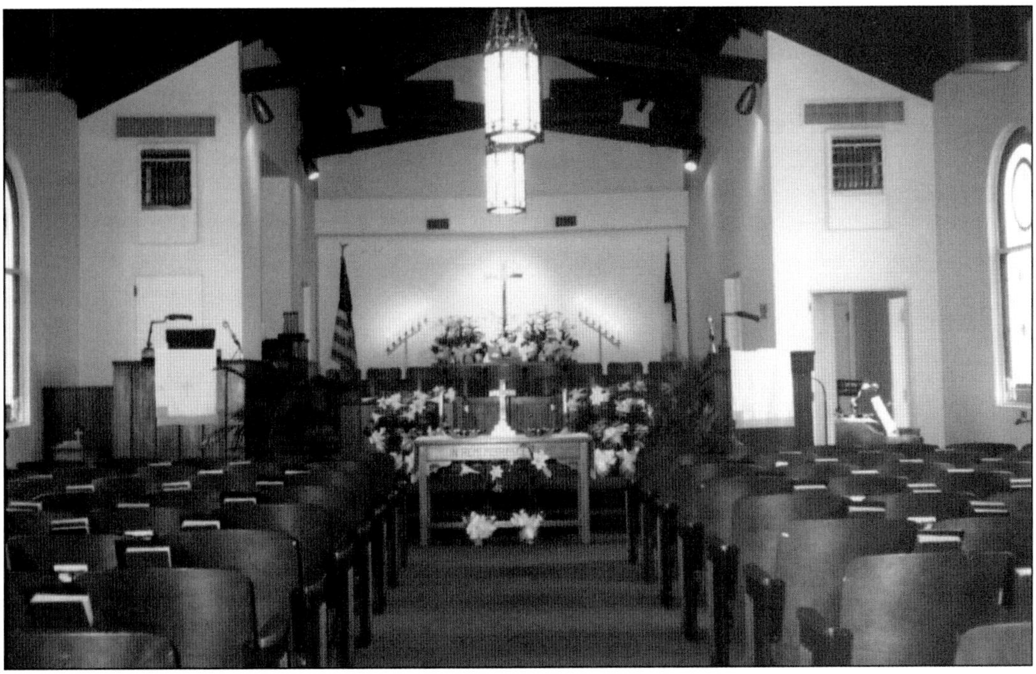

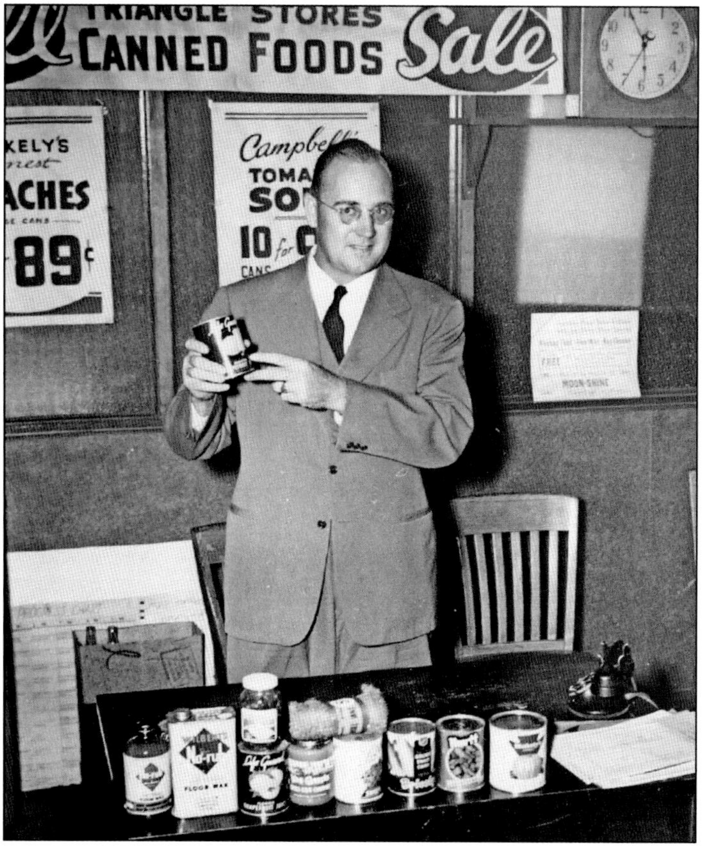

Gene Bruce, the sales manager of the Howey Company, created a plan to clear Northern grocery store shelves of last year's canned citrus goods by dropping prices to levels that attracted heavy buying by housewives. His campaign was marketed as a contest between the grocery stores, which further helped to move thousands of cases of Florida juice. Pilot Walter Schanz flew each winning grocery chain supervisor and his spouse in the Howey Company plane for a week's vacation at Miami Beach. (HH.)

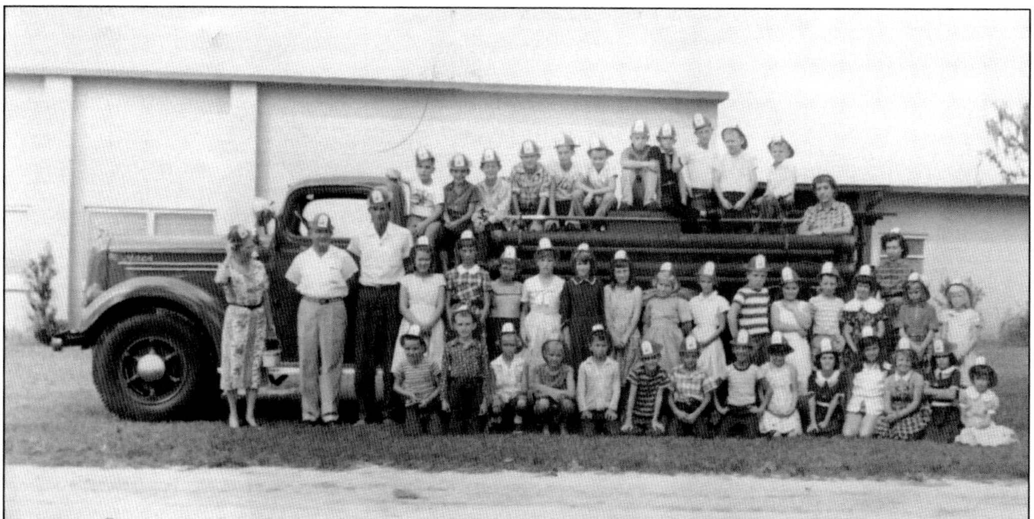

In 1946, Mack built 122 red fire engines for the US Army Corps of Engineers. A year later, to the delight of the children of Howey grammar school, the Howey-in-the-Hills Volunteer Fire Department acquired one as army surplus. In 1991, when the squad disbanded, the trusty firefighter went to the county, only to be returned a few years later and meticulously restored by volunteers for special events. (HH.)

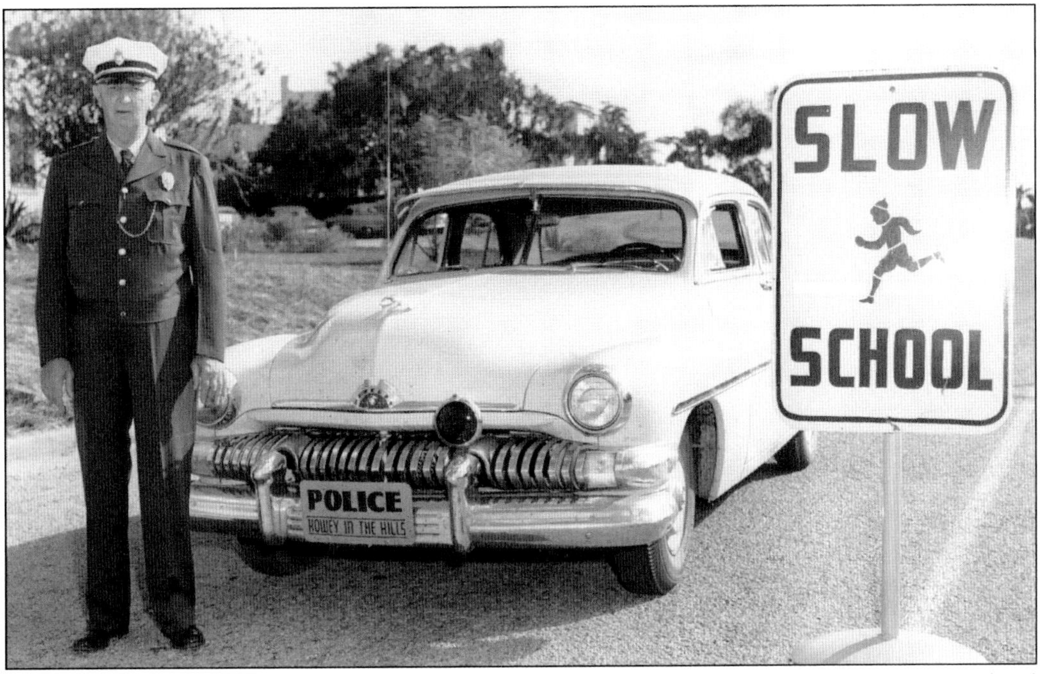

Before Howey-in-the-Hills had a police force, a town marshal patrolled the streets. When school was let out in the afternoon, he helped children cross the street, particularly at the town's single flashing yellow light. While duty was light in those days, the town marshal was still a welcome sight. (HH.)

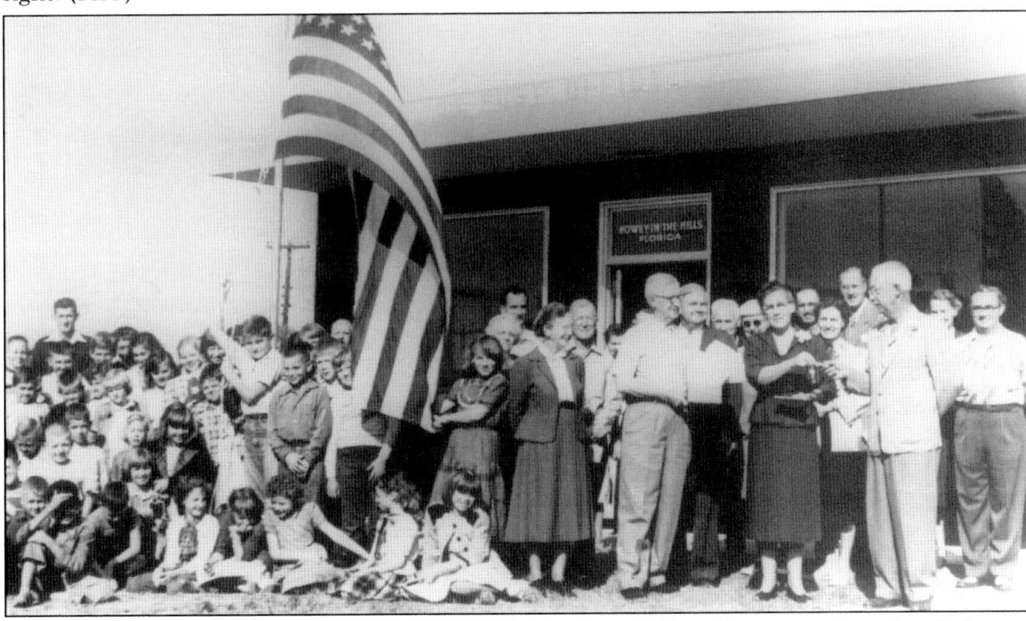

This building was the third location for the Howey Post Office. Patrons gathered and chatted in front during the old days, when individuals were assigned wooden mailboxes. Marguerite F. Matthews, the new postmaster, attended this grand opening on Palm Avenue to receive her key to the new facility. To the left of Matthews (holding a box) is resident George Linn, founder of *Linn's Stamp News*, the largest weekly newspaper for stamp collectors. (HH.)

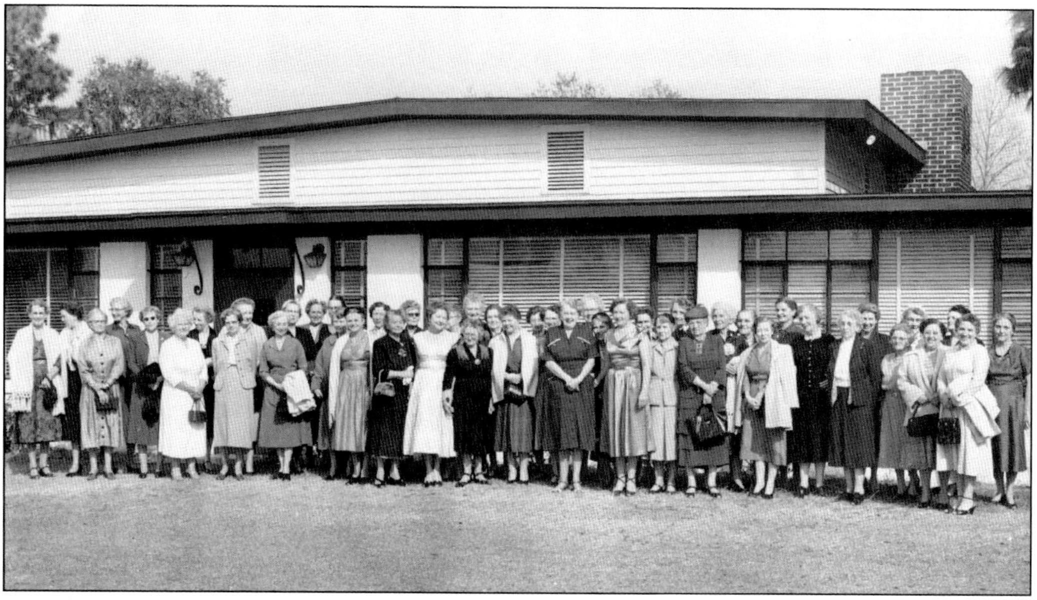

Founded in 1951, the Howey-in-the-Hills Garden and Civic Club's first president was Mary Taylor. Here, the women's club gathers in 1956 for a luncheon and cards at the clubhouse of the Floridan Country Club, across from the Howey Mansion. Peter VanEss, a former Howey mayor and town grocery owner-operator, organized the first Howey Garden Club in October 1928 and was its inaugural president. (HH.)

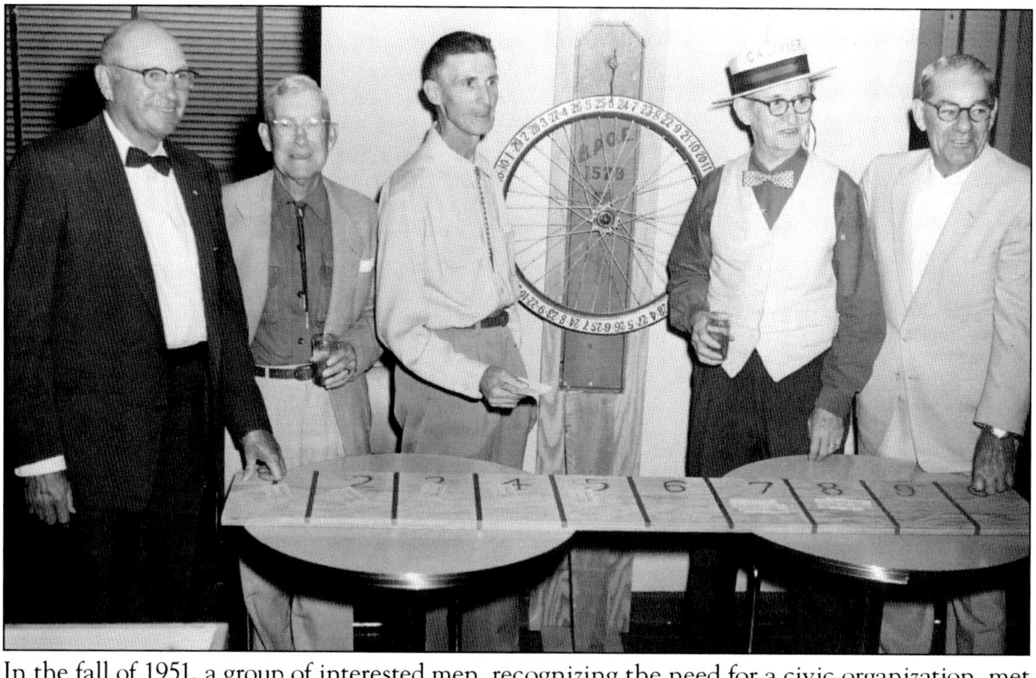

In the fall of 1951, a group of interested men, recognizing the need for a civic organization, met at the Floridan Country Club and organized the Men's Club of Howey-in-the-Hills. Horace L. Woody was the first president. A new civic center was a gift to the town from C.V. Griffin and was furnished by the generosity of Grace Howey. From left to right are Carol Chalk, Art Colvin, Mayor Edwin Hazelton "Haze" Ketchum, George Linn, and Al Smith Sr. (HH.)

Six

FLORIDA'S INLAND PLAYGROUND

Howey-in-the-Hills is located at the northern end of Florida's famous ridge section, an area of unsurpassed beauty and bounty that was once known to thousands of Americans as the nation's pier, an incomparable playground.

Investors arriving on specially conducted tours were provided accommodations at the Hotel Floridan, where complete hotel service was available. Visitors were shown over the far-reaching Howey properties, where producing groves exemplified the methods employed in raising quality fruit. "Take a trip to Howey" was the company salesmen's catchphrase, and what awaited those who took advantage of the offer was a true sportsman's paradise.

The surrounding countryside abounded with quail and dove, while ducks and other waterfowl were in abundance in area lakes. Deer hunting in the "big scrub" appealed to the more experienced hunters. And no finer bass fishing existed in the country than in the hill and lake section of Lake County. Practically all the 1,400 county lakes were well stocked with game fish, making Howey-in-the-Hills a utopia for fish and wildlife.

A fan of the game, Howey built one of the sportiest golf courses in all Florida. Each of the holes was hilly and rolling, and many featured natural water hazards. A $40,000 cabin cruiser was popular for Lake Harris sightseeing trips, while surreys transported guests to the golf clubhouse and beach.

The dude ranch put on rodeos for 2,000, and the stable of 45 Saddlebred horses provided the horsepower for equestrian lessons and trail rides through the groves.

Outdoors, the hotel offered shuffleboard courts and bowling lanes. Indoors, there were card games, nightly lectures, and social gatherings. Dances were hosted regularly, and when social director Mickey got behind the "mike" or mic, guests were recruited into the next act or singing group. There was a time when the hotel's bookings were so solid that reservations were limited to three-night stays.

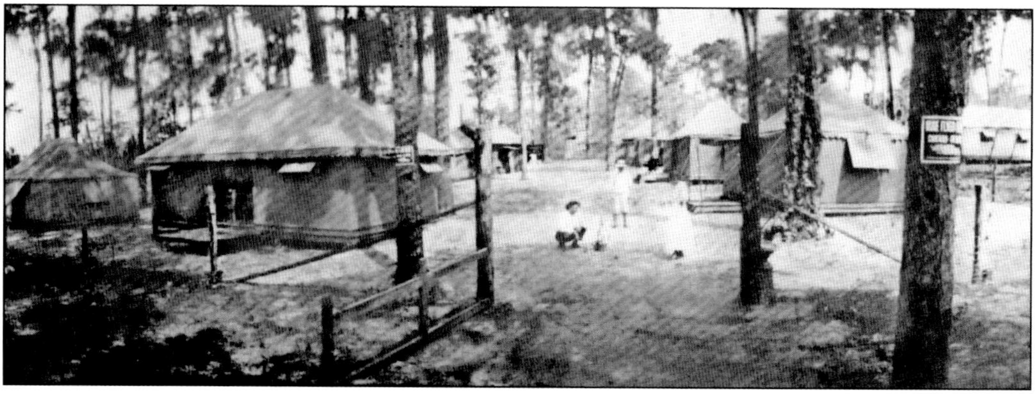

Howey's promotion for land opportunities attracted thousands in the fall of 1916. Available resources were tapped when Tent City was erected with aboveground tents of three-foot-high wood plank sides, drop-down netting that flapped in the breeze (if there was one), and wooden roofs. Residents entertained themselves in the social hall, dancing the jig and Virginia reel to toe-tapping sounds from the player piano and attending booster picnics every few weeks. Bathtubs retrieved from the Bougainvillea Hotel fire rubble were recycled. When customers with children arrived, a schoolhouse was provided in a tent. Dropped pencils often fell through wide cracks between flooring planks to the earth below the Schoolhouse Tent, only to be snatched by wild hogs seeking shelter from the weather. After school, mothers picked hog fleas from the ruffles and seams of their children's clothing. (Both, HH.)

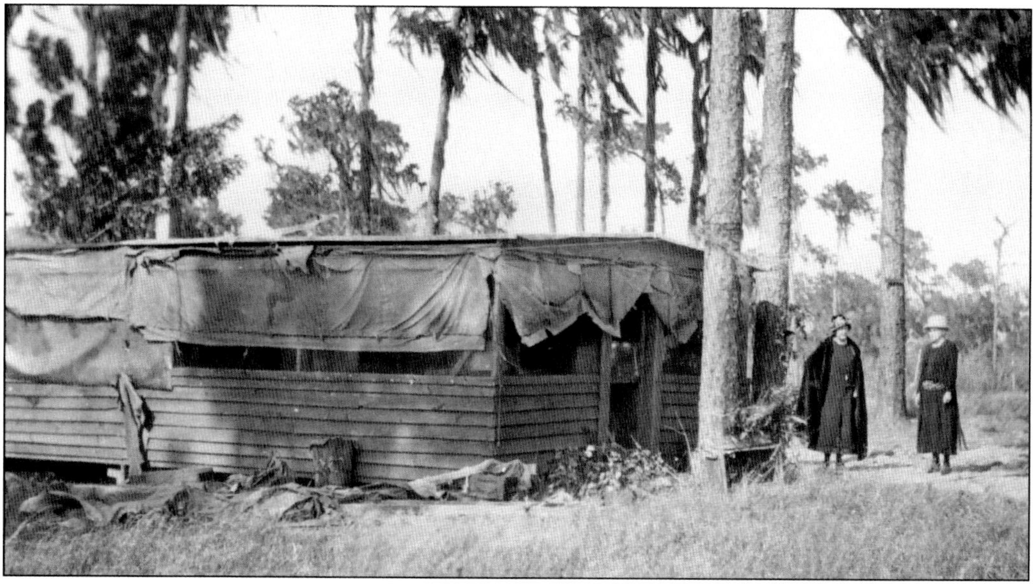

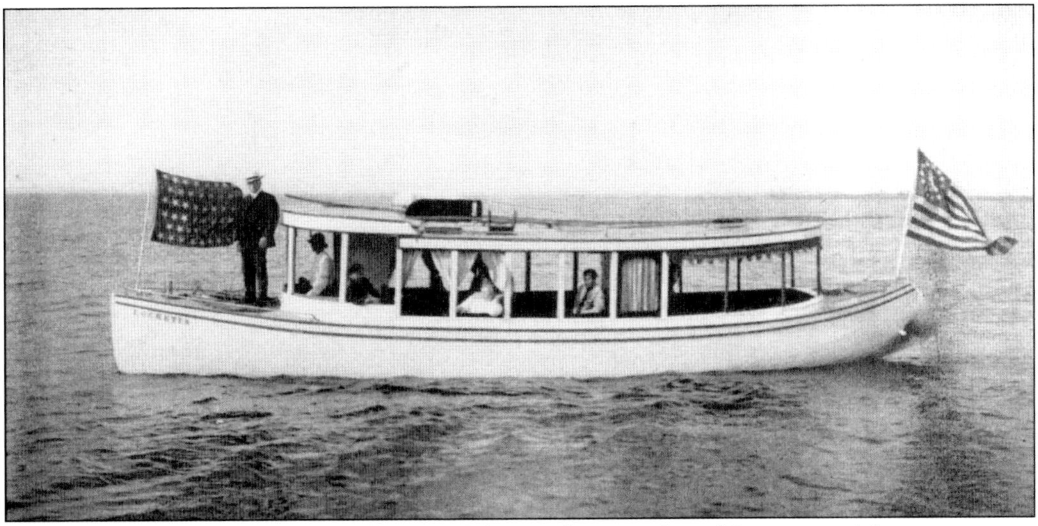

The Harris chain of lakes provided hours of pleasure boating aboard *Lucretia* and discovering rare water scenes of moss-covered cypress. The great lakes of the highlands are connected by streams, which were passable at the time by boats up to the size and draft of a small cabin cruiser. The tropical waterways about Howey were in sharp contrast to the rolling beauty that best characterized most of its landscape. Nearby Echo Glen was once part of the Howey enterprise. (LCHM.)

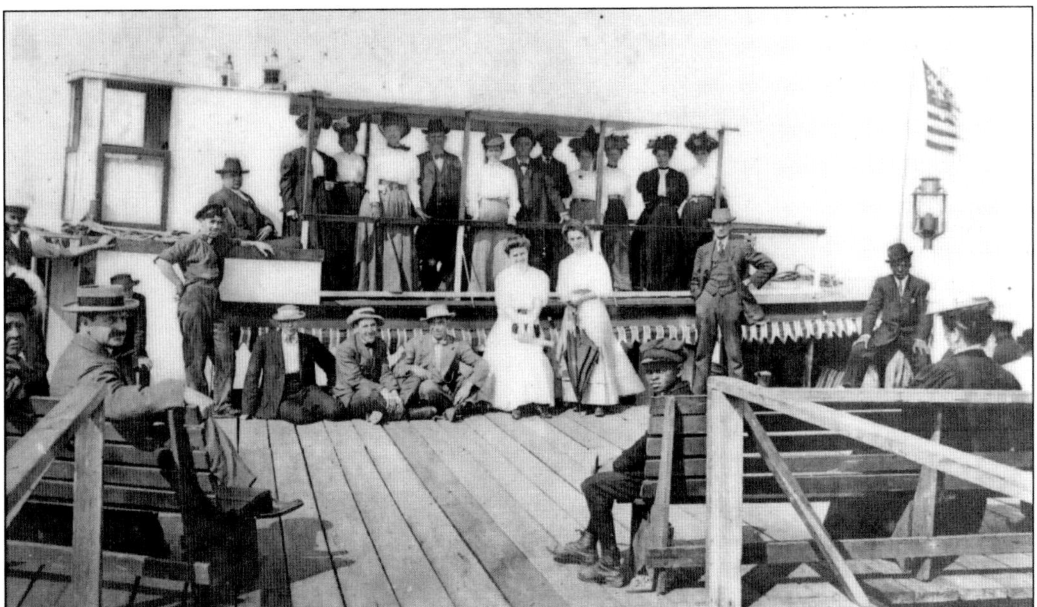

For these passengers, their destination was worth the adventurous trip. The closest public dock was on Lake Harris's south edge, approximately eight miles west of Howey. When the first investor-guests disembarked at the town of Bloomfield, wagons were sent for the passengers and luggage. When nearby Bloomfield became a ghost town, the town of Yalaha operated a dock where Howey shipped out citrus and the Howey Mansion furnishings arrived. (LCHM.)

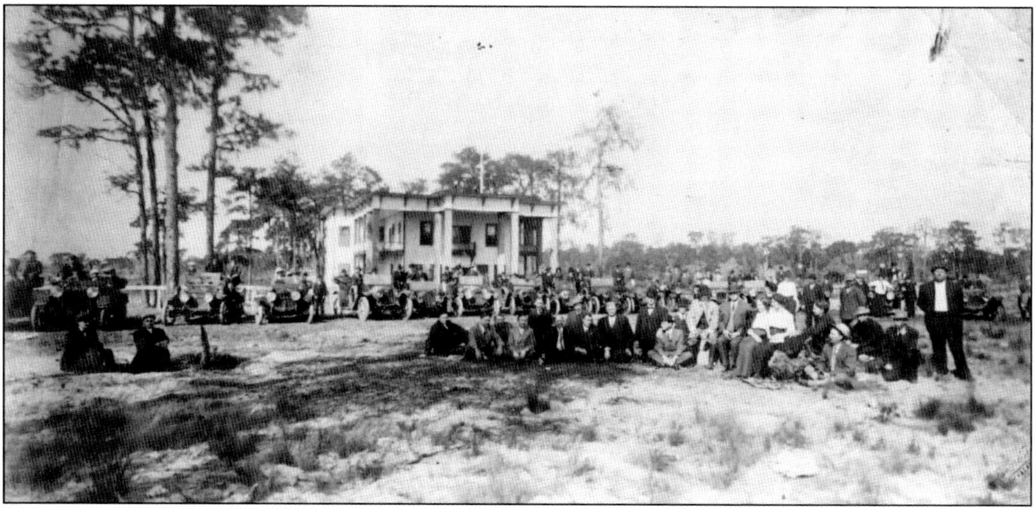

In 1917, Howey's first prospective grove investors were welcomed to the two-story boardinghouse the Bougainvillea. The hilltop frame structure was built on the same location as the future golf clubhouse, across from William and Grace Howey's destined mansion site. While the sand parking lot was packed with customers, scenes like this one only lasted until 1920, when the Bougainvillea burned down. (HH.)

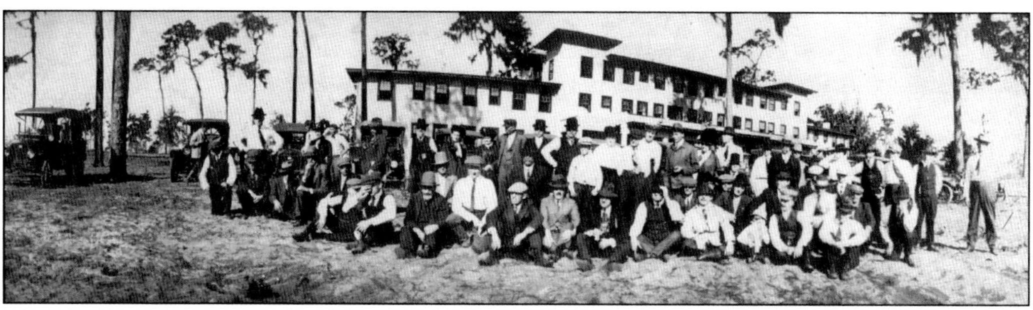

The Hotel at Howey was the first name applied to the multi-story lakeside inn that William J. Howey built for potential investors and existing grove owners. Driving on soft, rutted sand roads, past few gas pumps, travelers arrived road-weary, with many having run out of gas or broken axles. W.J. Howey was so charismatic and convincing that he drew thousands to his Hotel at Howey in 1920. (HH.)

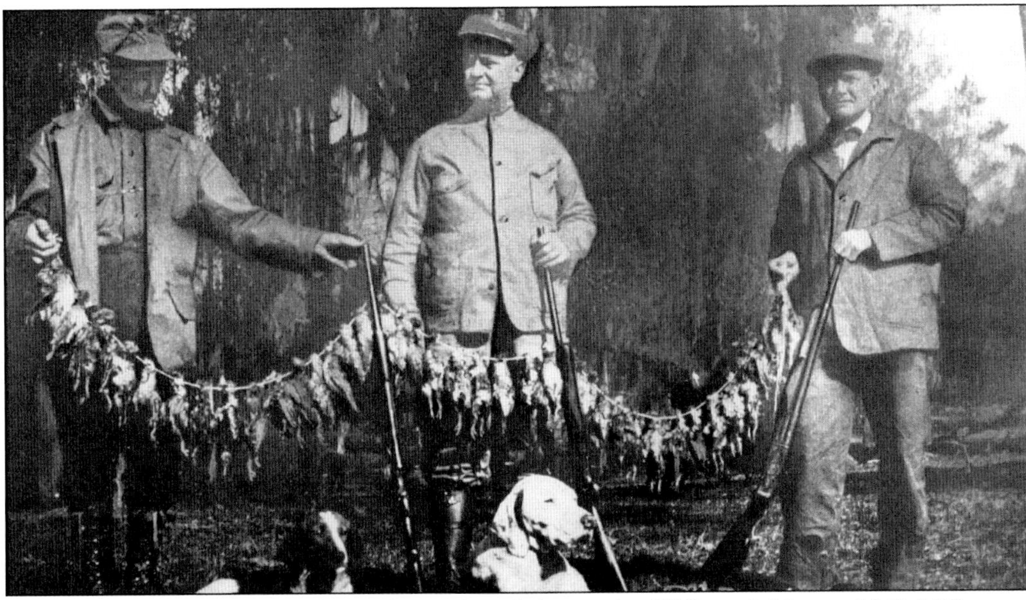

Flaunting the result of a few hours' hunt, from left to right, William J. Howey, H.G. Miller, and noted physician and surgeon Dr. William E. Bell of Terre Haute, Indiana, stand with their hunting dogs and spent shotguns. Howey lands were proven hunting grounds, a paradise for nimrods of the sport. Between patients, Bell found time to purchase 80 acres of Howey grove land and visit often for fishing and hunting. (LCHM.)

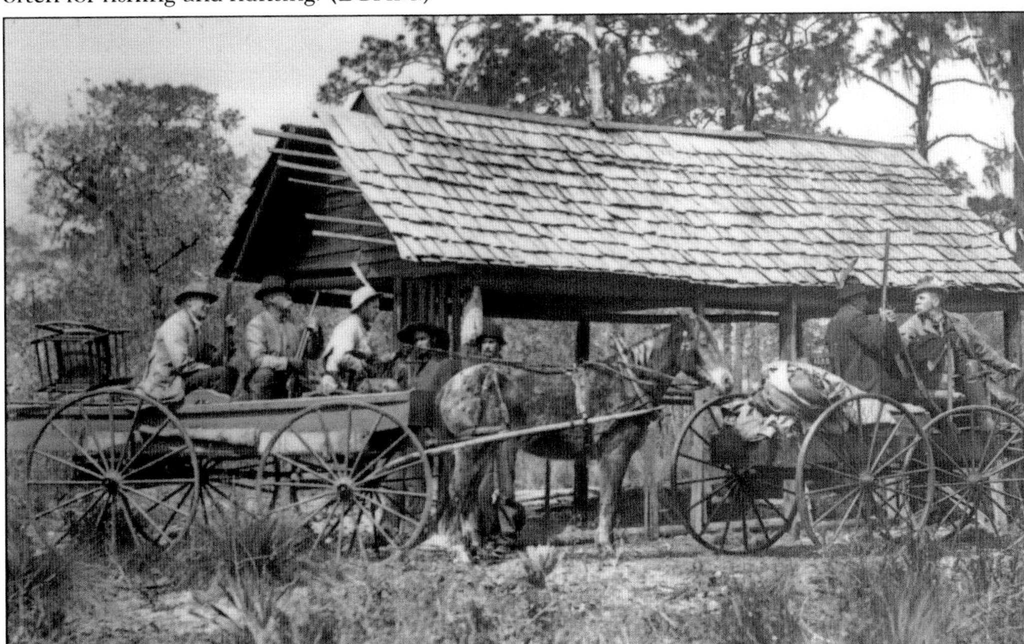

In the early days of Tent City and the town, groceries and provisions were purchased from out-of-town stores. If early inhabitants did not live a self-sustaining lifestyle that included homegrown fruits and vegetables, chickens, and cattle, they traded with neighbors or made a daylong trip to the nearest store. The alternative was to do like this band of brothers and hitch the mule to the wagon and go out and hunt dinner. (LCHM.)

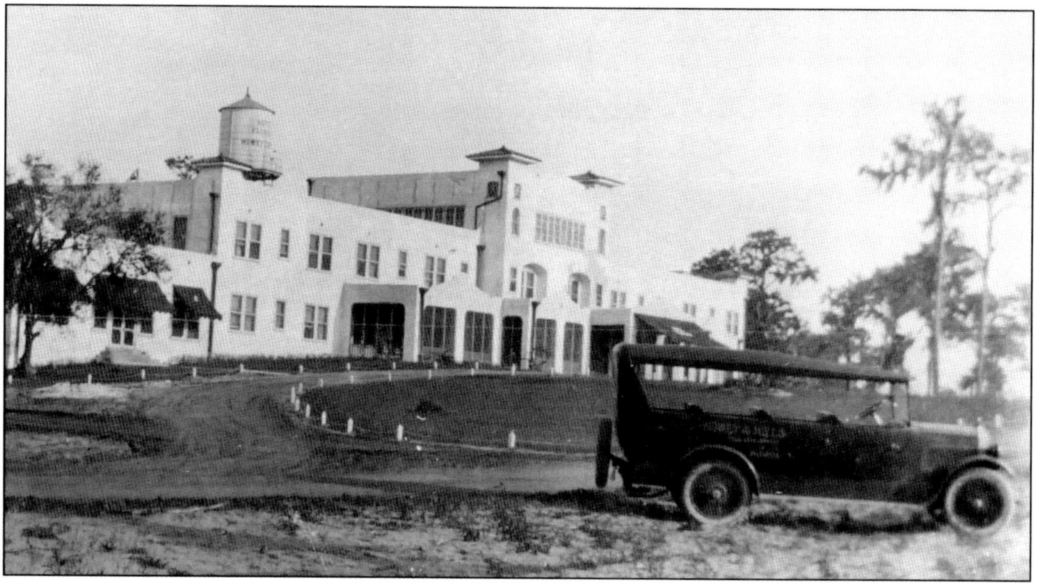

The Hotel Floridan was up and running by 1924, prepared to house and entertain potential investors in the successful Howey development. When the Howey offices were first built in the hotel's north wing (above left), visitors climbed across rafters to maneuver their way to the other side. Parked in the sandy, rutted drive, the vehicle out front displays the Howey-in-the-Hills development name on its side. The southern view of the two-story hotel shows the water tower and scaffolding (below right) for the hotel expansion. The third-floor section (center) above the lobby was the grand ballroom, where dances and special events were held until it was removed and building materials recycled for constructing the golf clubhouse. Note the construction truck in the foreground. (Both, CB.)

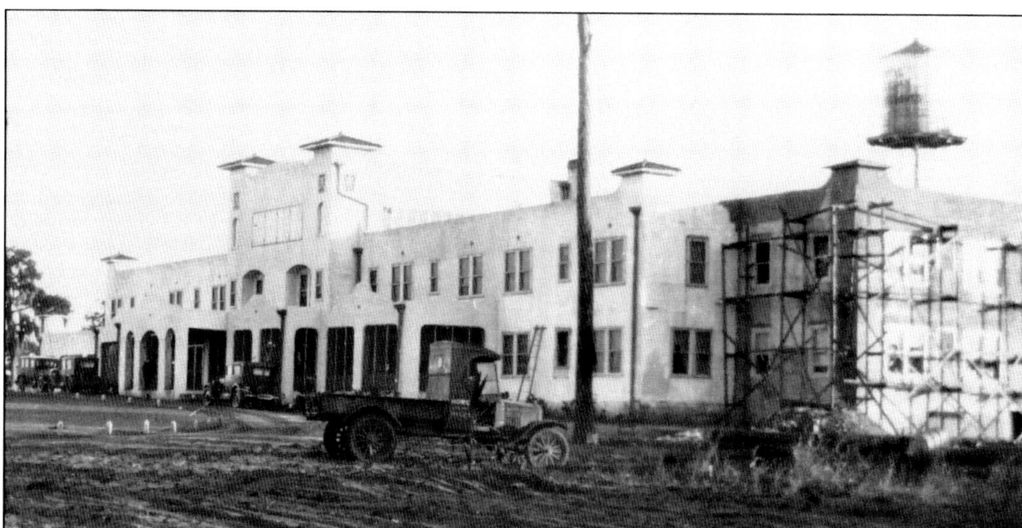

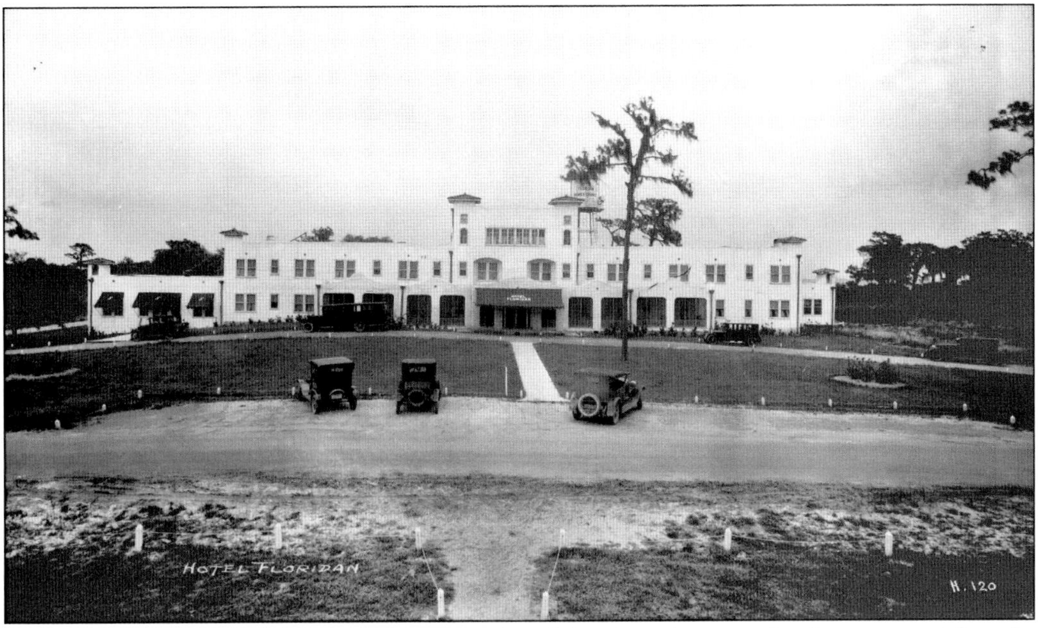

The impressive Hotel Floridan was envisioned and developed as an inland resort providing for all of the guests' needs and desires: comfortable overnight accommodations, recreation, social activities, fine dining, and plenty of fresh picked oranges and grapefruit. In front of the Howey Company office and hotel, the dust-covered automobiles are parked along the unpaved road that was later named Palm Avenue. (OCHC.)

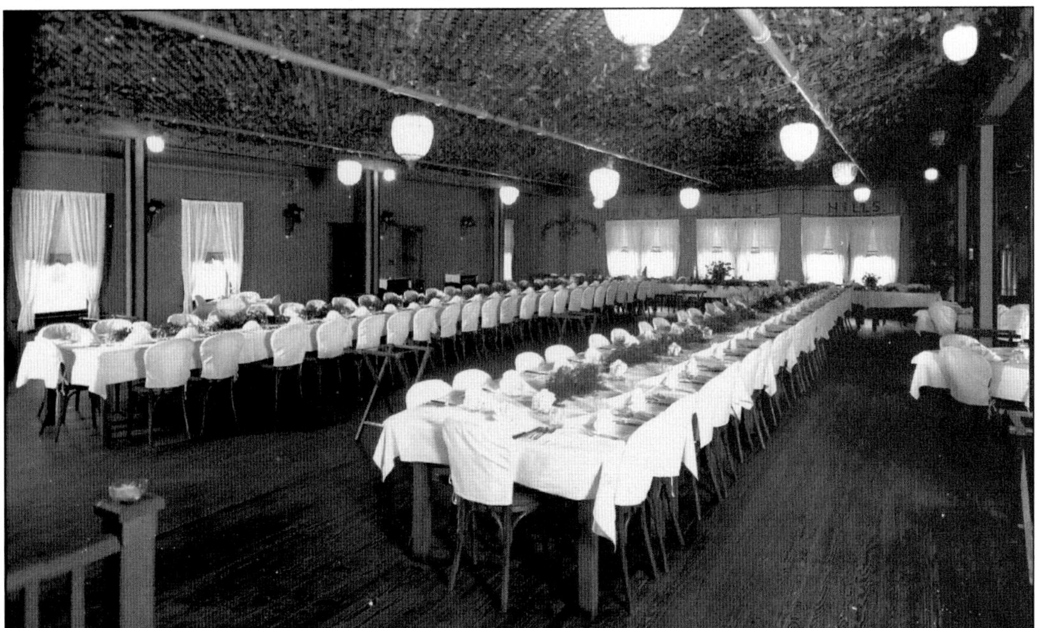

Howey's prestigious events, such as visiting politicians, golf groups, and the 1930 Home Welcoming for author Opie Read, were held in the expansive hotel banquet room. Convened from dozens of states, the team of 200-plus Howey Company sales members utilized the open room to conduct sales seminars. (OCHC.)

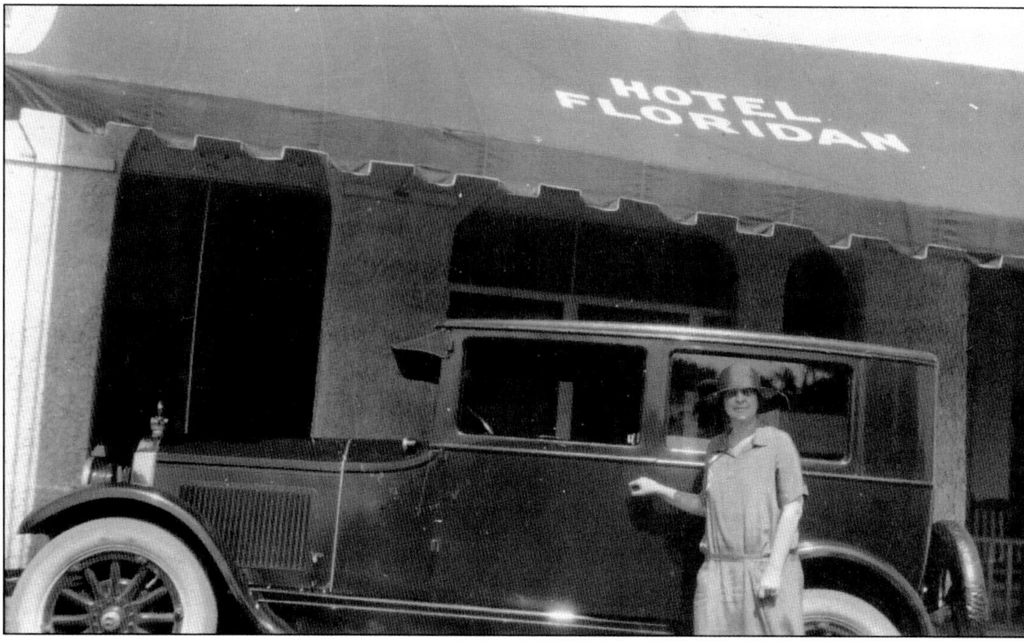

In various city newspapers, the Hotel Floridan advertised vacation getaways that included convenient train travel to nearby depots where guests were met by motor coach. This program proved successful, especially with tour operators packaging special all-inclusive eight-day vacation promotions for $106. These packages covered transportation, lodging, meals, recreation, and more. The hotel operated in the red in order to attract potential buyers to the development. (CB.)

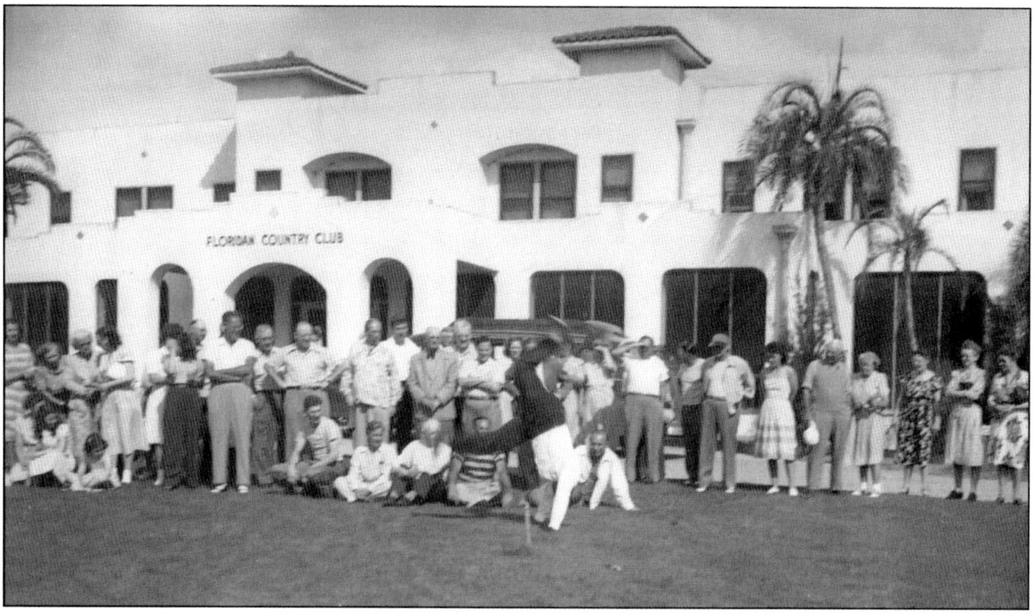

This Floridan Country Club employee entertained guests in the afternoons by walking on his hands from the lobby, down the stairs, and out to the front lawn. In 1926, hotel guests witnessed a sharpshooting exhibition by Gordon Apgar, the 13-year-old junior trap champion of the world. Apgar broke small marbles tossed in the air and then split a calling card with a rifle bullet while perched on his head. (HH.)

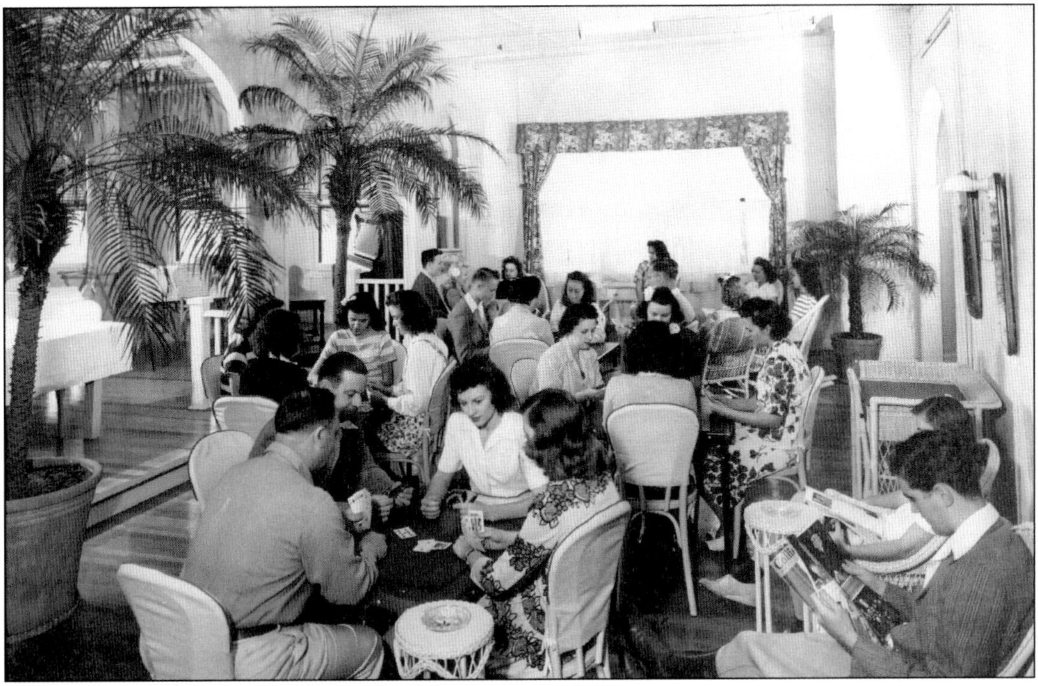

Day and night, the lobby's wicker chairs and tables set the scene for card playing, table games, or relaxing with a favorite magazine. After absorbing several of the nightly hotel lectures, the women organized "the Poker Widows' Club." Any woman was eligible to membership whose husband played poker or stayed out late at night. (HH.)

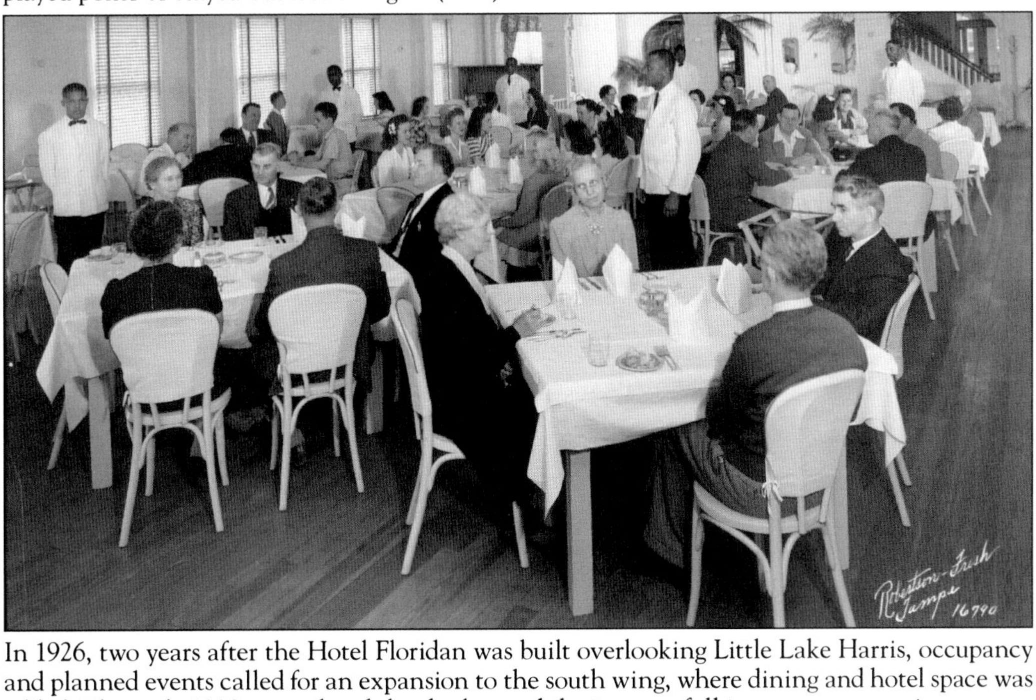

In 1926, two years after the Hotel Floridan was built overlooking Little Lake Harris, occupancy and planned events called for an expansion to the south wing, where dining and hotel space was added. The early 1920s roared with land sales, and the inn was full in season, prompting rates to be raised in 1928 from $3 nightly, all-inclusive, to $4 with very few extra charges. (HH.)

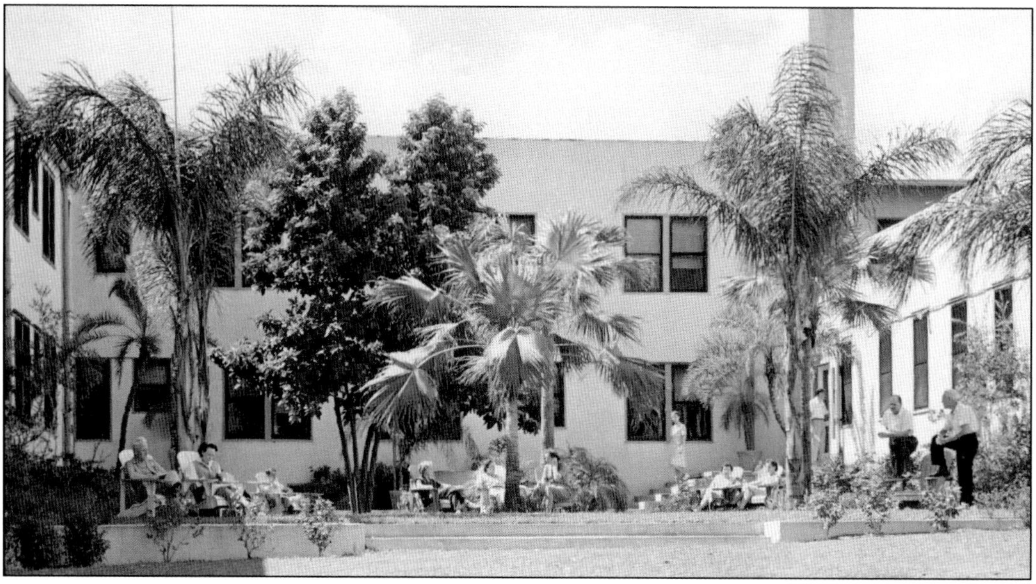

One of the best places to sit back and relax in shade or sun was the hotel's court overlooking Little Lake Harris. Here, freshly squeezed orange and grapefruit juice was served, and baskets of just-picked citrus were always available. Guests watched boating and beach activities as well as horse-drawn surreys and slow-motoring tourists catching the sights. (HH.)

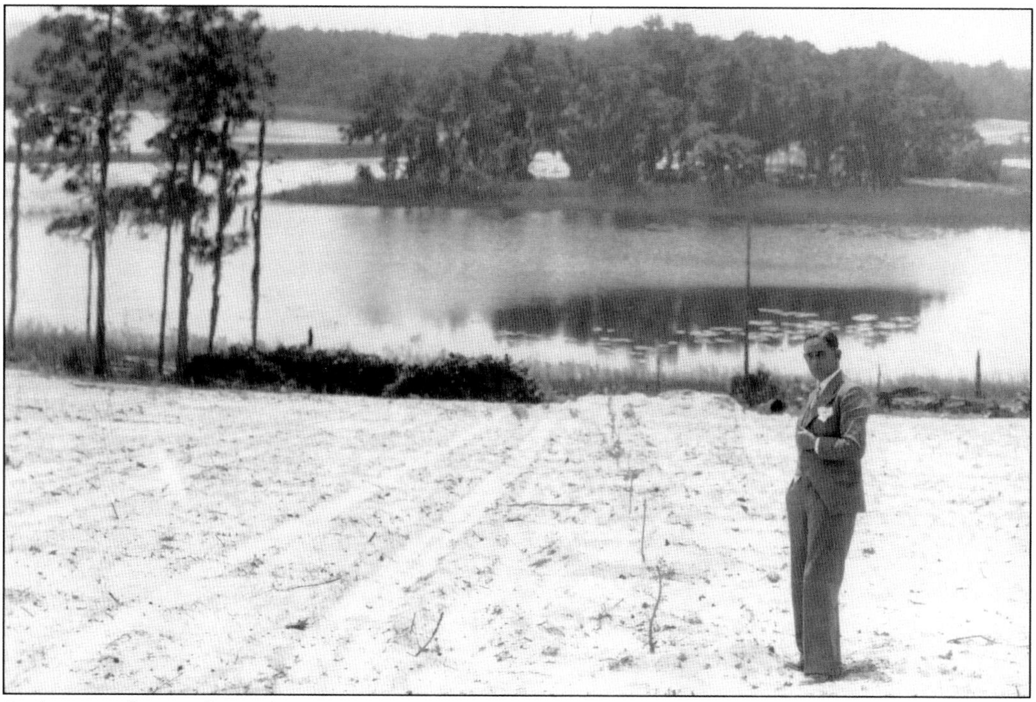

Seeking seclusion from the strain of public life, Albert E. Doman presented his wife, Madame Elisabeth Rethberg, a world-famed prima donna of New York's Metropolitan Opera Company, a 35-acre hillside Howey grove overlooking beautiful Lake Shepherd for Christmas in 1926. The German-born couple found perfect harmony in their new winter haven. Howey offered Rethberg rest and relaxation and Doman the opportunity to establish a truck farm. (LCHM.)

Seven

THE CELEBRITY RED CARPET

William J. Howey always rolled out the red carpet when celebrities accepted his invitation to enjoy his hospitality and tour the world's largest citrus empire. Traveling over velvet highways through endless rows of citrus trees laden with the perfume of millions of orange blossoms, Howey was at home behind the wheel giving private tours of his territory.

Headlining the list of Howey's celebrity invitees were former US presidents Calvin Coolidge and Herbert Hoover and state governors Ralph O. Brewster of Maine and Alfred "Alf" Landon of Kansas. Other dignitaries who frequented the town were Lord Bathurst of England; H.B. McNeal, the publisher of *Golfer's Magazine*; golf master Chick Evans; Frank and Jane Gibson Phillips of petroleum fame; numerous stage and silver screen stars; opera singers; and acclaimed physicians and research scientists.

Madame Elizabeth Rethberg, a world-famed prima donna of the Metropolitan Opera Company; Katherine Cotheal Budd, one of the first female architects of the nation and New York designer of the Howey Mansion; Madame Annie France-Harrar, a distinguished Austrian writer and scientist; and Baroness de Beckendorff were all visitors. Landscape architects M.B. Foster and A.O. de Leon not only executed projects on the grounds of the US Naval Academy in Annapolis and the White House and Capitol Building in Washington but also completed the Park surrounding the Howey Mansion as a Florida showplace in exquisite year-round bloom.

Grace Howey was a soft-spoken hostess with tremendous attention to detail. For celebrated guests, she often hosted teas, luncheons, and ballroom dances and provided midnight suppers at the mansion. Mary Grace Hastings Howey enjoyed raising roses in her garden and arranging floral centerpieces for the ballroom-sized drawing room. Between gubernatorial campaign events of 1928 and 1932, Grace and Bill Howey entertained at the hotel and mansion. Celebrities arrived by private plane, streamliner train, or car. No matter their means of travel, W.J. Howey greeted all guests, investors, and celebrities with a red carpet of welcome.

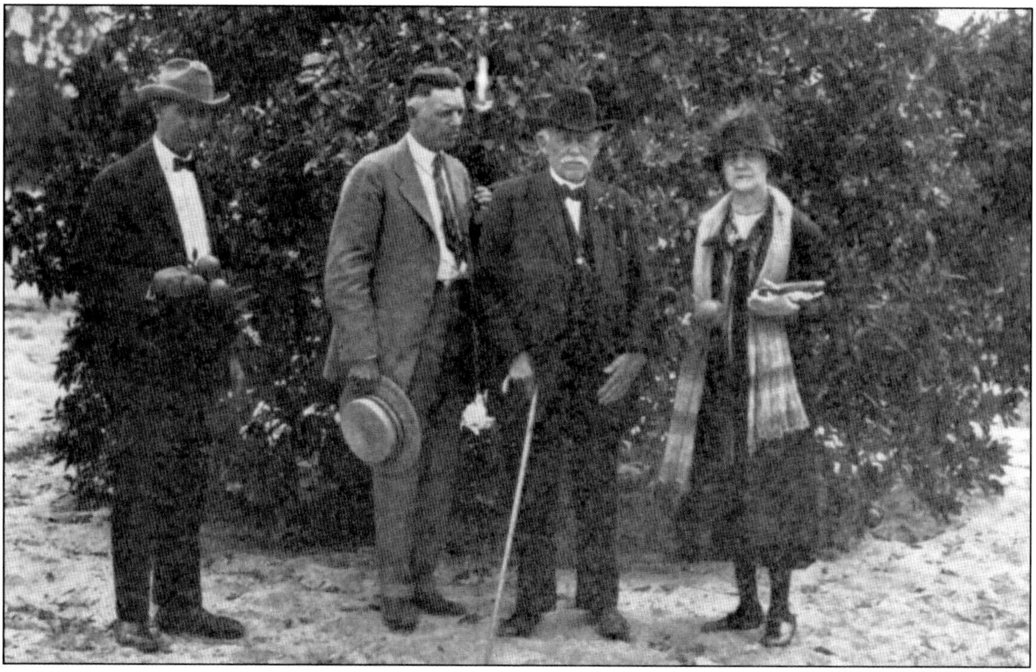

The winter months of 1926 were a buzz with activity at the Floridan Hotel in Howey-in-the-Hills, welcoming loyal guests, golf groups, and celebrities. Touring the grove on what must have been one of the cooler days are Dr. George T. and Phoebe Harding, parents of the late president of the United States Warren G. Harding. With favorite straw hat in hand, W.J. Howey acted as honored tour guide. (MIR.)

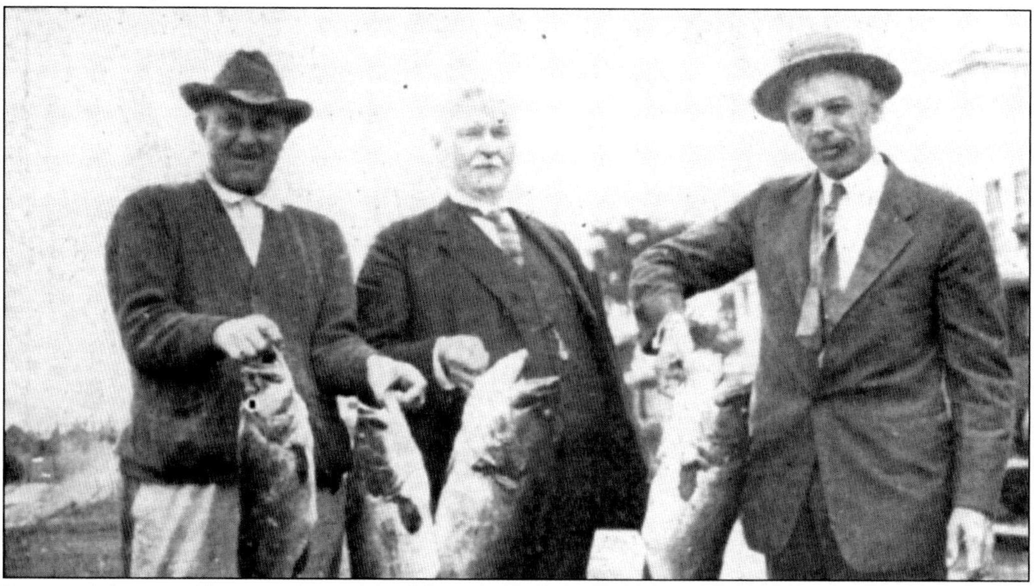

Pioneer fishing tackle manufacturer and famous angler Joe Pflueger (center) of Akron, Ohio, hailed Howey's lakes as America's best bass fishing grounds following an April 1926 fishing expedition. Pflueger brought numerous new baits to test in the company of C.E. Baxter (left), the local Izaak Walton League president. After landing a 14.75-pound black bass, measuring 27 inches long, Pflueger named the victorious bait after his cigar-smoking host, W.J. Howey (right). (LCHM.)

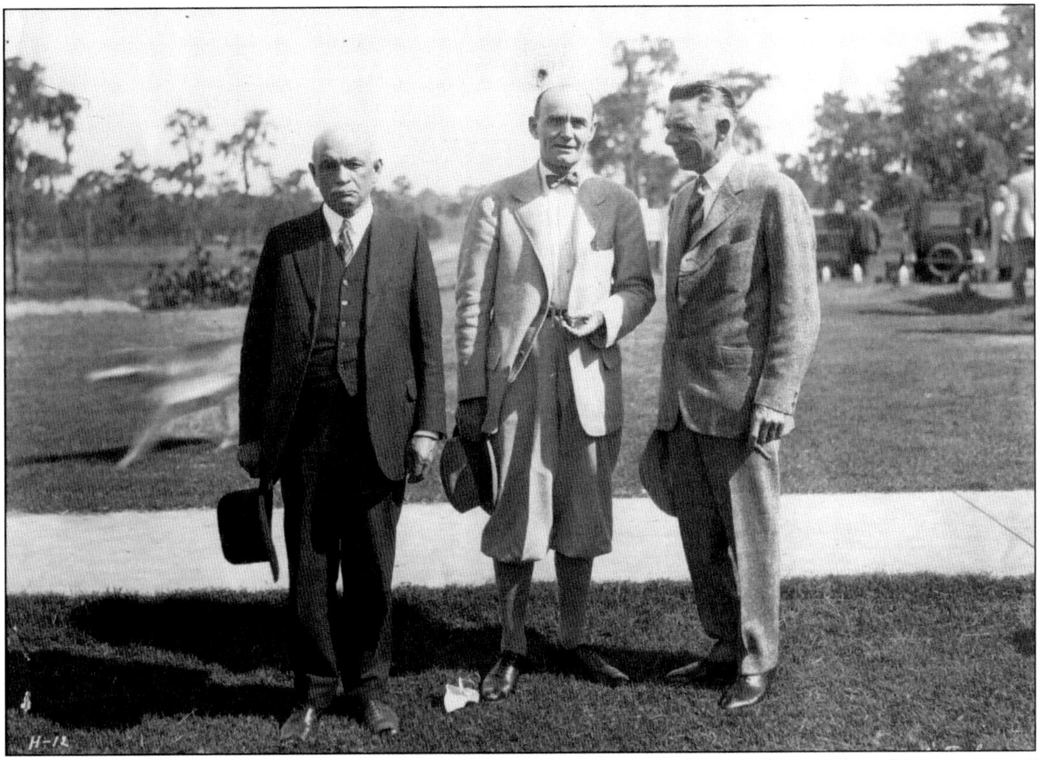

Wearing knickers, William M. Jardine (center), US secretary of agriculture, placed his stamp of approval upon Florida's agricultural practices following his May 1926 Howey tract inspection. In proportion, he stated that growth would follow the wealth made out of soil, instead of first selling lots. W.J. Howey (right) and the stern Charles S. Barrett (left), the American Farm Union president, agreed with the cabinet officer that quality fruit and cooperative marketing were vital. (HH.)

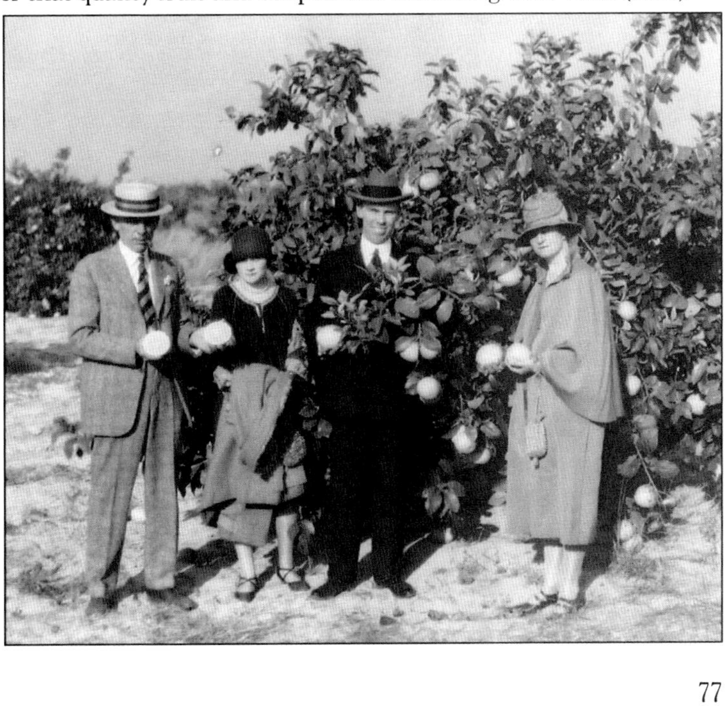

W.J. and Grace Howey (left) hosted 160 representatives of Maine, headed by Gov. Ralph O. Brewster and Dorothy Brewster, on February 13, 1926. The Maine to Southland Pilgrimage was organized by Maine's citizens to acquaint Southerners with its resources as an industrial, agricultural, and summer resort state. The delegation embarked on a 34-mile tour through the Howey citrus tract aboard Howey motor coaches before attending a banquet at the Floridan Hotel. (OCHC.)

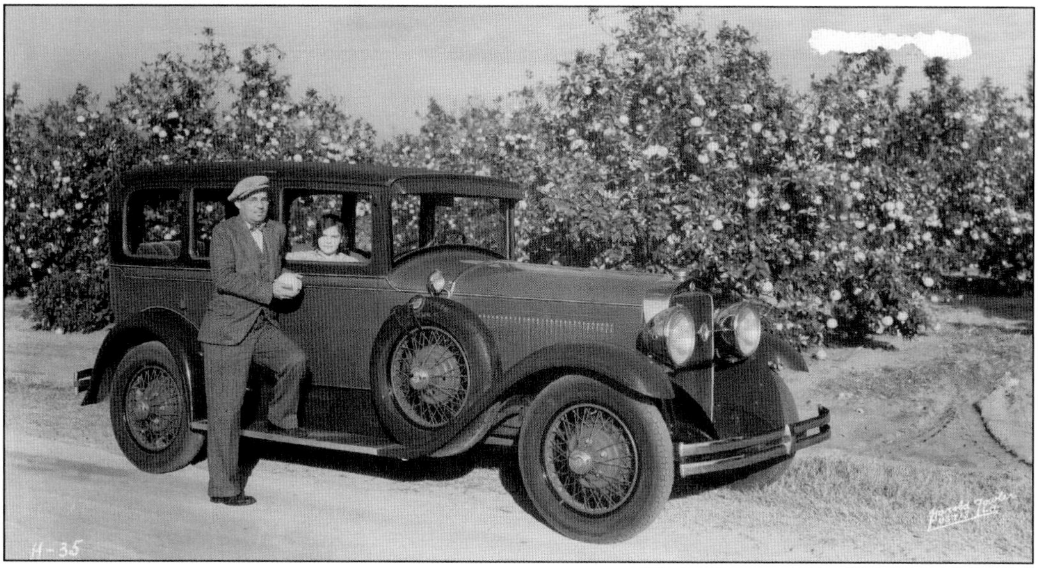

Too far to walk and too important to miss, Lucy Johnson's father put on his three-piece suit and donned his favorite cap to chauffeur his daughter to Howey, where she had an assignment of presidential proportion. She was selected to handpick grapefruit for future president of the United States Herbert Hoover. No prouder task had been assigned. This special occasion called for the best dress, friendliest of smiles, and a motorcar that shined. (HH.)

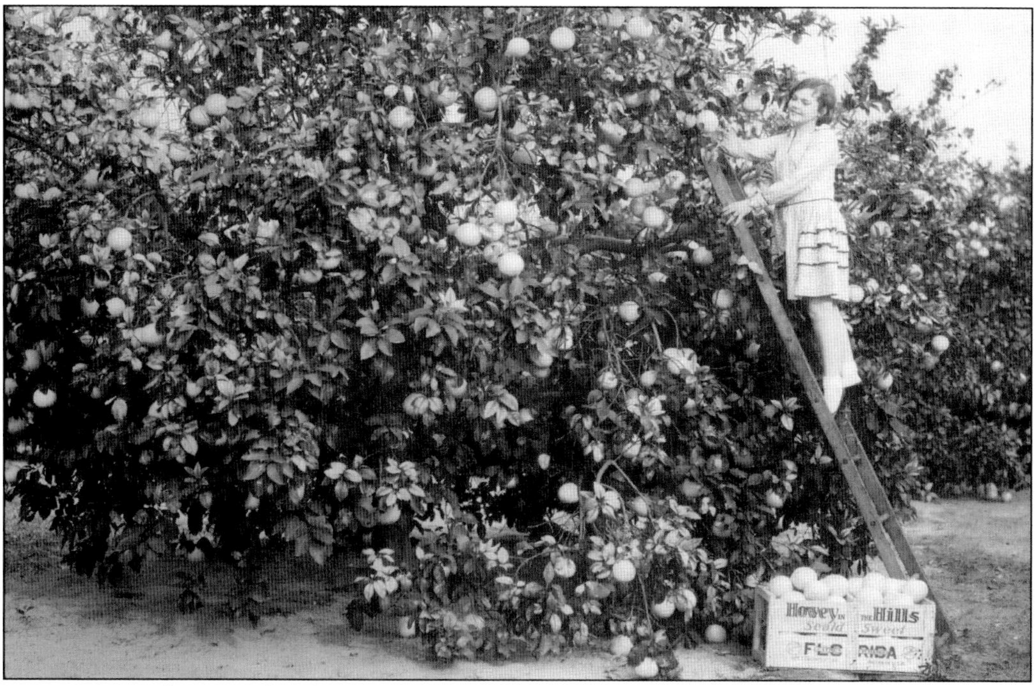

Dainty Lucy Johnson, a local schoolgirl from nearby Eustis, was handpicked to climb the rungs of the wooden ladder and pinch the finest Howey grapefruit fresh off the tree for shipment to a very special customer in Miami. J.C. Penney, at whose south Florida estate President-elect Herbert Hoover sojourned in 1929, ordered a large consignment of citrus from the area growers' association. (HH.)

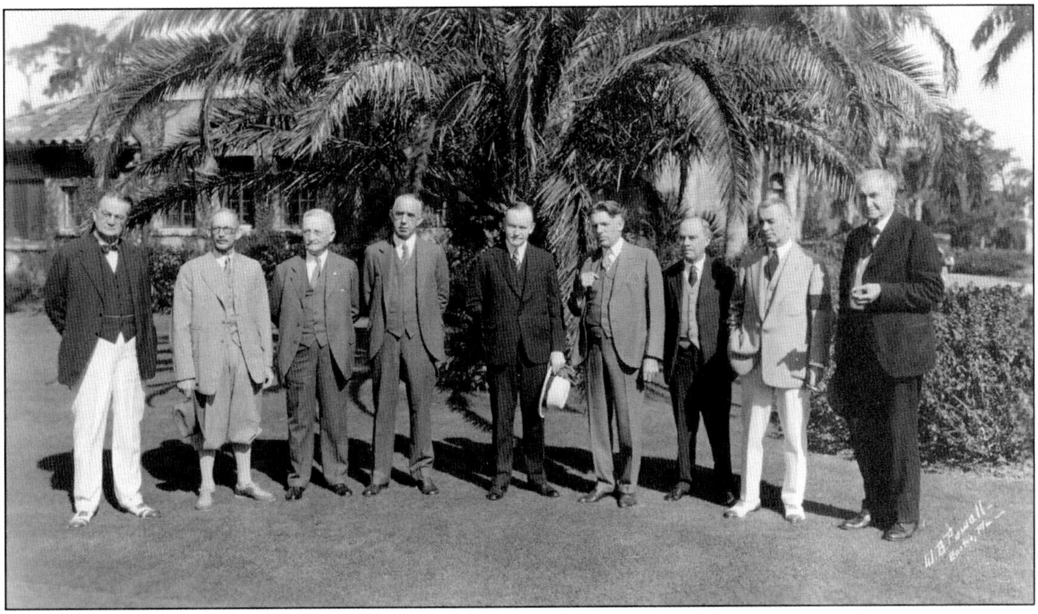

Calvin Coolidge, who succeeded Warren G. Harding as president of the United States, toured the extensive Howey properties, sauntered through the fruit packinghouse, inspected the juice canning plant, sucked an orange, posed for pictures, ate squab at a Howey home noonday stag luncheon, and beamed his approval of it all. In February 1930, "Silent Cal" Coolidge stands white hat in hand, with W.J. Howey to the right of him. (HH.)

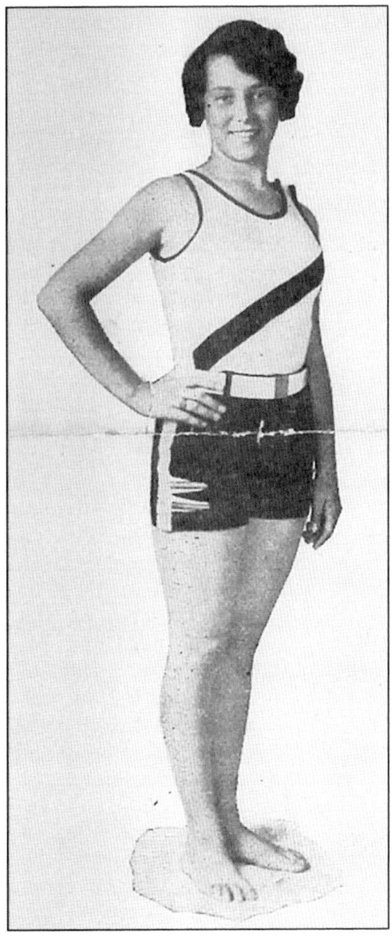

Lake County's Florence Smock was presented in Chicago as the Nation's 4-H Club Champion Health Girl for 1930. Popular and modest, the 17-year-old local Eustis High School athlete ate Howey grapefruit daily, exercised routinely, and never smoked, danced, or applied lipstick. Following graduation, Smock planned to attend the all-girls' college at Tallahassee, now Florida State University, to specialize in physical education. Smock's figure and health were envied by all. (HH.)

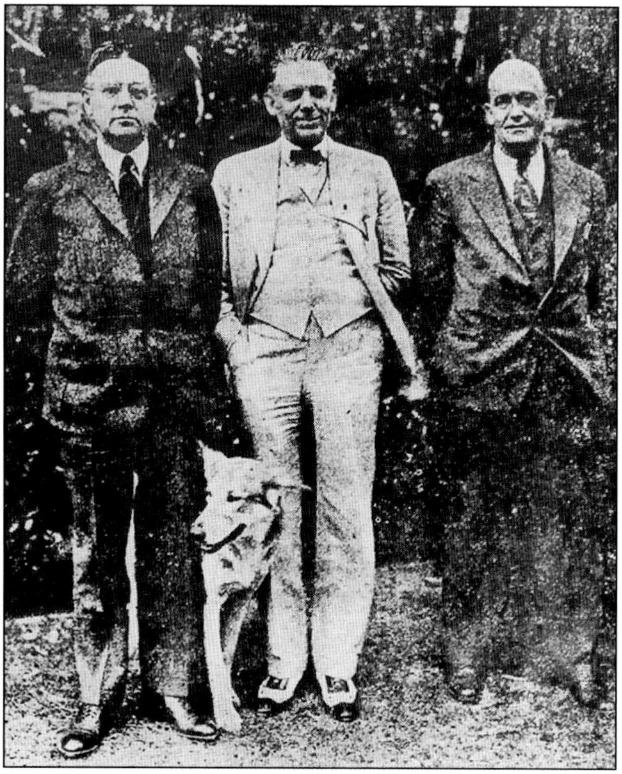

Postmaster General Walter F. Brown and his wife, Katherin Hafer Brown, were graciously entertained at the Howey Mansion during a May 1931 Florida vacation. From left to right, the US postmaster general; Bill Howey, wearing the light colored suit; and E.L. Pryor, a Tampa chairman of the Republican State Committee, pose with Mr. Howey's four-legged sidekick Big Boy, who warmed up to the cabinet officer like everyone else in Howey-in-the-Hills. (HH.)

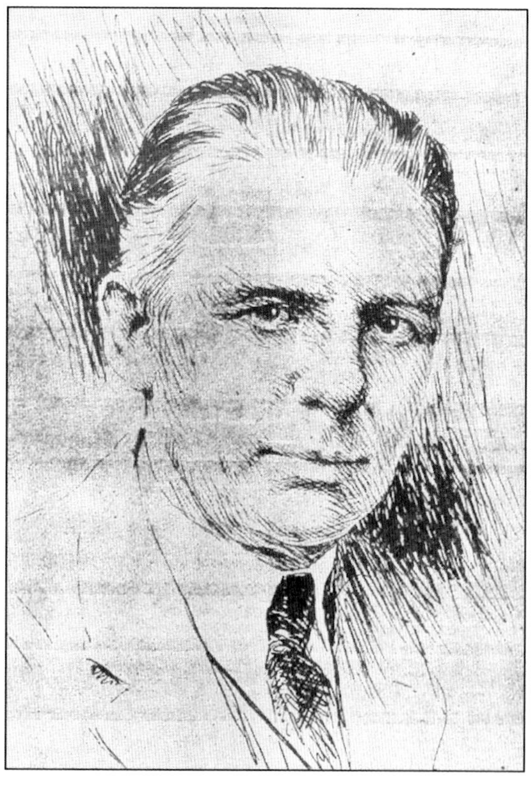

Dwight C. Sturges, an illustrator for the *Christian Science Monitor* who occupied an exalted position in the realm of art, executed this etching of W.J. Howey in 1931. Sturges, who was born in Boston and became a pupil of Cowls Art School in Boston, received numerous lifetime achievement awards. Here and abroad, in private collections and in fine art institutes and museums, Sturges's etchings are coveted strokes of genius. (HH.)

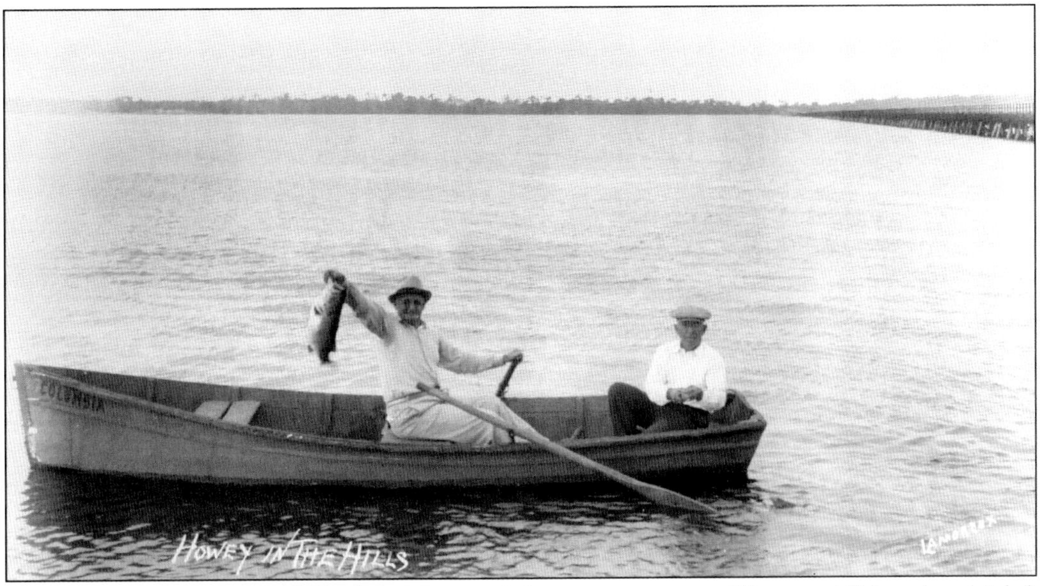

Town resident Jacob Wolfe (right) convinced former governor of Kansas Alf Landon (right) that bass fishing would be effortless on Little Lake Harris on November 11, 1938. Posing for the camera with his catch held high, Landon, a satisfied angler, rowed back to his Floridan Hotel accommodations telling tall tales of the one that got away. To the right is the wooden short-route bridge linking Howey and Astatula. (HH.)

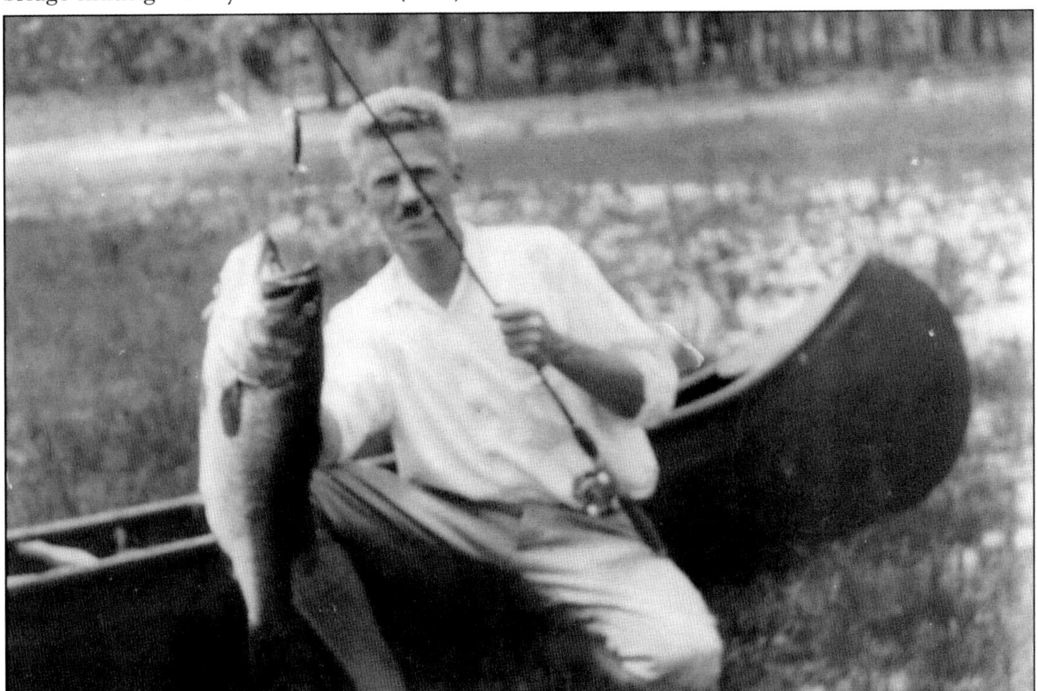

David M. Newell, a well-known artist and writer on outdoor topics, caught this fine black bass in the Howey lakes one winter day in 1929. The ink had just dried on Newell's new children's book of verses on American animals before coming to Howey for a well-deserved afternoon in a canoe. (LCHM.)

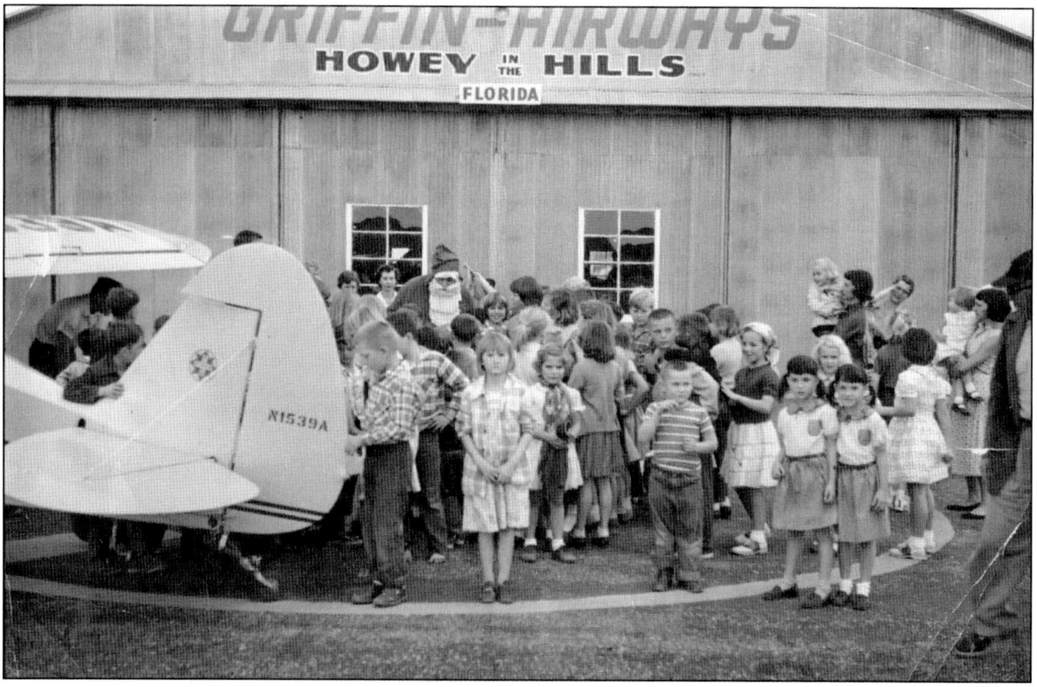

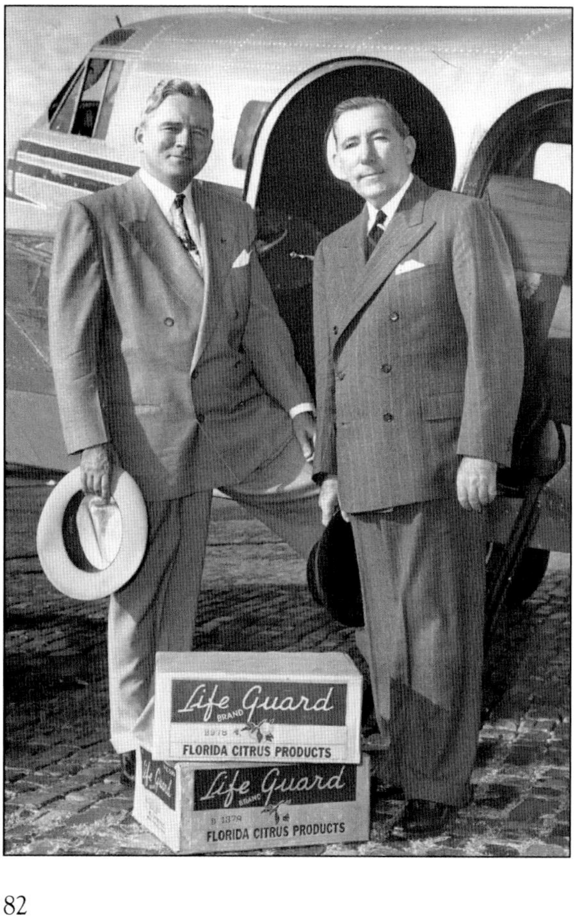

Of all the arrivals witnessed at Griffin Airways, none was as exciting as Santa's in the early 1950s. Wally Schanz, C.V. Griffin's personal pilot, flew the jolly man, played by teacher Sam Commander, to see Ruth Sullivan's fourth-grade Howey Elementary class. Keeping an eye on the twin girls, Kerry Wrobel is pictured slightly to the right of the center of the photograph. In the background, Rose Livingston (third from right) is seen holding her daughter Aileen, and her sister Wilma Livingston Dell (far right) is pictured carrying Becky. (GLT.)

When Fuller Warren (left) ran for governor of Florida in the 1948 election, C.V. Griffin was campaign manager and reportedly covered one third of Warren's campaign costs. As the elected transportation governor, Warren expedited the construction of the State Road 19 Memorial Bridge over Lake Harris and the expansion of County Road 27 near Howey. Warren and Sen. Claude Pepper (right) brought Life Guard brand juice back to Tallahassee. (LCHM.)

Eight

Now That's Entertainment

At Howey-in-the-Hills, near Orlando, in a fairyland of lakes, groves, and rolling countryside, the answer to the vacationer's dream of "fun and sun" laid waiting to be rediscovered. By the 1940s, the establishment was hopping again and advertised at less-than-prewar rates. This delightful resort, never publicized as a glittering spa, was conducted on the pattern of a private club. The 65-room guesthouse on the shore of Little Lake Harris was spacious and carefully furnished for comfort and rich living. Here, guests found niceties that made the perfect vacation: attentive service of a thoughtful management, a cuisine for which the club was justly famous, and interesting, congenial members. Life was easy and informal at the club, and evening dress was out for the duration.

Vacationers could occupy every minute outside if desired. They could partake in a round of golf on the tricky nine-hole course, a daily canter on one of the club's fine Saddlebred horses, a secluded pool of wily bass, a cruise on Florida's inland waterways, and many other activities, or they could just bask in glorious sunshine on the sundeck.

And best of all, at the end of a stay, guests were not faced with a lengthy bill for "extras." With exception of caddy fees, fishing bait, and gratuities, the original payment took care of every expense because a full Floridan Country Club membership was extended to each guest arriving on the all-expense arrangement.

The land cruise plan promoted eight full days, including transportation and meals aboard deluxe streamliners departing daily from New York, for $106.75, or if departing from Baltimore, Philadelphia, or Washington, the amount of $7, $3.25, or $9 was deducted accordingly.

The Country Club was promoted as an exclusive resort that was located against the background of beautiful hills and lakes and among the world's finest citrus groves. The idea behind attracting and entertaining a younger set with steady income to the hotel was a greater likelihood of converting a land sale.

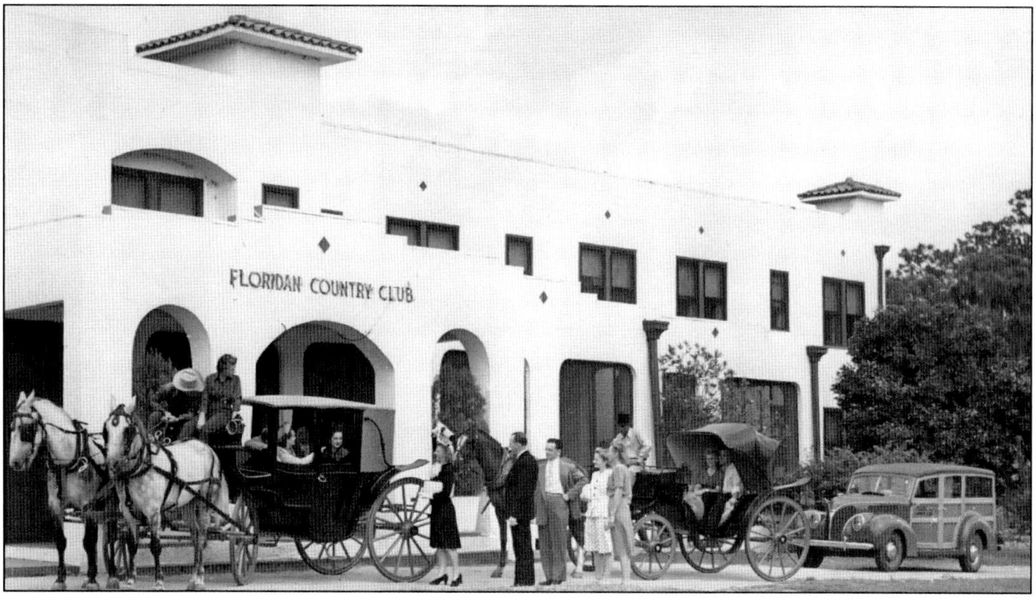

The hotel maintained an entire fleet of authentic horse-drawn wagons, surreys, and coaches, which were truly unique for the resort. Guests were swept away at a leisurely pace along the lakefront or Palm Avenue, from the Floridan Country Club at the town's southern entry point northward to the golf clubhouse. The wood-sided station wagon takes third place behind the horses that wait patiently on guests and their transportation needs. (HH.)

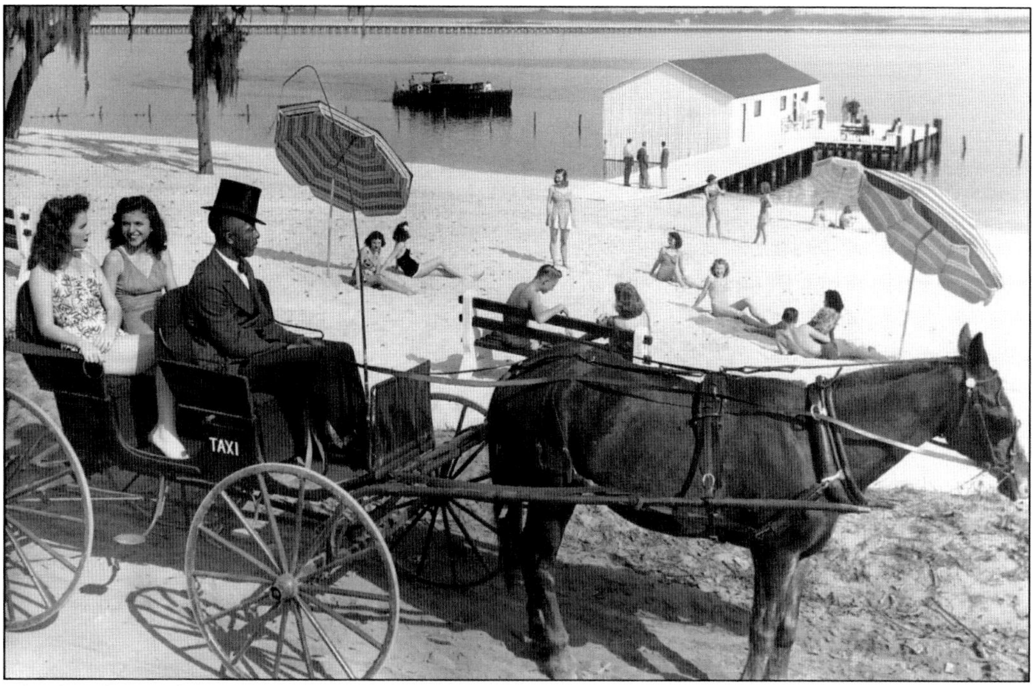

This beach taxi driver was only too happy to don his top hat and take guests to the Floridan Country Club beach and boathouse. In the 1940s, this was a typical scene of guests soaking up the sun in a variety of ways. Captains of larger boats waited for Charlie Ard to hand-crank the wooden bridge's middle section open in order to access the other side of Little Lake Harris. (LCHM.)

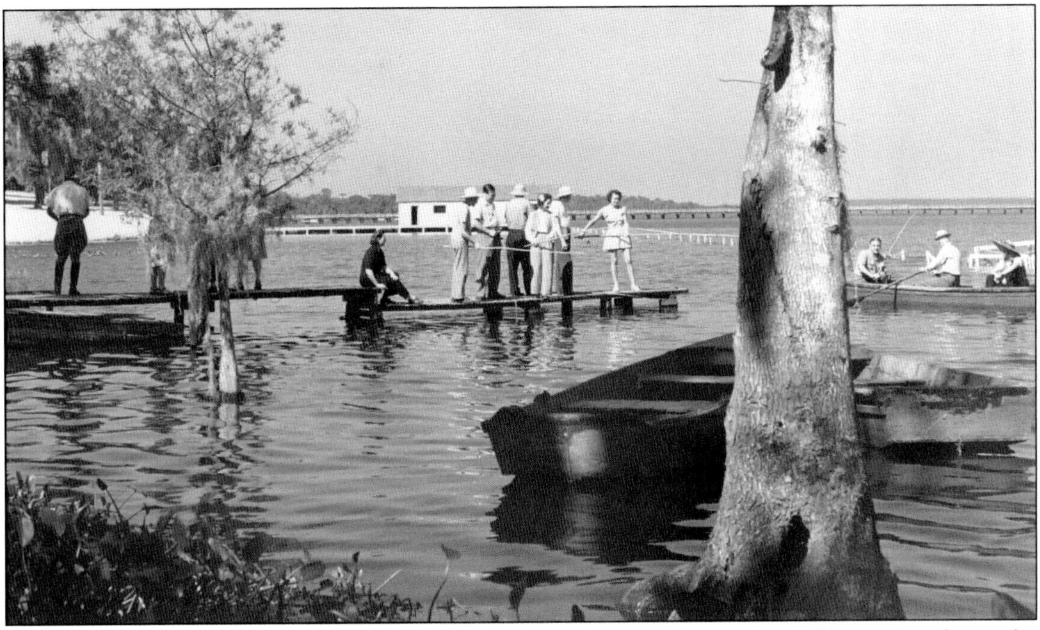

The use of fishing boats and tackle was included in the hotel's daily rate, with an extra charge for bait only. This Lake Harris chain of lakes was a fisherman's paradise, brimming with black bass and other local fish that never failed to be tempted by hook and reel. Special fish fries and hush puppy parties held near the wooden bridge were favorite outdoor dinners among guests. (HH.)

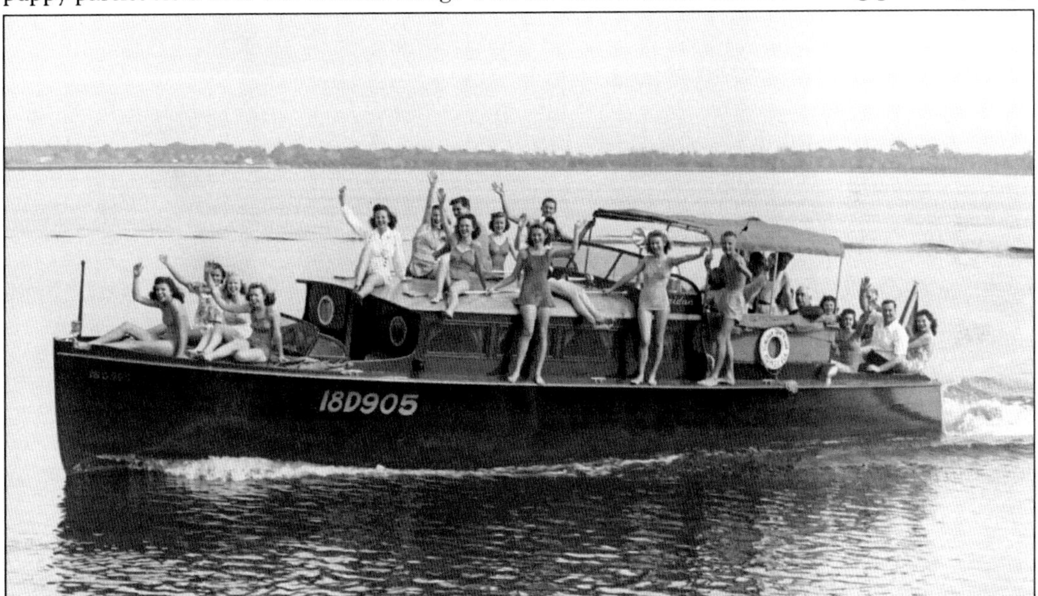

C.V. Griffin stored his personal cabin cruiser in the beachfront boathouse at the Floridan Country Club until he sold it to the hotel for guests to cruise the tropical waterways of Little Lake Harris and beyond. The girls cover the deck of this ship, with only a few good men aboard. While afloat, sightseeing in a bathing suit was the fashion for bringing home that souvenir golden tan. (HH.)

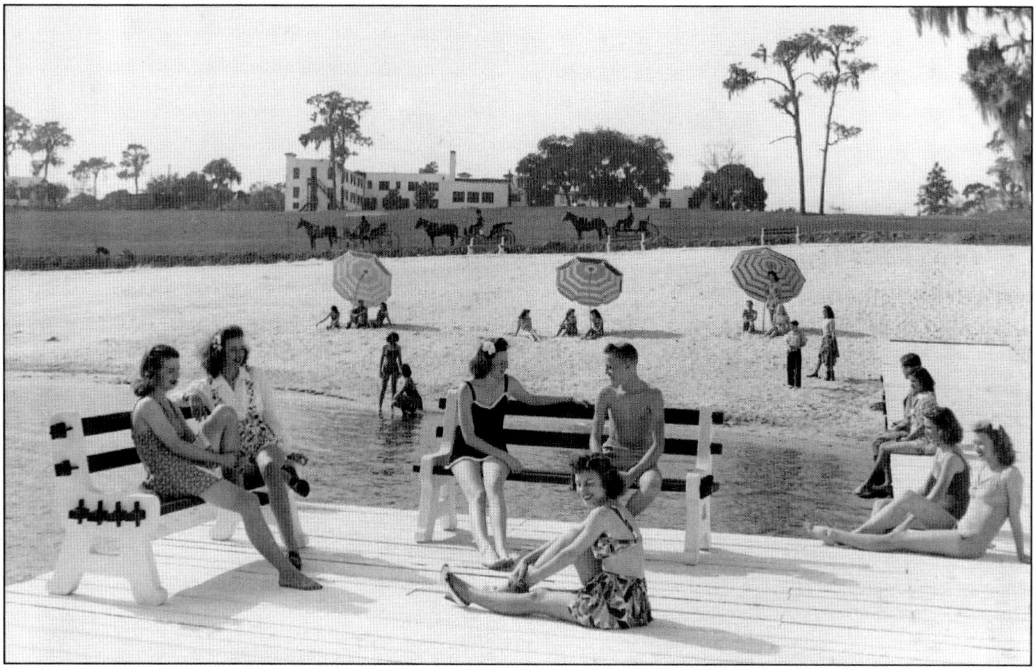

When gas, batteries, and tires were rationed, the horse-and-buggy taxi operation of the Floridan Country Club was considered patriotic. An advertisement in the *Philadelphia Inquirer* dated May 21, 1944, offered a "honeymoon package" that included a round-trip railroad fare from Philadelphia with reserved streamliner seating, transfers to the club, room and meals, swimming, golf, riding, and fishing for $103.50 for eight days. (HH.)

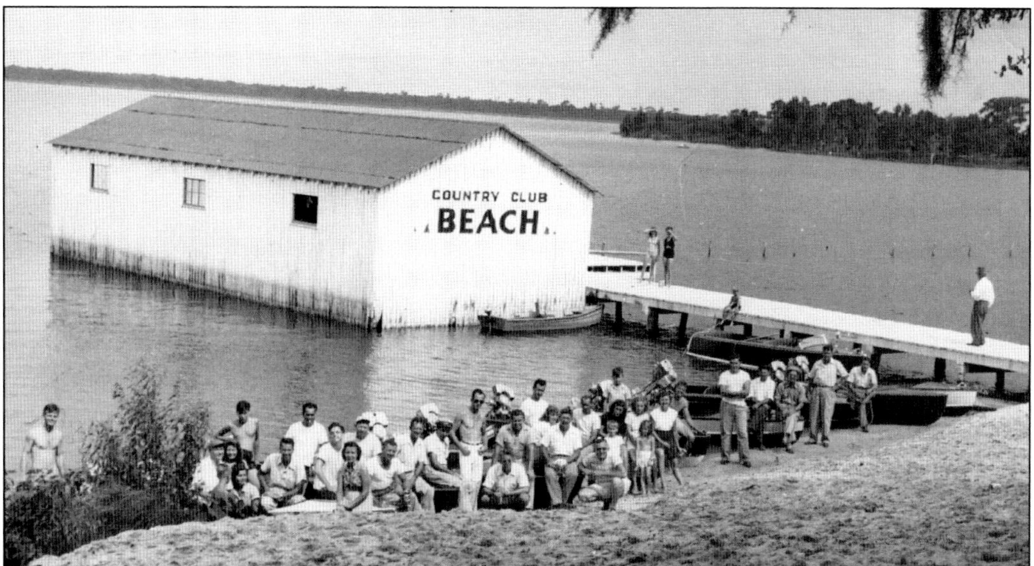

Young speedboaters gathered on weekends at the boathouse for racing the smooth waters of Little Lake Harris. During the Howey Academy years, boys' crew team members rowed daily, in addition to practicing cross-country and doing plenty of exercises. In 1968, the academy's nine-man team represented Florida among the top 38 high school teams at the Schoolboy Rowing Association meet on Philadelphia's Schuylkill River. (HH.)

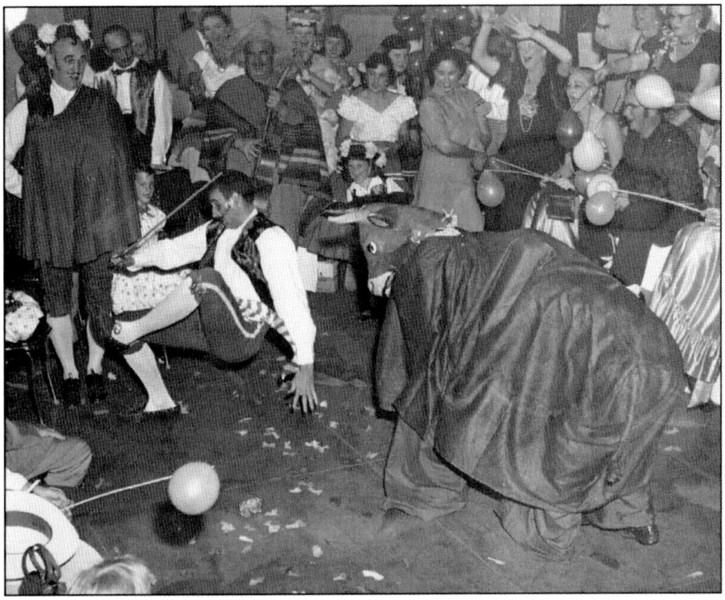

According to issues from the 1950s *Howey-Hi-Lites* club newsletter, Mickey, the club's zealous social director, kept guests and residents busy and laughing. On costume night, it was anyone's guess who might appear in make-up and what character they would impersonate. On this evening's program, the bull and bullfighters were out to entertain. One Howey resident especially tickled by it all was little Ginny Livingston (behind the bull with flowers in her hair). (GLT.)

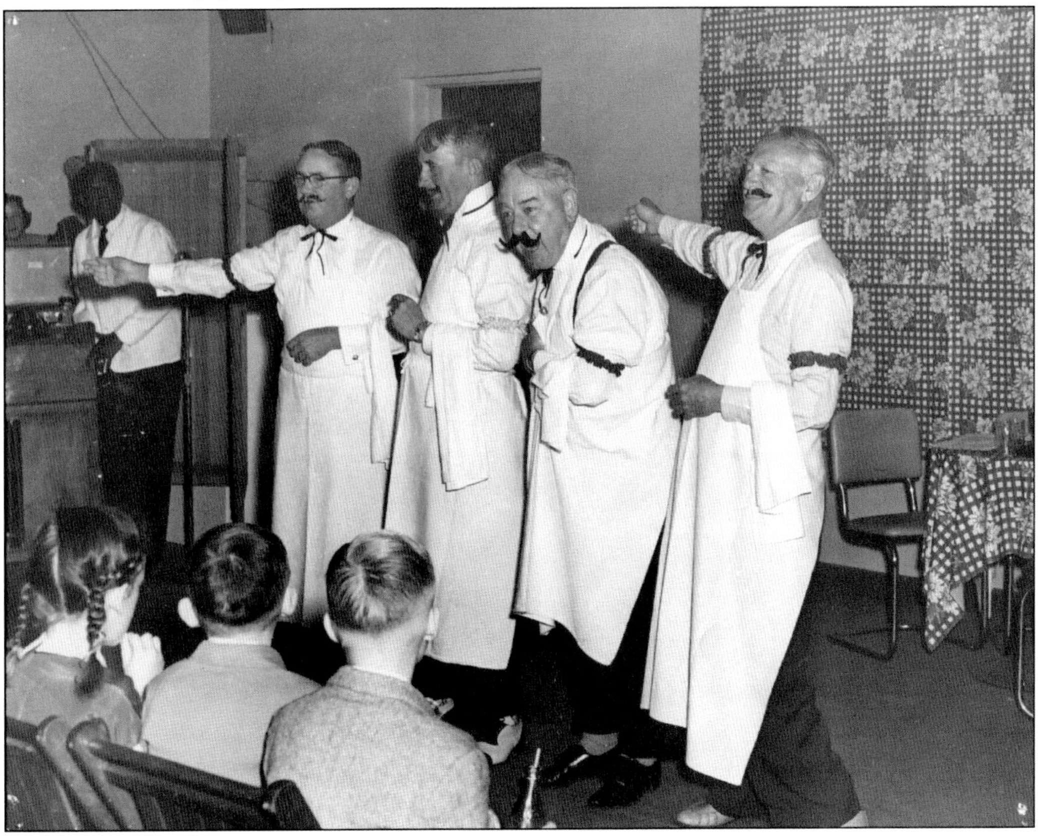

This barbershop quartet was a cast of characters. Standing on the left, Howard Matthews may have sung for his supper on this particular night, but by day, he worked for Peter VanEss's grocery store. When he made home deliveries, children liked to follow along with him from house to house. (AS.)

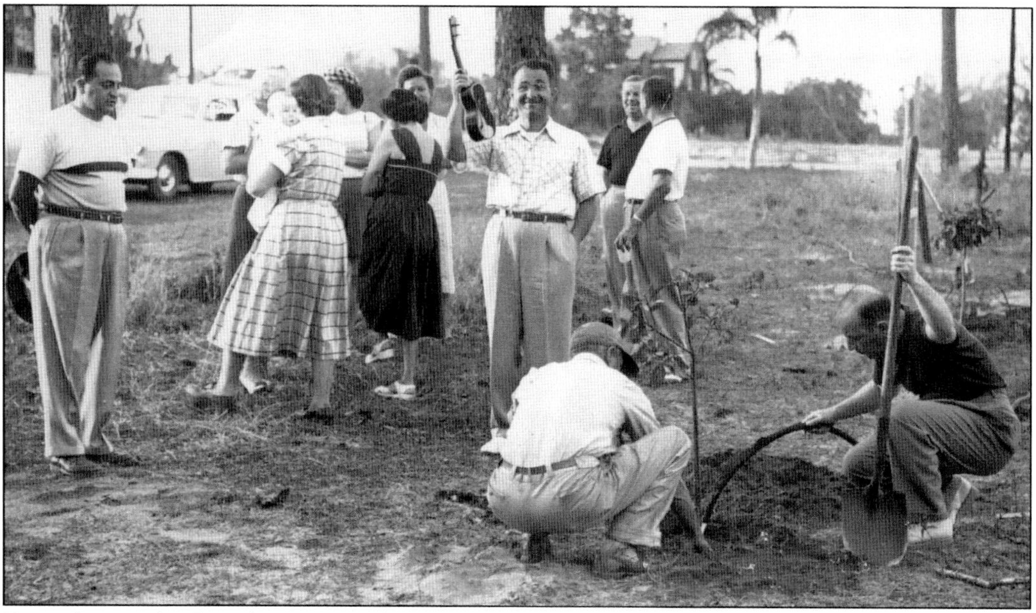

Even planting backyard citrus trees became a social activity for winter residents of Howey. Many town residents grew vegetables in their yards, keeping their homes supplied with fresh produce. Holding a ukulele, the man overseeing the planting prepares to lead the group in song. (HH.)

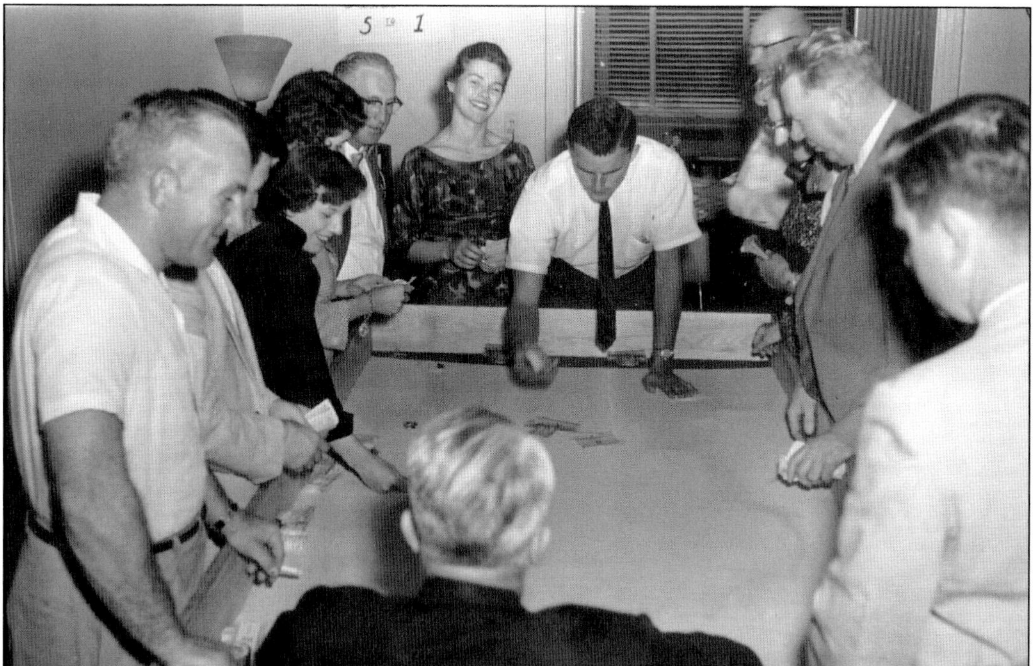

In the 1950s, casino nights were popular with club members and Howey residents. C.V. Griffin is seated with his back to the camera watching his son Rodney handle the bet while Howey police chief Walter Notz (left) watches and Ann Linn Griffin stands beside her husband, Rodney. Howey evolved as a model of small-town America, where residents were so close-knit that everyone was known on a first-name basis. (AS.)

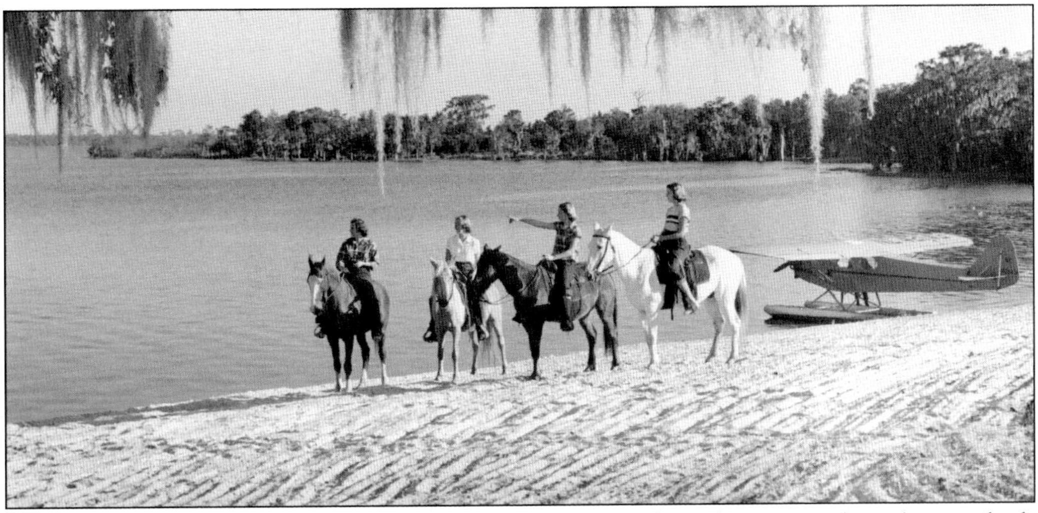

The Little Lake Harris beachfront was popular with sunbathers, boaters, and seaplanes, which flew guests to the Howey hotel. Little Lake Harris was a favorite direct route by boat between water-connected cities Leesburg and Howey. The only time this was interrupted was during the days of war restriction. Horses made getting around town fun for these young ladies, including Sue (left) and Mary Jane Taylor (second from left). (HH.)

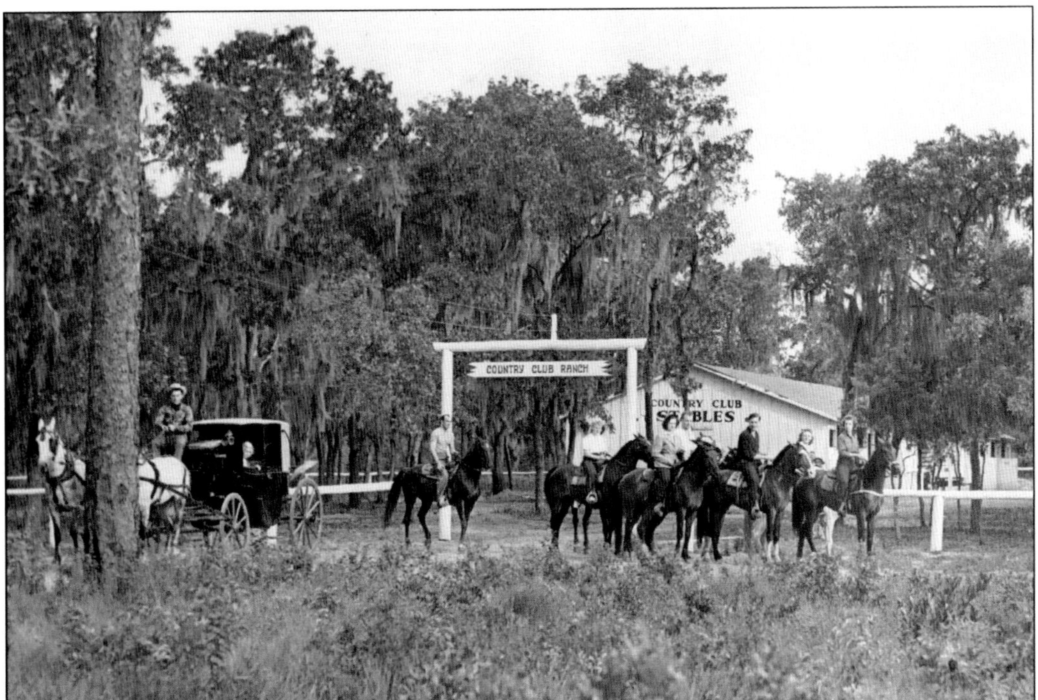

The Floridan Country Club dude ranch, run by Florida cowboy and accomplished horseman Red Simpson, became the preferred guest amenity. It offered a stable of 45 fine Saddlebred horses for surrey rides, trail rides, foxhunts, rodeos, and lessons. Scenic trail rides meandered for miles through the Howey Company's vast citrus groves over hills and past lakes. Simpson was known for his ability to put novice horse riders at ease. (HH.)

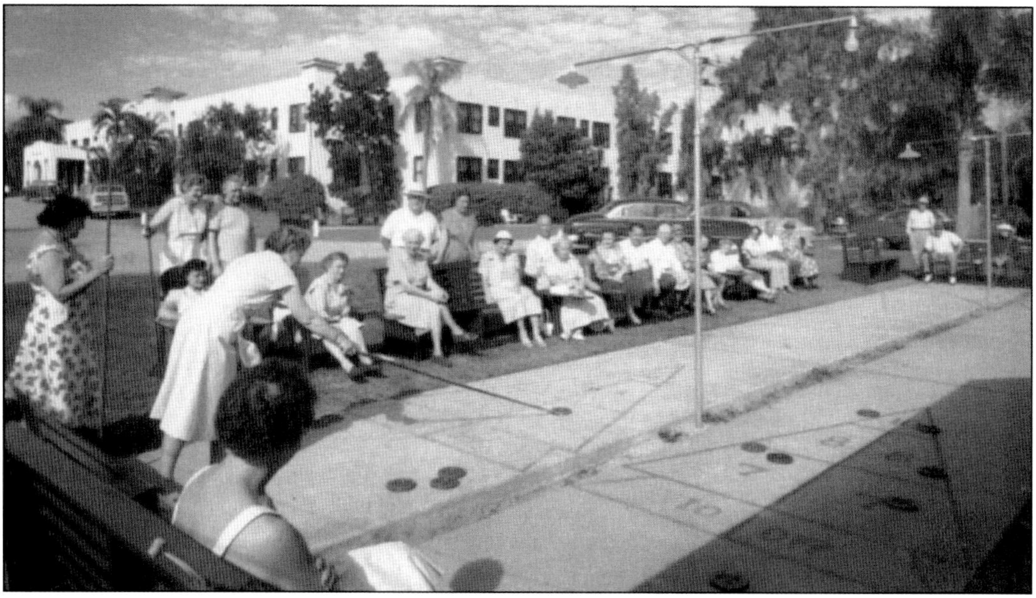

The shuffleboard courts were adjacent to the outdoor bowling lanes at Howey's Amusement Club and were illuminated for evening play. The price for shuffleboard was 5¢ per game. At one time, shuffleboard was so popular with residents in town that a much larger set of courts was built adjacent to the town hall. (CB.)

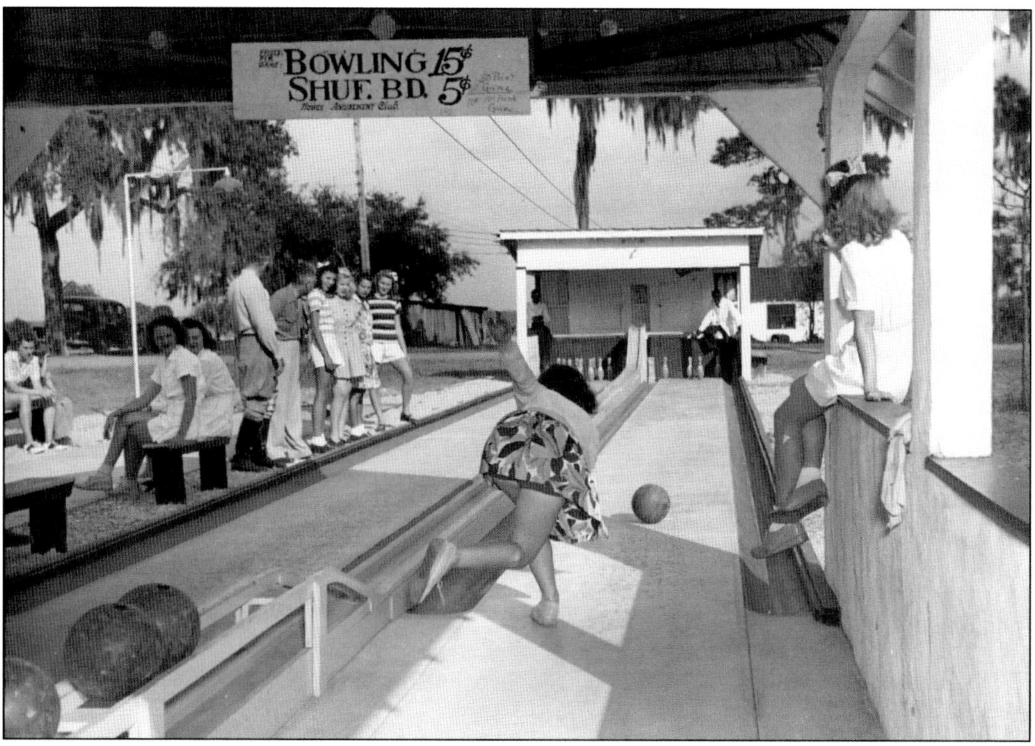

The Howey Amusement Club was located at the Floridan Hotel along Palm Avenue, which, at the time, was not a very busy street. Each of the two bowling lanes had its own uniformed attendant to return the ball. Guests paid 15¢ per game. (HH.)

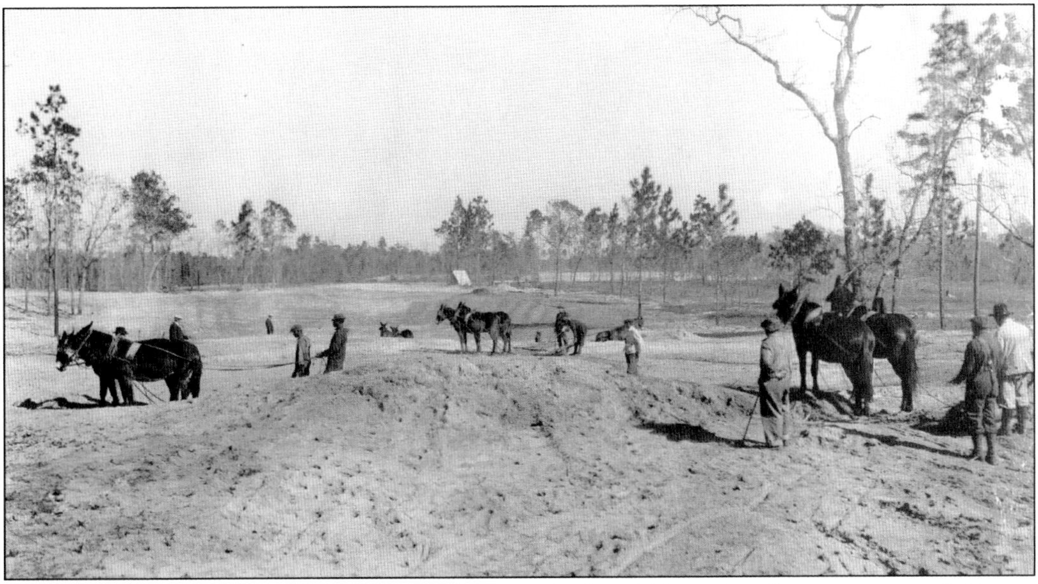

Groomed by men and mule teams, the first nine holes of Howey's hilly course were laid out, graded, and sown in Italian rye and featured grass putting greens, which were rare below the Mason-Dixon Line. Upon completion, George O'Neil said that the course would be one of only two regulation-length courses in the state and would attract nationwide professional and amateur golfers to the sportiest layout in the Land of Flowers. (OCHC.)

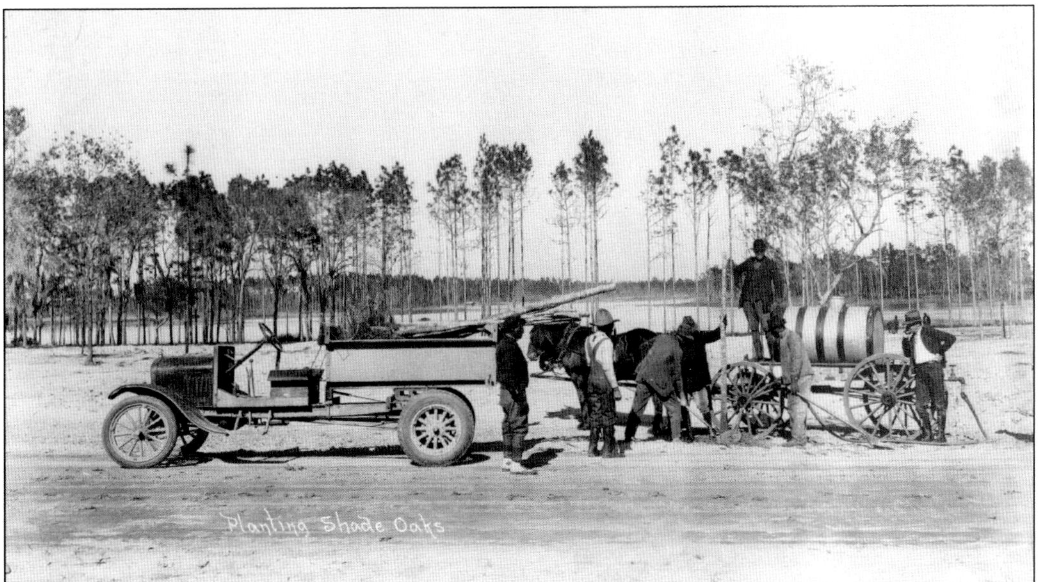

Shade oaks were planted throughout the new links by hand and immediately watered utilizing a portable irrigation system, shown on the right. In anticipation of George O'Neil's inspection, finishing course details were installed during the summer of 1917. At that time, fairways were rolled and flowers and shrubs were planted. O'Neil staked his reputation as America's foremost golf course architect on the Bougainvillea links and the layout's natural advantages. (OCHC.)

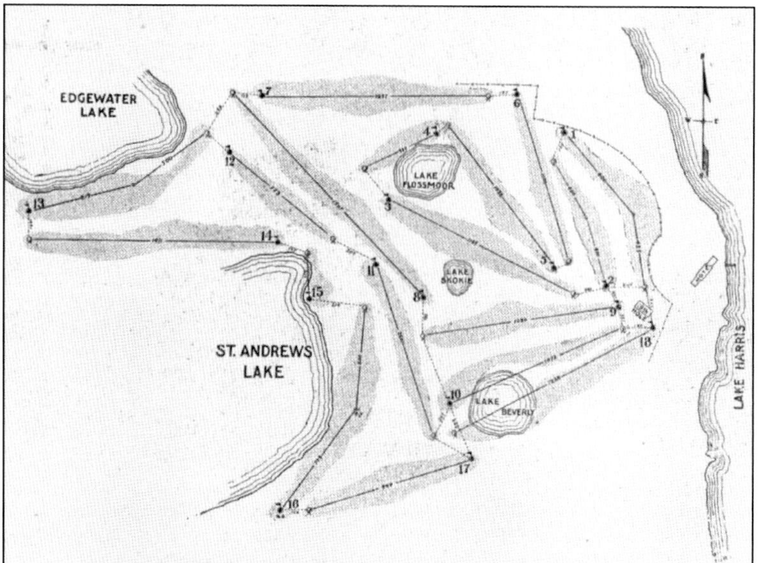

MAP OF THE CHAIN-O'-LAKES GOLF COURSE, HOWEY, FLORIDA. NOTE THE LAKES.

William J. Howey commissioned America's foremost golf expert, George O'Neil of Chicago, to design an 18-hole golf course adjacent to Howey's hilltop hotel. In a 12-page, colored yardage book, O'Neil illustrated the Chain-O'-Lakes Golf Course, its lakes (named for cities in Illinois), and the Bougainvillea Hotel in 1917. "This will be America's most famous course in a very short while," O'Neil stated. (LCHM.)

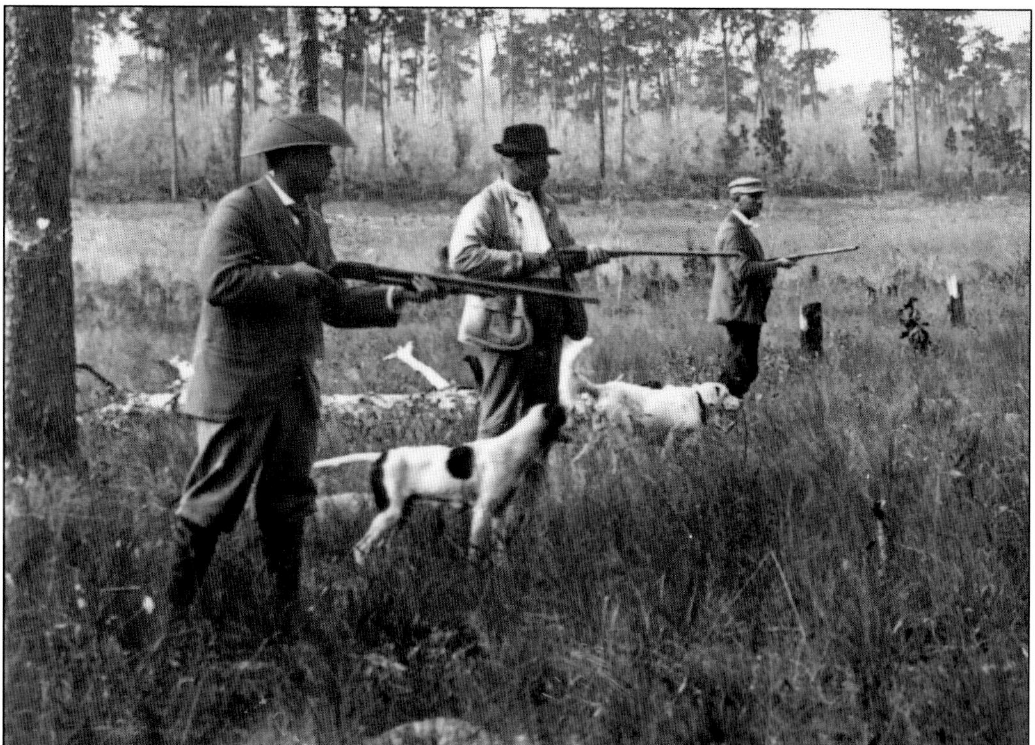

In 1930, a fox chase was filmed in Howey-in-the-Hills for sound newsreel distribution. A pack of trained foxhounds and mounted hunters left the mansion and chased the red fox across the golf course after its release from the tee on the second hole. The fox dashed for its life across the fairway toward cameramen before its final capture in nearby woods. Prior to becoming a golf course, hunters traversed this wooded land. (LCHM.)

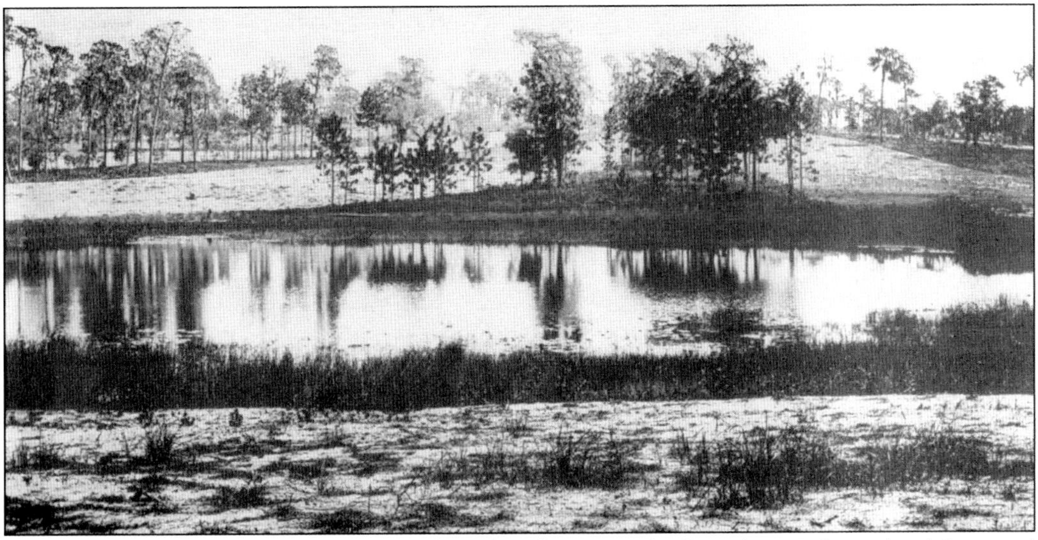

Pictured are two challenging golf holes that played across Lake Beverly to either side of the stand of trees. These holes were very much like the holes that are played today. In a 1920 brochure, this golf photograph promoted Howey as a destination for land investment, overnight recreation, and year-round or seasonal residence. Howey's 6,250-yard course capitalized on the best golfing ground in the country, utilizing only a select portion of an undulating 250-acre site. (LCHM.)

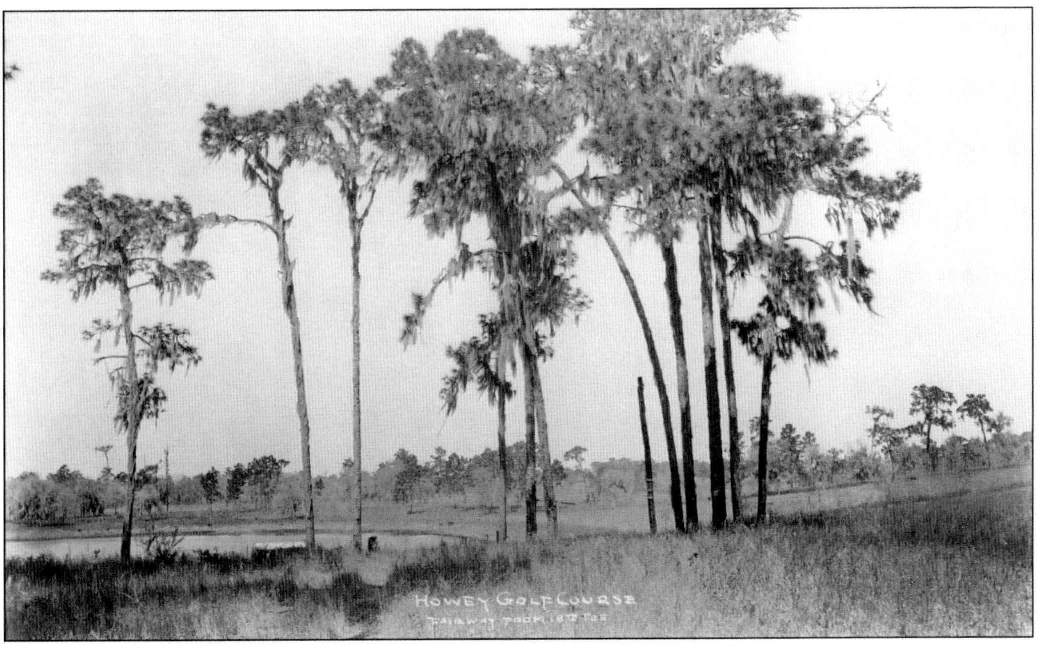

The 18th hole was more difficult and steeper than the ninth hole and carried 160 yards over water. The original fairway is seen in this image, taken from the 18th tee. A golfing innovator, course architect George O'Neil was the originator of the Indoor Golf School in Chicago in 1911 and wrote instructive golf articles for the *Chicago Daily Tribune*. He was also the first to hire women greens keepers. (HH.)

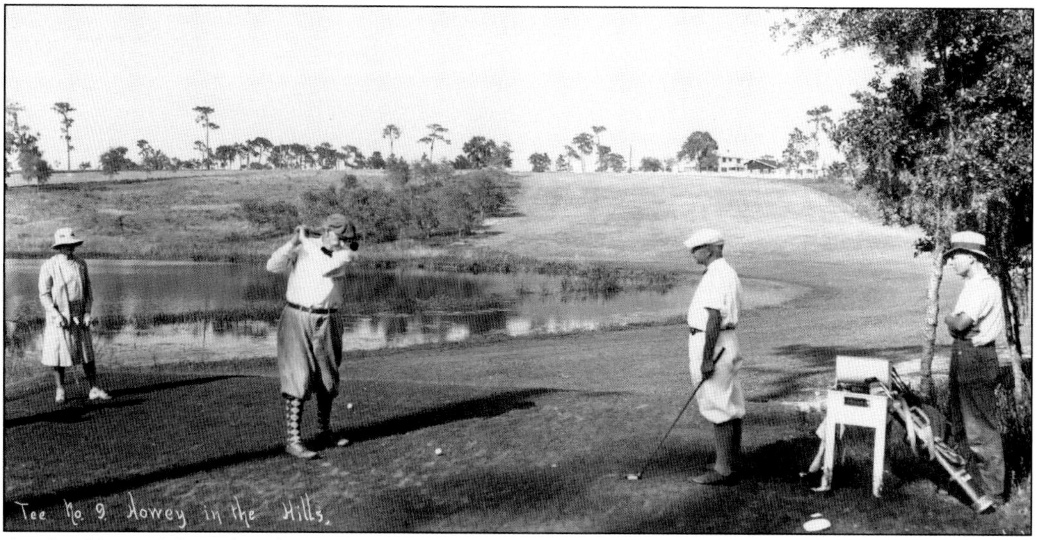

Avid golfer and famed author Opie Read tees off the ninth hole, accompanied by golfing partners and a caddy. In the 1917 golf course yardage book, club officers were listed as W.J. Howey, the president and treasurer; George A. O'Neil, the vice president and manager; and Charles "Chick" Evans Jr., an advisory board member. The book noted that golf course offices were located in Chicago and Howey. (OCHC.)

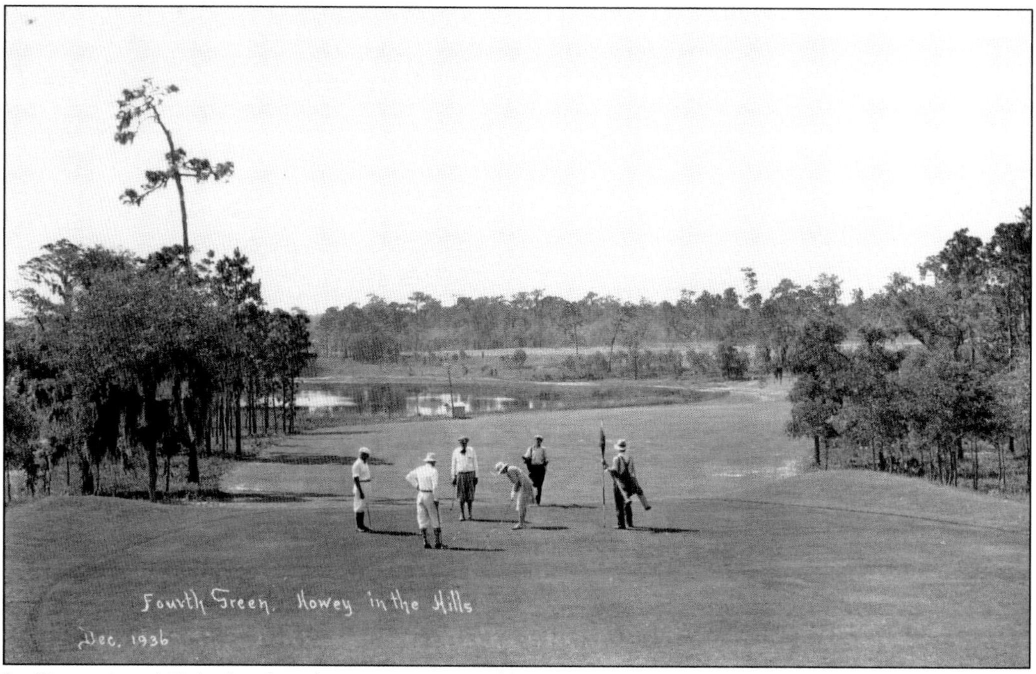

In December 1936, the fourth green was a golfing test to this foursome, which included Opie Read wearing the dark-colored knickers (third from left). Two caddies toted clubs and tracked errant golf balls. Today, this same hole is the seventh hole, with Mission Inn Resort's hotel in the background. (HH.)

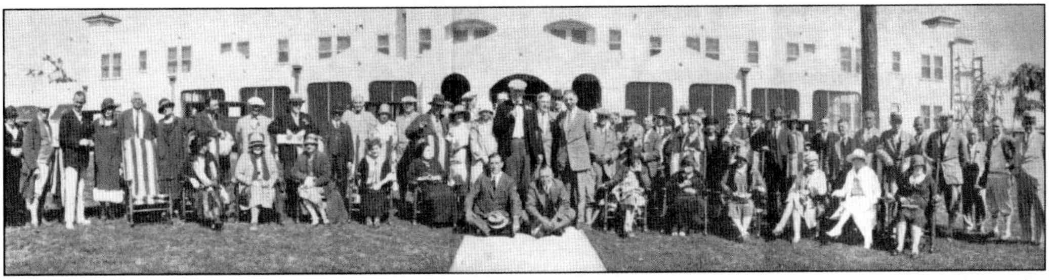

The Dixie Golf Pilgrimage, sponsored by C.B. MacMeals, the editor of *Golfers' Magazine*, brought 100 golfers from Chicago and other Midwest cities to the Floridan Hotel on March 9, 1926. After lunch, outing members toured the Howey citrus tract and inspected the golf course, which was 85 percent complete. Chick Evans, former American Amateur and American Open golf champion, declared George O'Neil's design the sportiest in Florida. (MIR.)

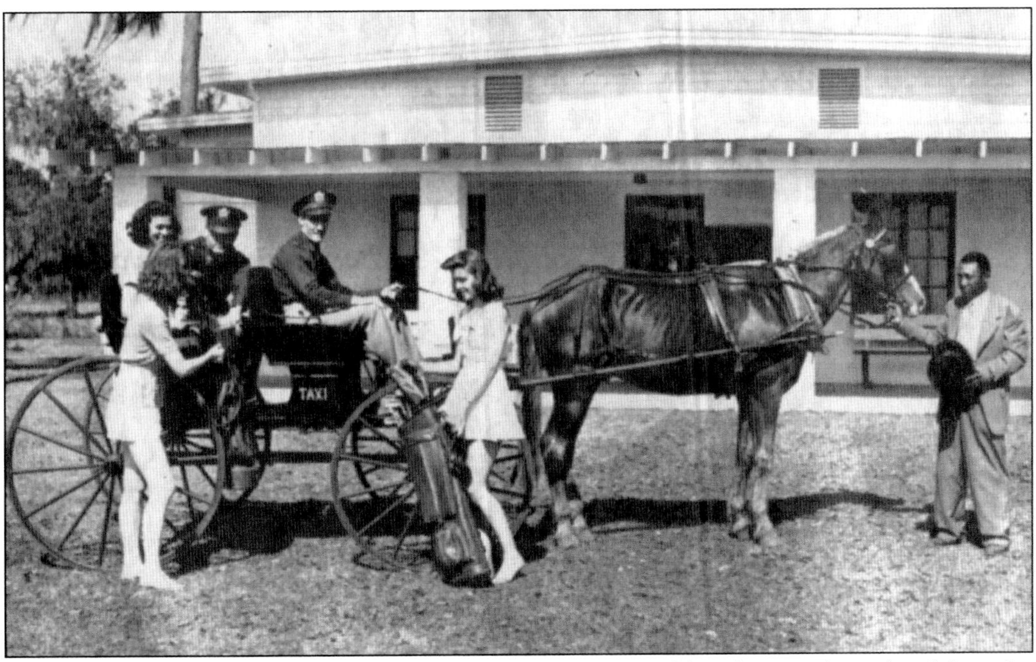

Gasless and tireless, this Floridan Country Club taxi conveyed hotel guests from the club to the golf course. Coachman Boykin, who stands to the right holding the reins and a top hat, piloted the horse-drawn carriage. Here, Julia Atwood (left, standing), Betty Kilgore (seated), and Alice Colglazier (right, with clubs) of Orlando accompany Lts. John Bull (left) and Bud Baker (right) to the course for a challenging round. (HH.)

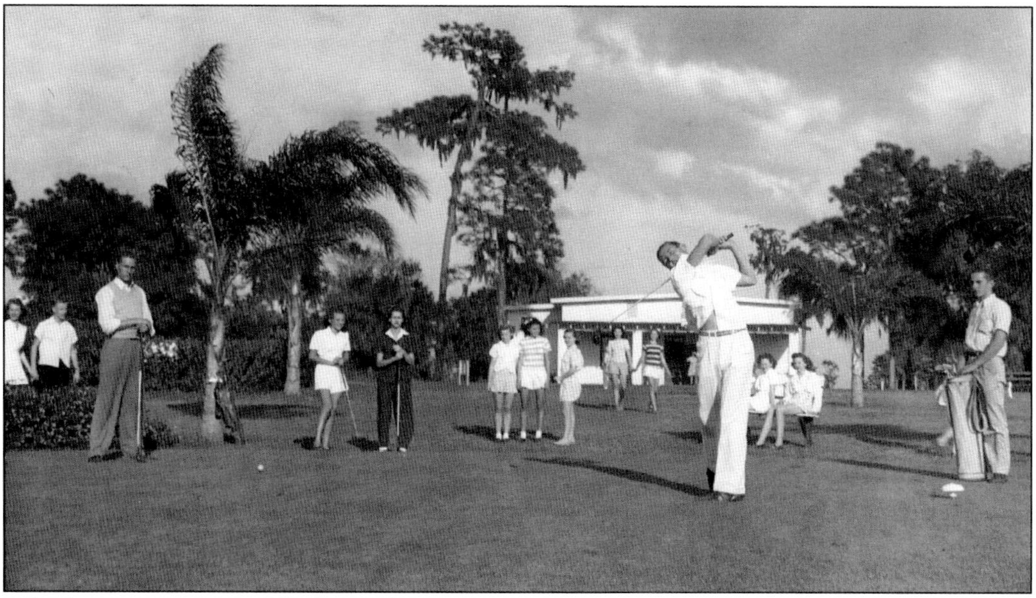

Whether visitors arrived by horse-drawn surrey in the early years or later by car, the Howey-in-the-Hills golf clubhouse and links remained a social center for all age groups residing in and around Howey or vacationing at the Floridan Hotel and Country Club. Famous golfers drawn to Howey's hotel and links during the 1920s, 1930s, and 1940s included the following: Ben Hogan, Patty Berg, Babe Zaharias, Beth Jamison, and trick-shot artist Joe Kirkwood. (HH.)

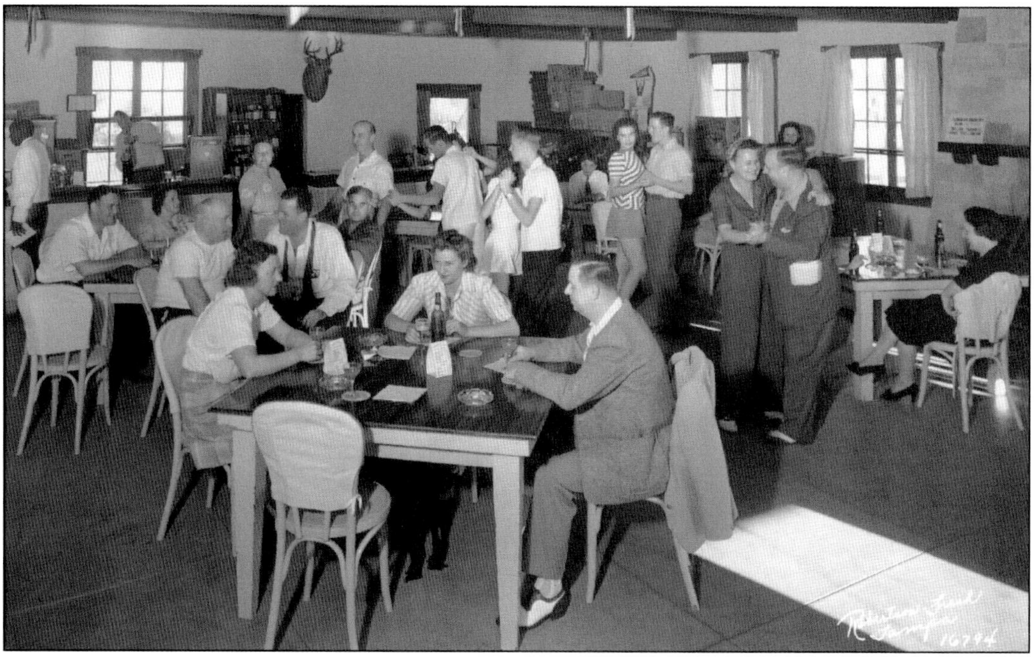

For decades, the clubhouse was located across Palm Avenue from the Howey Mansion on the highest point of Howey's in-town property. With golf and sunset views, the Floridan Country Club's clubroom became the place to convene for dances, dining, meetings, and cooling off after a round. Nick Beucher razed this original structure, making way for hilltop condominiums, and in January 1992, he opened a second 18-hole golf course and a grand new clubhouse. (HH.)

Nine

C.V. Griffin to the Rescue

While historians credit William J. Howey as the architect of Howey-in-the-Hills, Clarence Vaughn Griffin Sr. was surely its greatest savior. Born in Canton, Illinois, on October 16, 1903, his family moved to Kansas while he was still a toddler. An entrepreneur from the very beginning, he obtained a franchise to sell ice cream from the president of the local railroad at the tender age of 15.

In 1924, Griffin accepted an offer from his uncle to finance his education at the University of Florida. After one year of studying diligently, Griffin's entrepreneurial spirit lured him away to pursue quick profits in the Florida land boom. Not all was lost with his brief college career, as classmate Fuller Warren played an important role later in Griffin's life.

Like any sizzling real estate market, the explosion extinguished as fast as it started. Griffin soon began a citrus shipping business. W.J. Howey offered the 25-year-old a lucrative citrus-packing contract if Griffin built a plant in town. Within five years, he was Florida's second largest fresh-fruit shipper.

In 1936, Howey approached Griffin with his crumbling dream. Howey's citrus empire was mired $450,000 in debt. After Howey's death in 1938, Griffin assumed the debt and inherited the 1,500 acres that made up the fledgling town in 1940. With real estate experience and the recently completed Memorial Bridge, Griffin held four auctions, selling off a total of 70 homes to jump-start the growth of Howey-in-the-Hills.

During 1956, Griffin helped establish the Howey Academy, a college-preparatory school for boys and girls, and sold several thousand acres of his groves. Griffin enjoyed flying around the country with his pilot, Wally Schanz, and raising Santa Gertrudis cattle. Before passing away on April 2, 1982, he was credited with establishing a foundation that fosters research into cold-resistant citrus.

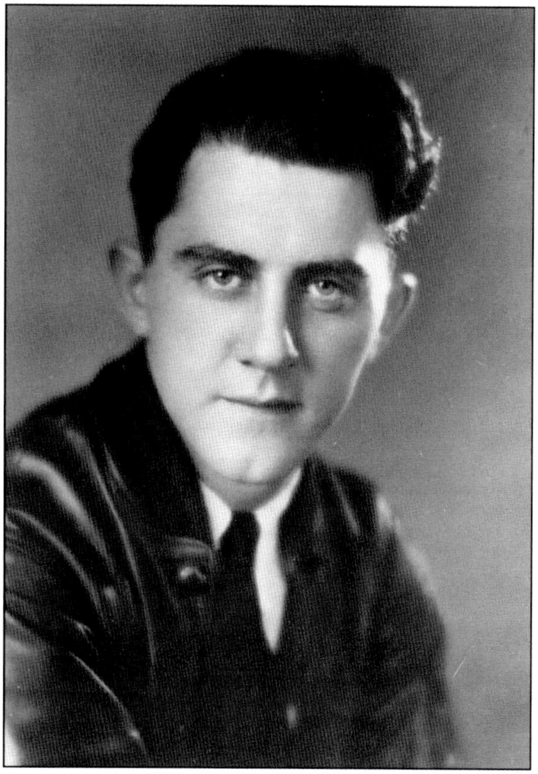

Griffin, at 27 years old, was deeply committed to making a success at whatever business he ventured into, as proven by establishing Florida's first single-strength citrus juice plant at Howey. Utilizing a spur rail line into Howey, he constructed the Vaughn Griffin Packing Company on the old Howey Juice Plant site, indirectly laying the groundwork for Silver Springs Citrus Cooperative to become one of the state's most successful. (HH.)

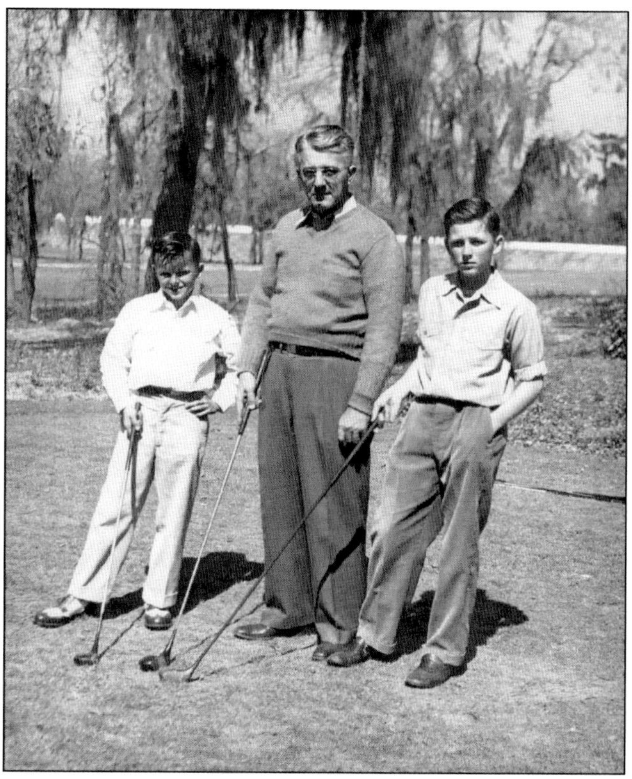

Between rounds of golf with his sons, Rodney (left) and C.V. Jr., Griffin ran Fuller Warren's successful bid for governor in 1948. Griffin became a powerful Democratic political force, counting US presidents Harry Truman, John Kennedy, and Lyndon Johnson among his personal friends. He helped establish the Florida Citrus Code of 1949 and the 12-member Florida Citrus Commission. (HH.)

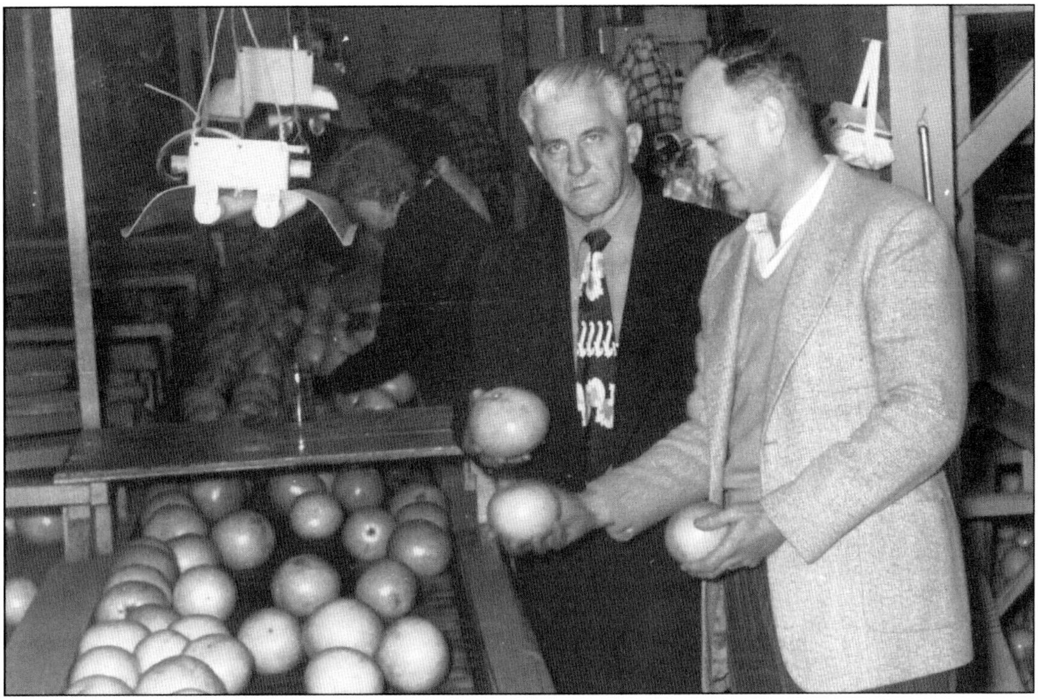

Griffin was one of the first to establish a truck line to distribute fruit to areas where primitive rail or boat transportation could not deliver perishable fruit. In 1937, Griffin and other grove owners met in Orlando and formed the United Growers and Shippers Association. C.V. Griffin (left) and Albin Crutchfield (right), vice president of Vaughn-Griffin Packing Company, inspect fruit inside the Howey plant. (HH.)

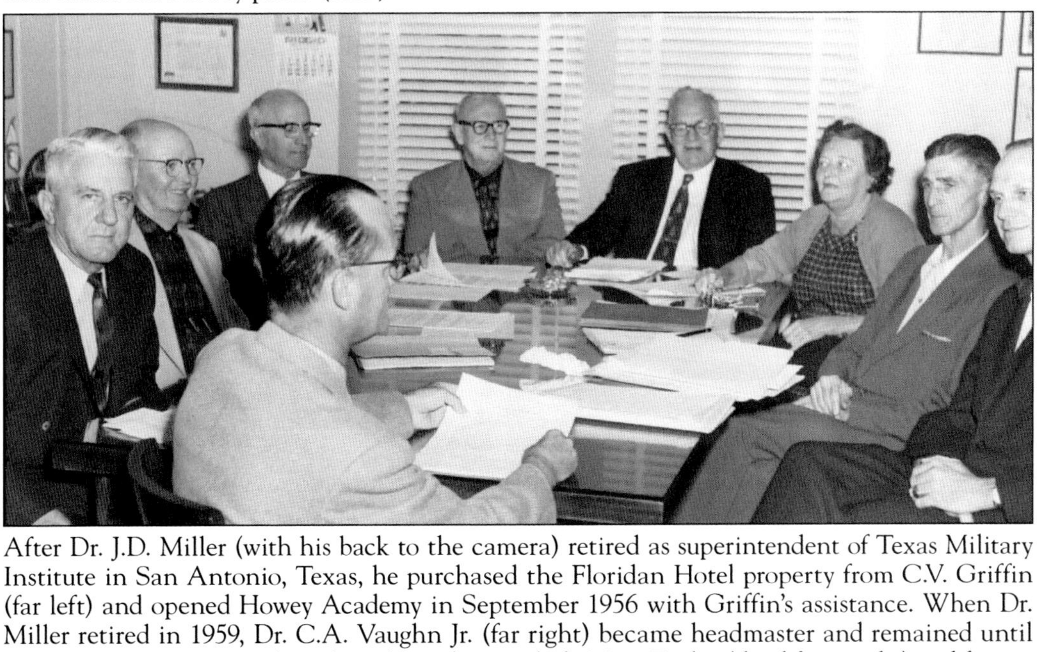

After Dr. J.D. Miller (with his back to the camera) retired as superintendent of Texas Military Institute in San Antonio, Texas, he purchased the Floridan Hotel property from C.V. Griffin (far left) and opened Howey Academy in September 1956 with Griffin's assistance. When Dr. Miller retired in 1959, Dr. C.A. Vaughn Jr. (far right) became headmaster and remained until 1973. Other meeting academy board members include Mary Taylor (third from right) and former mayor Edmund Hazelton "Haze" Ketchum (second from right). (HH.)

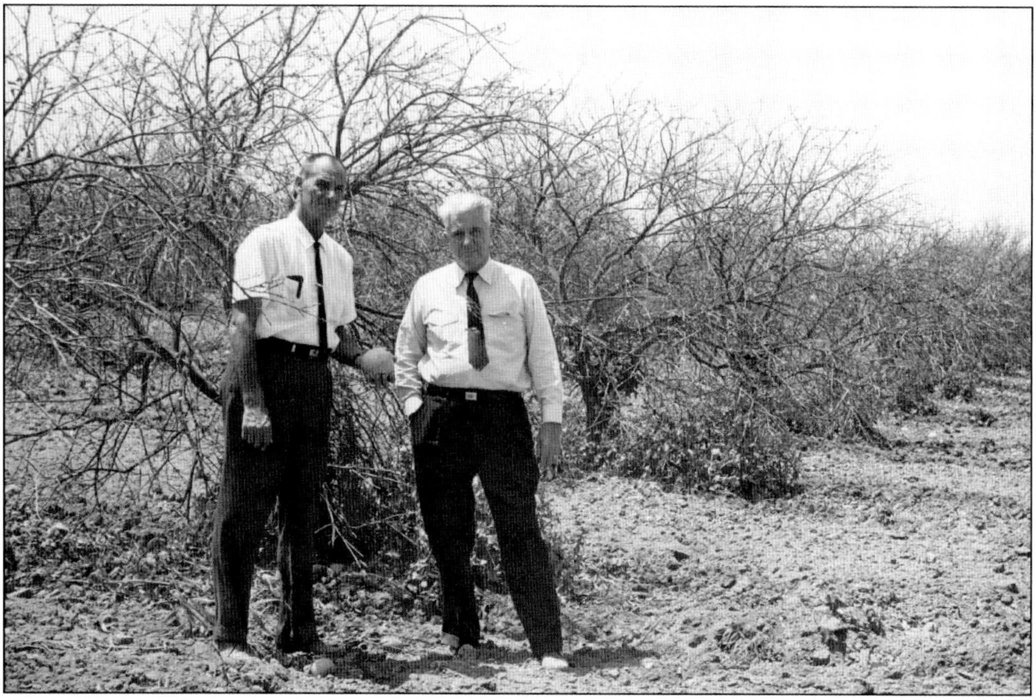

Operating on a shoestring after the land boom collapsed in the 1920s, Griffin (right) purchased and reconditioned broken-down, second-hand packinghouse equipment and started his first citrus shipping business. Griffin's success attracted the attention of W.J. Howey, who offered a 10-year contract if Griffin relocated his operation to Howey. In the 1950s, Griffin and his grove manager Terrell Holland (left) traveled to study damage caused by freezing temperatures in Texas. (HH.)

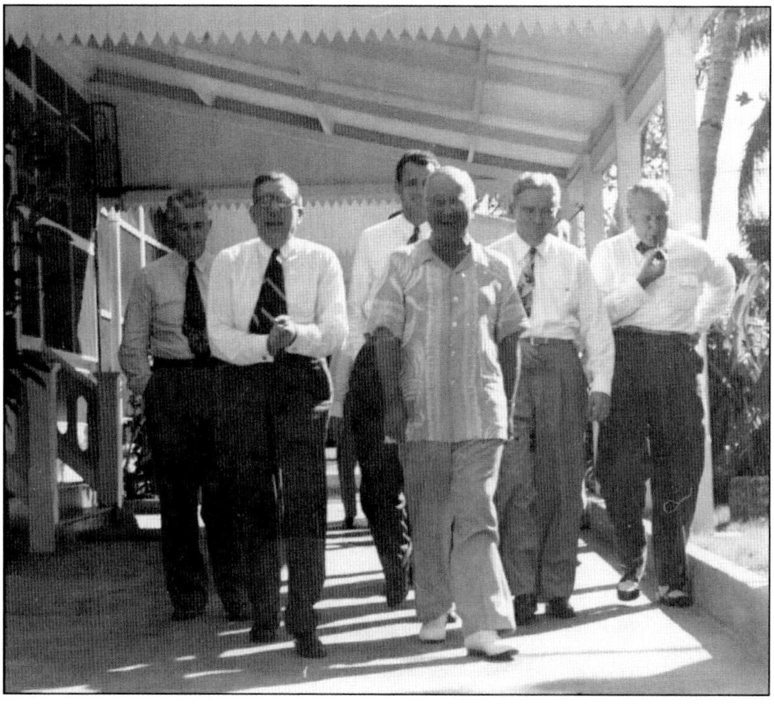

US president Harry S. Truman (center) enjoys a walk with friends and fellow politicians at his "Little White House" in Key West, Florida. President Truman is shown relaxing in his tropical shirt, while those around him are pictured dressed for business as usual. Those walking behind the president are, from left to right, C.V. Griffin, Sen. Claude Pepper, Sen. George Smathers Sr., Gov. Fuller Warren, and citrus grower Jack Fosgate. (HH.)

Born in Jackson, Michigan, in 1902, Dodge Taylor came to Florida in 1923 when he started as a sales manager for the Howey Company. He managed Howey's extensive citrus interests until Howey passed away in 1938. Taylor and C.V. Griffin purchased the assets of the town and Howey Company in 1940. Taylor's greatest achievement as executive of the firm was to bring both the town and company out of debt. (HH.)

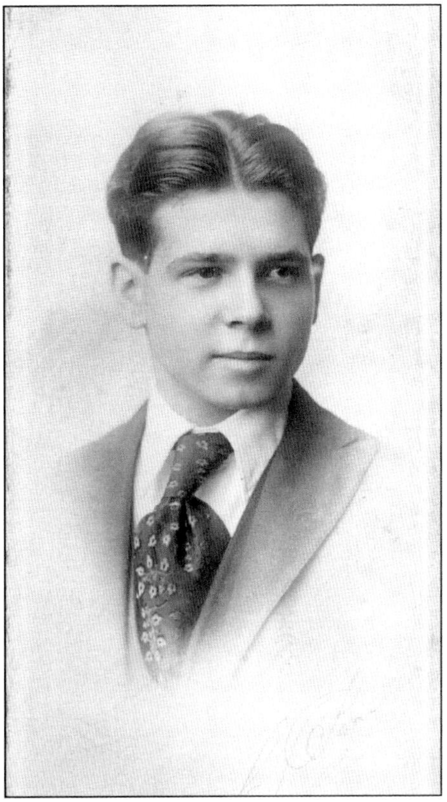

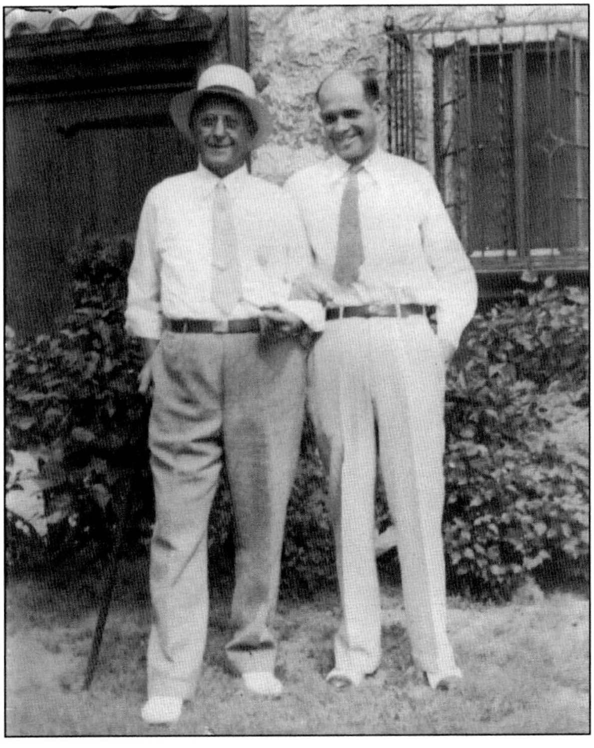

A graduate of Dartmouth College, Taylor was commonly referred to as "Mr. Citrus" for being one of the most aggressive citrus industry leaders over his 25 years. Taylor, who died at the age of 48, was active in the formation of the *Florida Citrus Manual* and served as chairman of the Florida Citrus Commission. Dodge Taylor stands with his father, Dr. Edwin Taylor, who researched the medicinal value of Howey grapefruit. (HH.)

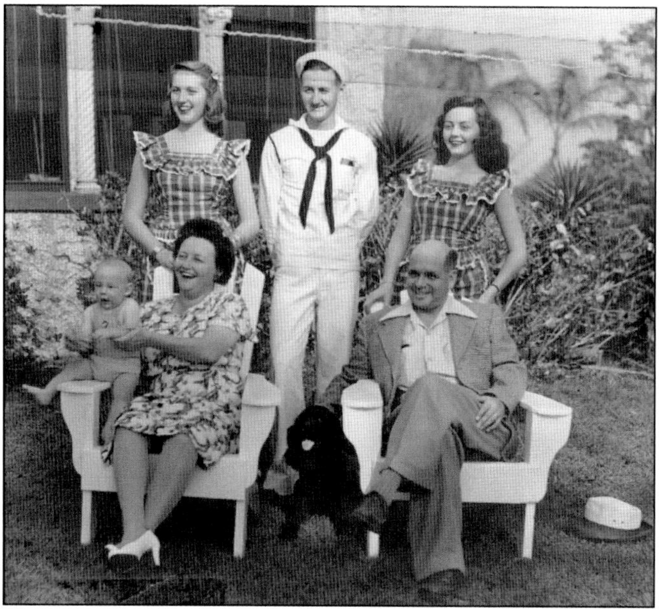

Dodge Taylor and his family are seen posing in front of their two-story home on Palm Avenue. Those pictured are, from left to right, (seated) Mary, holding baby Lane, and Dodge Taylor; (standing) Mary Jane, Bill, and Sue. After Dodge Taylor and C.V. Griffin sold most of their land, they operated a large grove care service, sold and shipped fruit, and operated the original Floridan Country Club. (HH.)

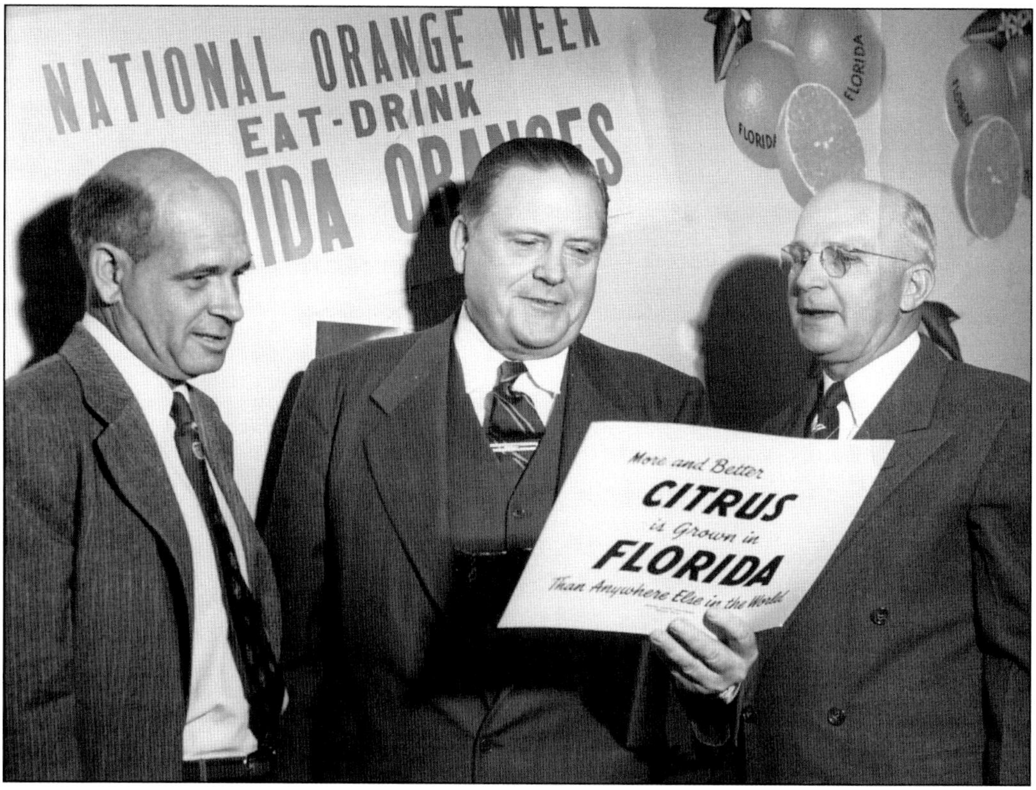

Dodge Taylor authored the citrus plank in Gov. Fuller Warren's campaign platform and conducted hearings after Warren's election that brought about the Florida Citrus Code of 1949. The code halted shipment of immature fruit, which guaranteed buyers quality citrus, and set high standards for frozen orange juice. While chairman of the State Improvement Commission, Taylor protected the code by refusing to allow crippling changes that would weaken the citrus industry. (HH.)

The producers of the Orange Blossom Rodeo were born in Florida and literally raised in the saddle; Red Simpson was from the cow capital at Kissimmee, and Odis Cowart was from the ranges of Volusia County. Simpson and Cowart's widespread acquaintances and contacts, among them performers and owners of stock alike, enabled the men to stage rodeos in Howey-in-the-Hills of as good a caliber as those found anywhere in the United States. (LCHM.)

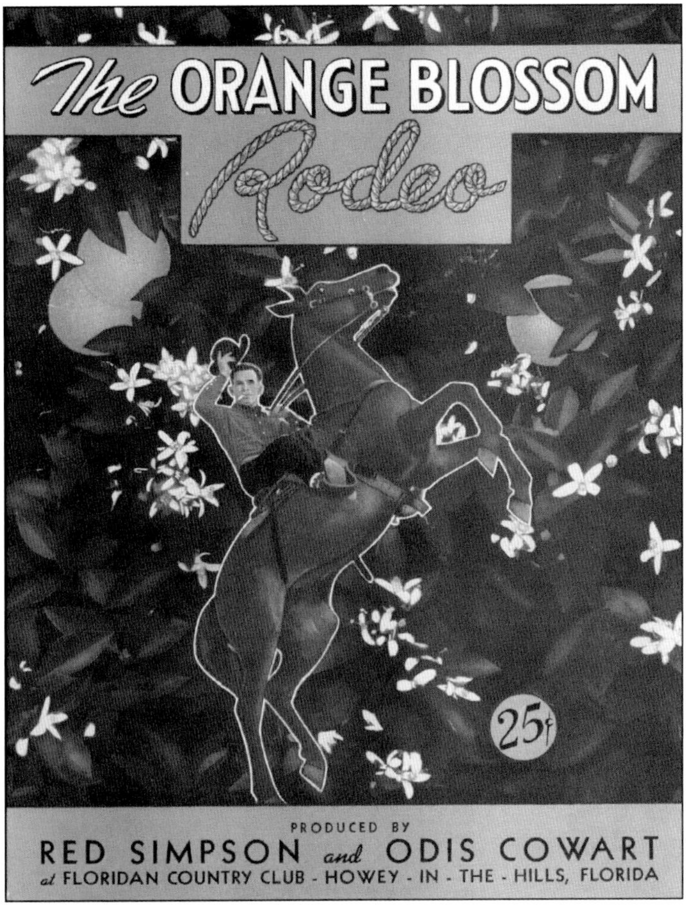

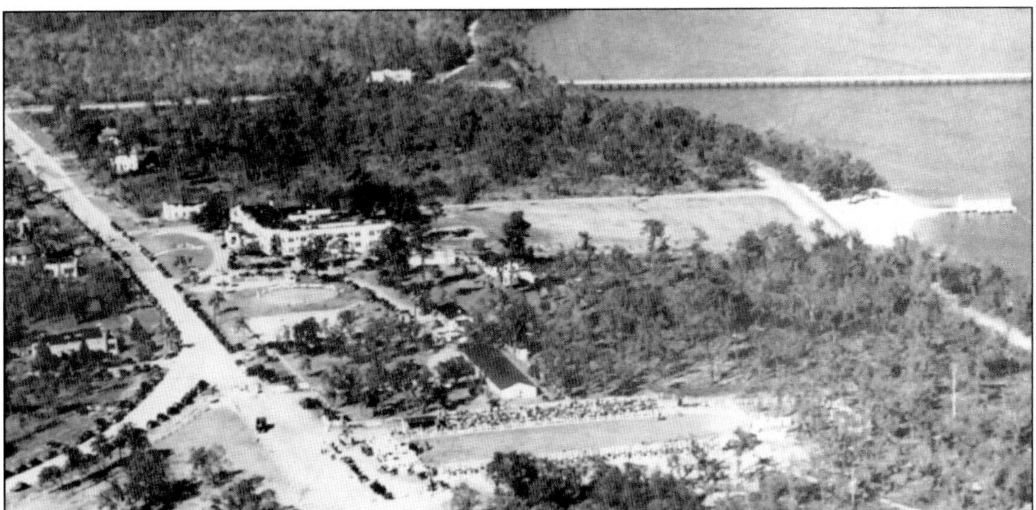

Looking north, this rare aerial view shows the Floridan Country Club's hotel, rodeo arena, and boathouse on Little Lake Harris in the 1940s. The wooden bridge to Astatula is toward the top, with Howey's Lakeside Service at the head of the bridge. On this day, the rodeo was a sellout event, lining the streets with black cars and filling the stands with would-be cowboys. (CB.)

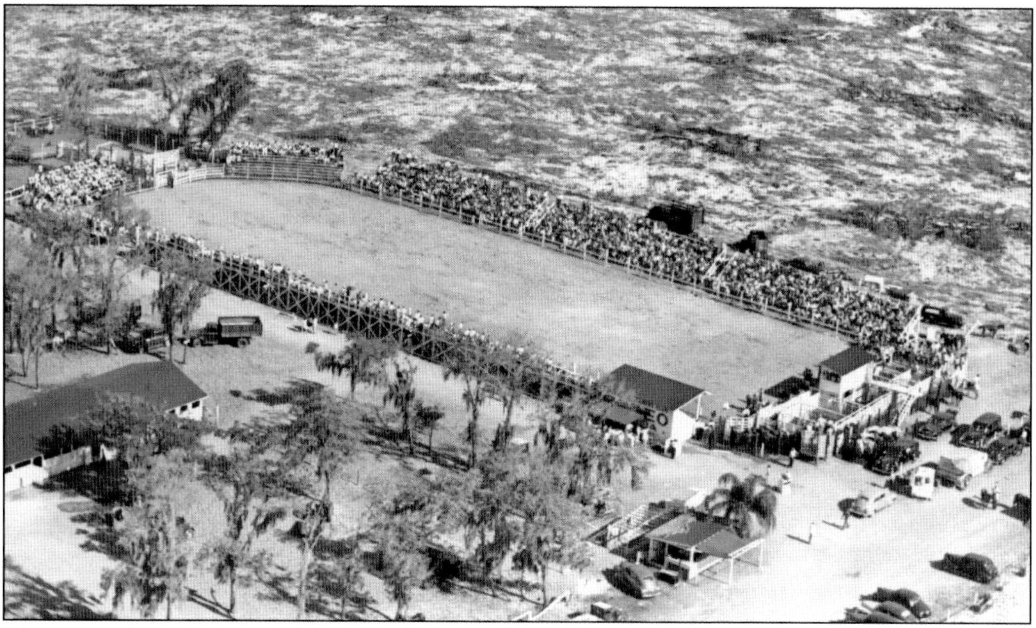

The Orange Blossom Rodeo brochure may have cost 25¢, but the rodeo was free to all, compliments of C.V. Griffin, who built the arena for 2,000 attendees to witness both man and animal. In preparation for grove planting or further expansion of the club facilities, the remains of cleared trees, located south of the area, are in neat piles at the top of the image. (HH.)

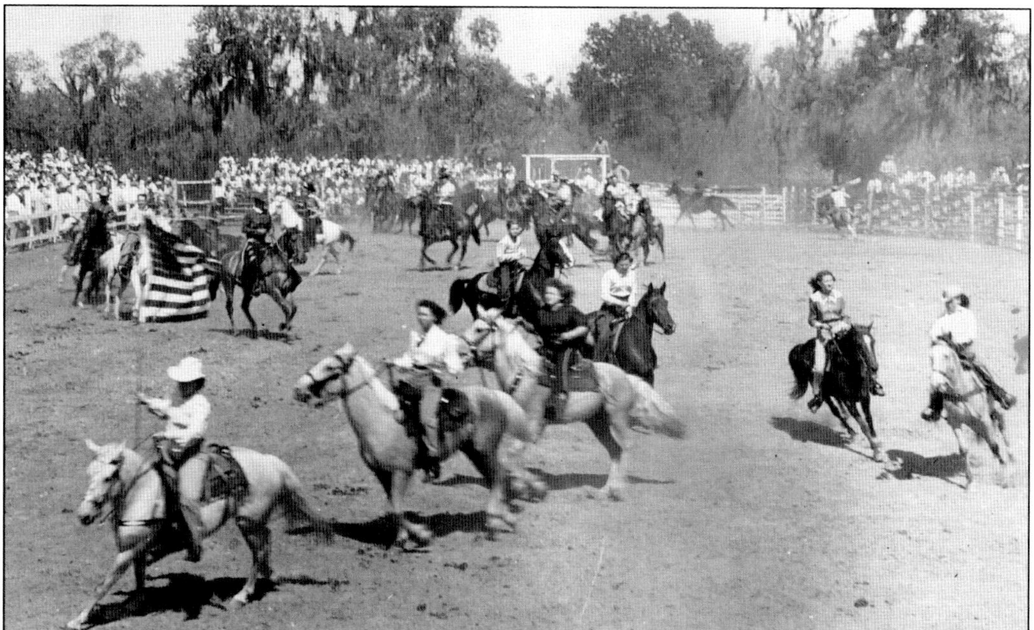

Some time during the 1940s, the grand entry and introduction of officials of the Orange Blossom Rodeo began stirring up dust at 2:00 p.m. Fourteen exhilarating events followed the American flag–bearing Quarter horse parade. From bareback bronco riding to trick roping and from steer wrestling to horse races, competitors came from as far away as Wyoming, South Dakota, and Texas. Norman Beasley and his Florida cowboys played Western music at the hotel. (LCHM.)

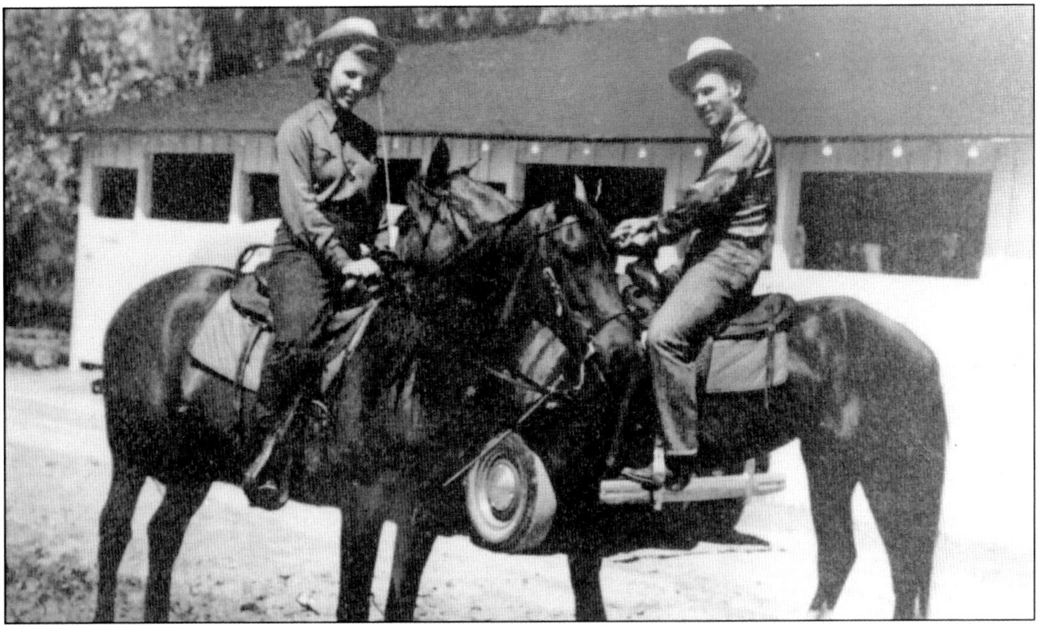

Red Simpson, horse trainer extraordinaire and rodeo competitor, appeared widely with his well-trained horse Cherry, who counted, added, and subtracted. Guests at the Floridan Country Club since 1942 knew Red not only for his skillful performances but also for his riding instructor expertise and ability to handle a horse. Under Red's management, with his wife Marcella's help, the ranch became the most popular adjunct to the Floridan Country Club. (CB.)

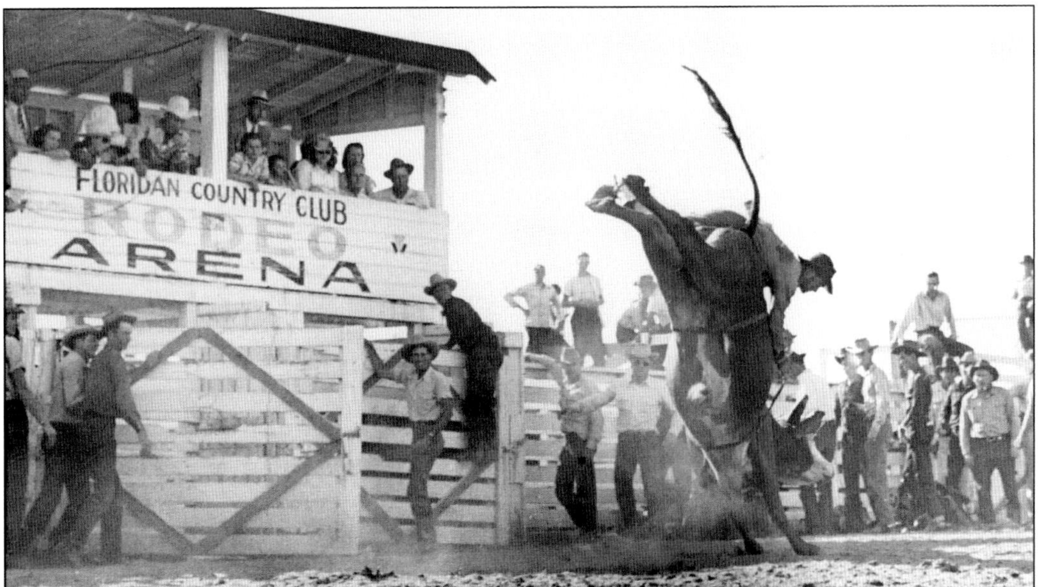

The first rodeo at which cash prizes were awarded was reputedly held at Pecos, Texas, on July 4, 1883. Five years later in Arizona, when an admission fee was charged for the first time, they became known as "Cowboy Tournaments." The name "rodeo" was applied more than 20 years later. The authoritative figures of this rodeo included producers Red Simpson and Odis Cowart, and the "Voice of Rodeo," announcer Bobby Murray of Fort Worth, Texas. (HH.)

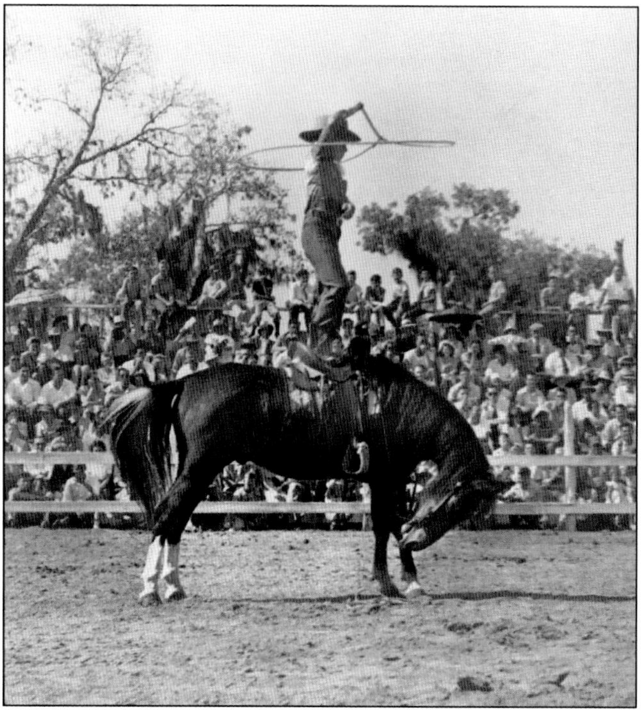

Two of the world's outstanding trick and fancy ropers, Dave Nemo and Bobby Boulter, performed in the same arena at the Orange Blossom Rodeo in Event No. 6 to the amazement of colleagues and attendees alike. Nemo and his wife, Dolores, another performer, came from Cheyenne, Wyoming. Boulter arrived from Rock Springs, Wyoming. In the 1940s rodeos, 40 chomping-at-the-bit contestants competed. (HH.)

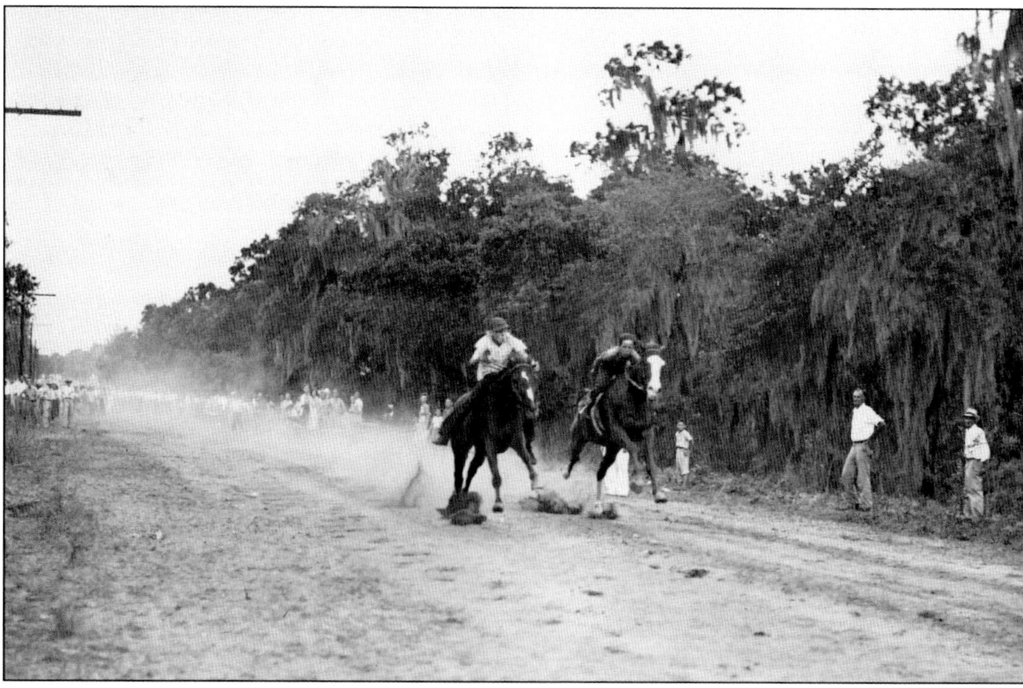

When the flag dropped, Jack Whitt (left) and Red Simpson's steeds took off in a cloud of dust galloping toward the finish line. Though many had wagered bets that day, the $100 stake between the two was as valuable as the honor placed on the victorious jockey. Whitt, who later became a dentist, was 16 years old when he dared the slightly older Simpson to race down Florida Avenue. (HH.)

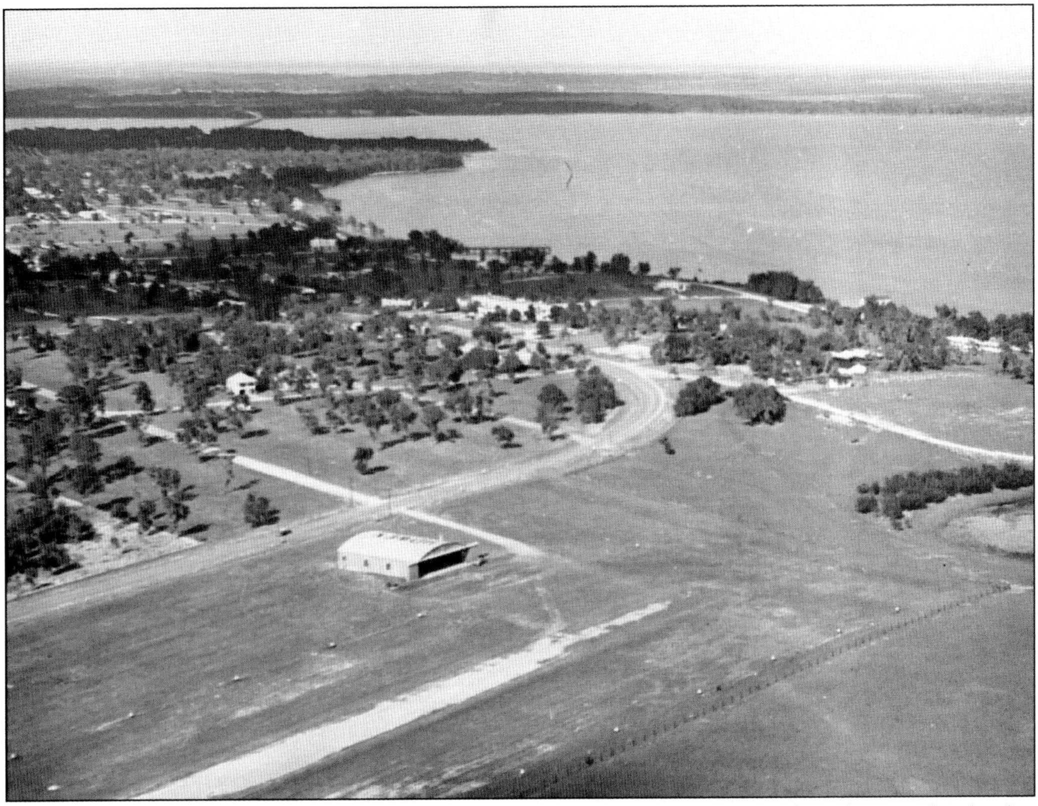

This aerial over southern Howey-in-the-Hills was taken in the 1950s, after the wooden bridge across Little Lake Harris at the town's center was demolished. Its million-dollar replacement, Memorial Bridge, is at the north, and many of today's homes are not yet built. Griffin Airways opened adjacent to the Floridan Country Club in 1947 and provided a travel convenience for vacationing hotel guests. (HH.)

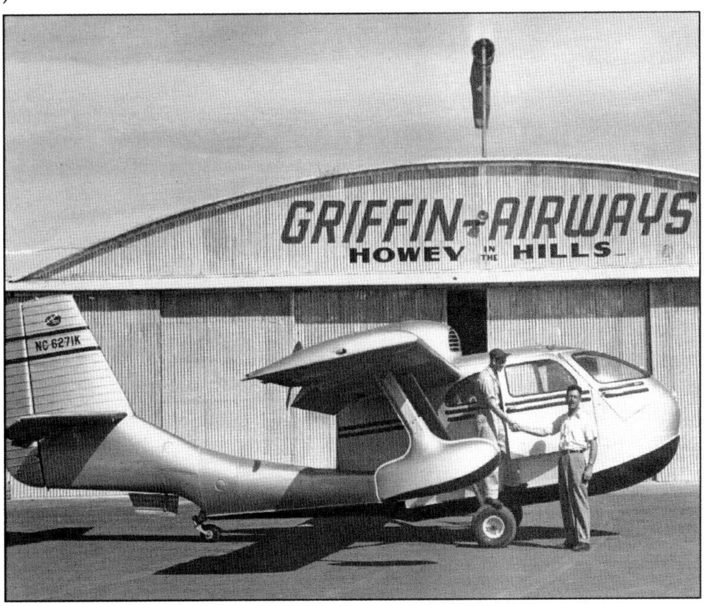

Wally Schanz, the private pilot for C.V. Griffin, welcomed this state-of-the-art amphibious plane to Griffin Airways. "Griff" used his own four-passenger Piper Clipper or twin-engine Beechcraft to peruse the citrus groves he purchased from Howey's widow, Grace, in 1940. Together, he and Dodge Taylor brought the town, hotel, citrus groves, and plant back from unstable financial ground. (LCHM.)

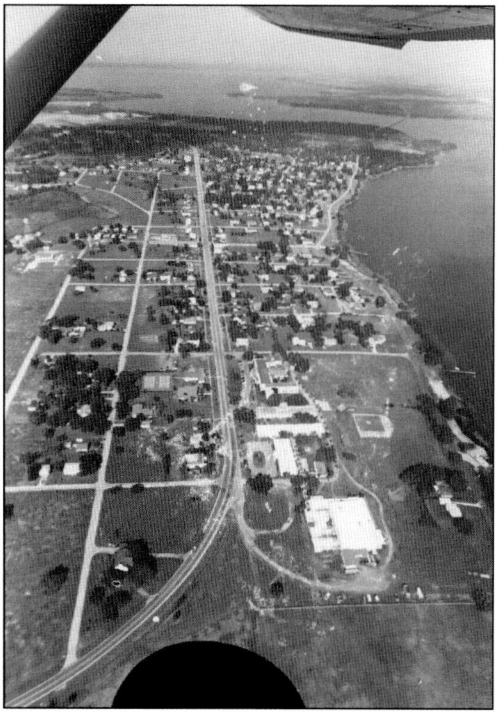

While the town of Howey-in-the-Hills had grown over the years, many lots were still vacant. This aerial provides a south-to-north view of Palm Avenue, the town's main street. To the right of the slight curve is the Howey Academy, formerly the Floridan Country Club hotel and grounds. The large white-roofed building was the school gymnasium. (LCHM.)

Happy were the vacationers who chose to fly by charter or private plane to Howey-in-the-Hills. Griffin Airways was just three short convenient blocks away from the Floridan Country Club, which provided transportation for guests and their luggage and sports gear. The single commodious hangar, clear approaches, smooth unpaved runways, and supply of gasoline for refueling made flying the right choice for these guests. (HH.)

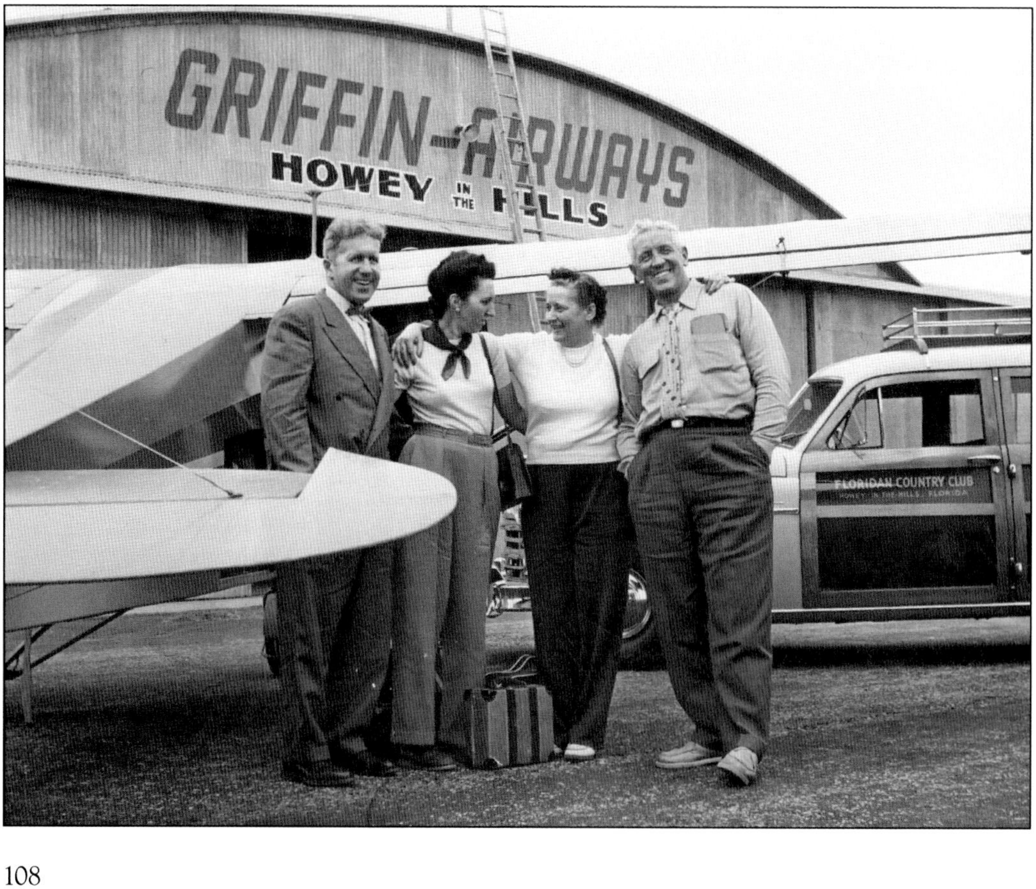

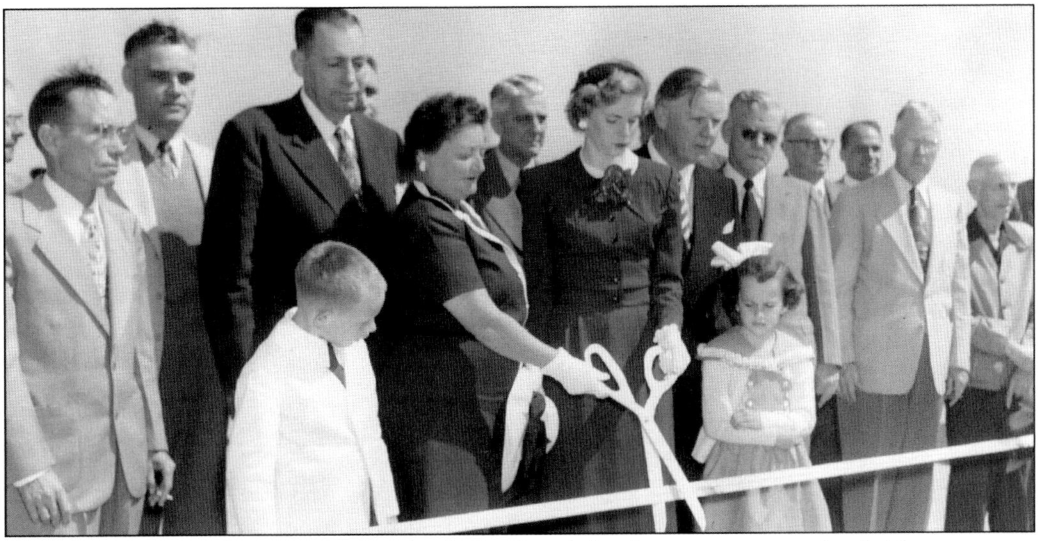

Dedicated in 1950, the new concrete bridge replaced the deteriorating wooden bridge spanning Little Lake Harris. Mary Taylor of Howey-in-the-Hills (holding scissors at left) and Alice Hocker of Tallahassee (right), the granddaughter of the late Florida Supreme Court judge W.A. Hocker, wore white gloves to cut the ribbon and officially open the Memorial Bridge, while young Lane Taylor (left, in white jacket) and Cheryl Griffin (right) were bearers of the ceremonial scissors. Numerous officials attended, including Sen. J. Edwin Baker, master of ceremonies. The bridge was a memorial to Mary Taylor's deceased husband, Dodge, and to the late town founder, William J. Howey. C.V. Griffin (between Mary Taylor and Alice Hocker) used his influence with friend Gov. Fuller Warren to expedite getting the new bridge built. For years, fishermen and their lanterns dotted the bridge walkways each evening. (Both, LCHM.)

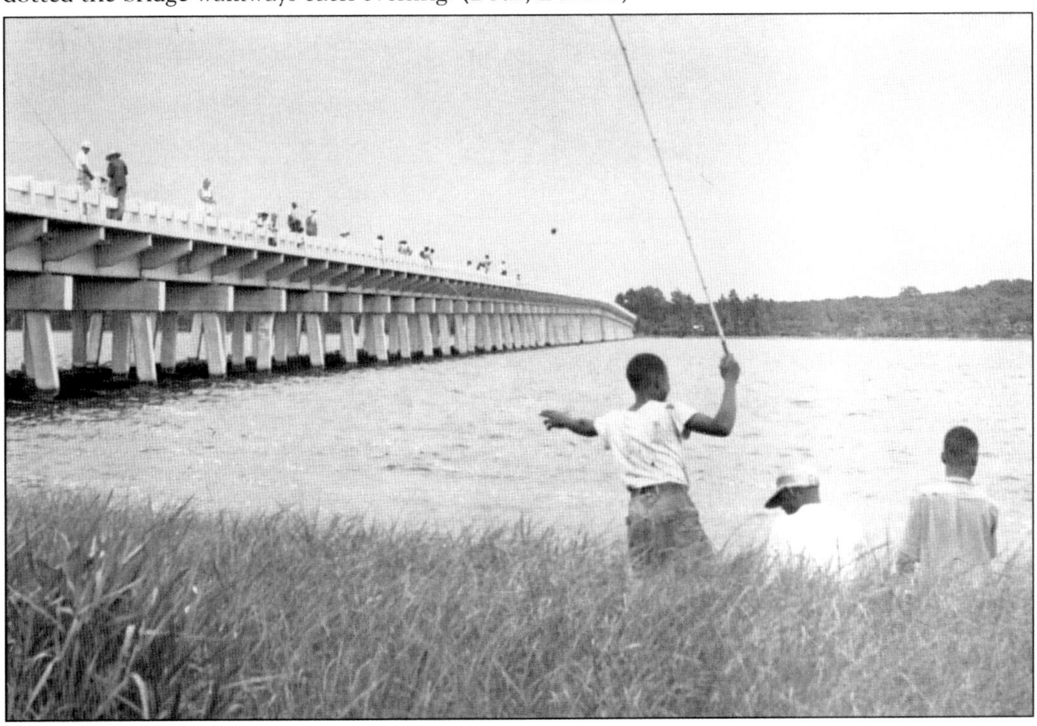

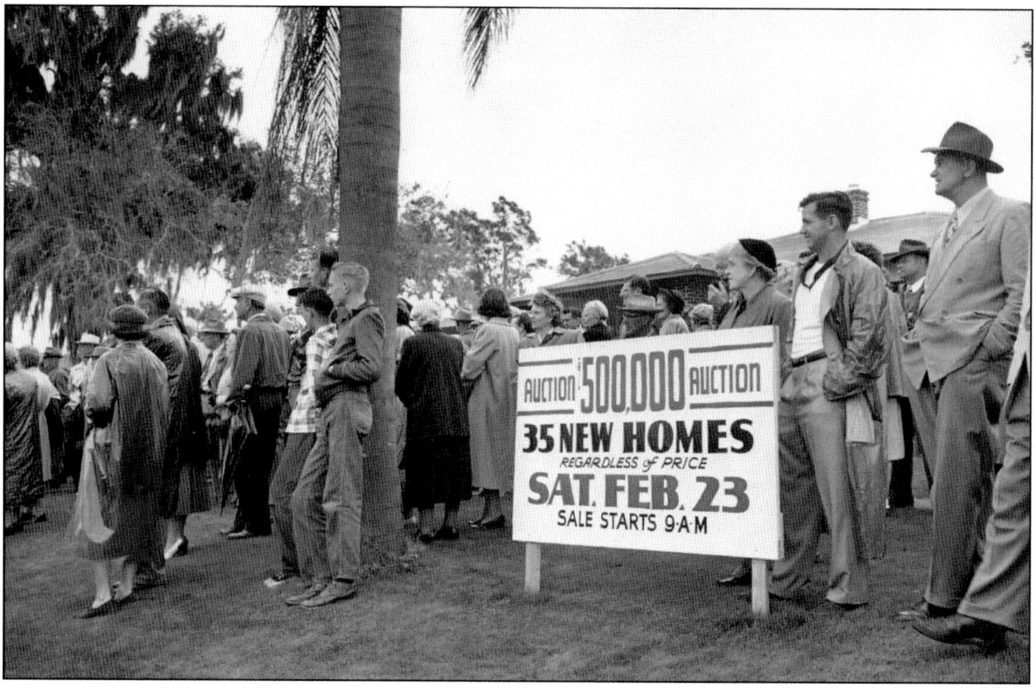

In order to generate interest in home sales with immediate impact to the town, C.V. Griffin hired Hansbrough, a national realty company, to sell 35 new homes at live auction. The promotion was valued at $500,000, and homes sold to the highest bidder, regardless of final price. As the sign indicates, bidding opened promptly at 9:00 a.m. on February 23, 1952. Buyers came in droves, despite the rain. (HH.)

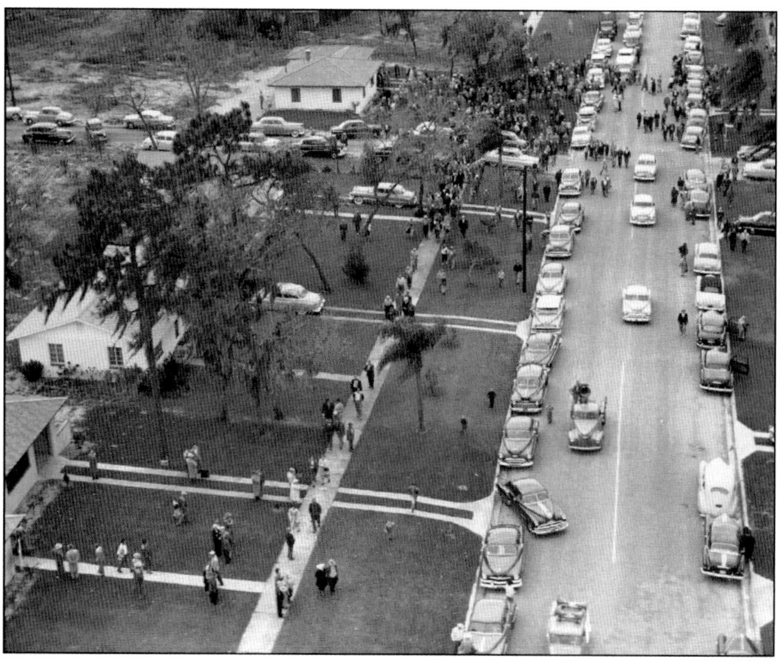

C.V. Griffin knew his idea drew buyers when a thousand people came to Florida's vacation wonderland to find their dream house in Howey-in-the-Hills. The Life-Bilt homes came fully furnished, with country atmosphere and city conveniences. Terms were inviting, the beautiful homes modern, and the auction the fair way to buy and sell. (HH.)

Eager to bid and secure their future in Howey-in-the-Hills, crowds gathered on the lawn of their first choice. As advertised, the sale lasted until all houses sold, rain or shine. Never again would there be such an opportunity, but actually, C.V. Griffin had four home auctions. In addition to the homes, choice lots for homes or businesses went under Griffin's hammer in the 1950s. (LCHM.)

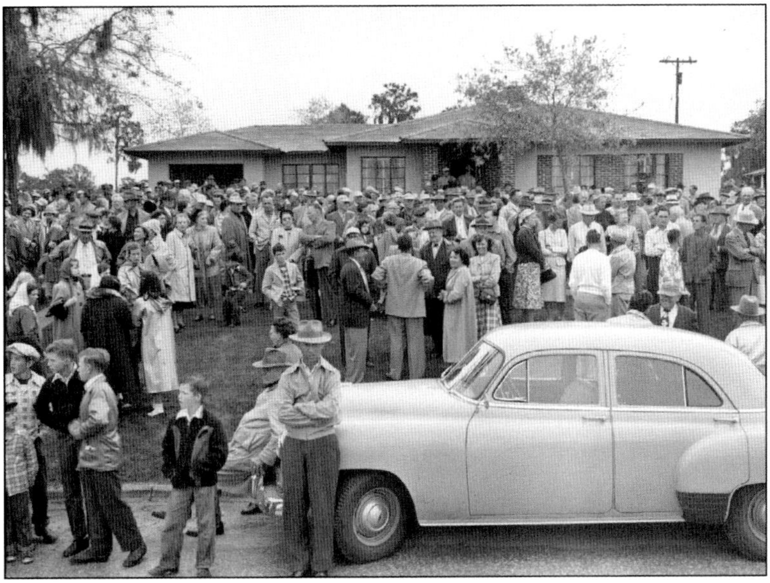

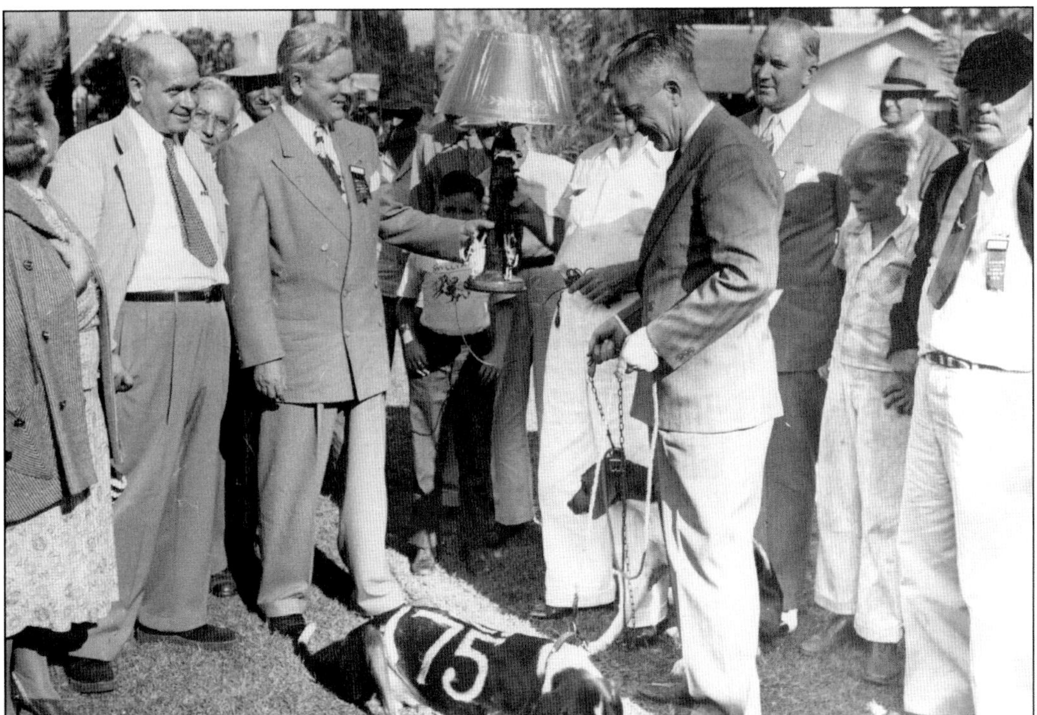

At the auction, Gov. Fuller Warren receives a souvenir lamp with a fox hunt theme as C.V. Griffin holds a dog marked with the number 75. These may have been gifts exchanged between the two longtime friends. Meanwhile, Dodge Taylor stands to the governor's right, getting a kick out of partner C.V. Griffin's actions. (HH.)

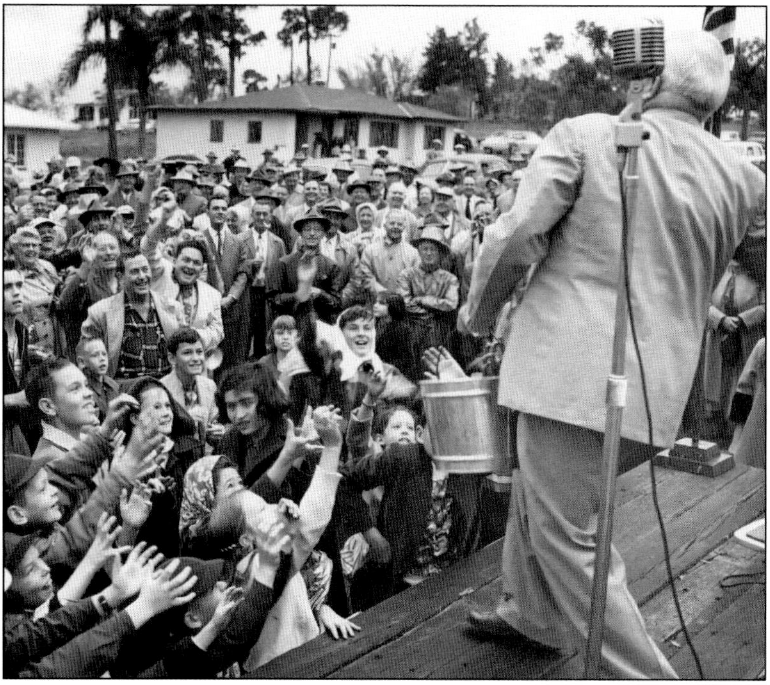

According to real estate broker and auctioneer company Hansbrough, this was the first auction ever held in Florida of brand new houses. Devised to attract more residents to Howey, the Griffin event was advertised in newspapers throughout Florida as well as in Kentucky, Georgia, Alabama, and Pennsylvania. Most unique to this auction was when thousands of silver dollars were tossed from a bucket into the crowd. (HH.)

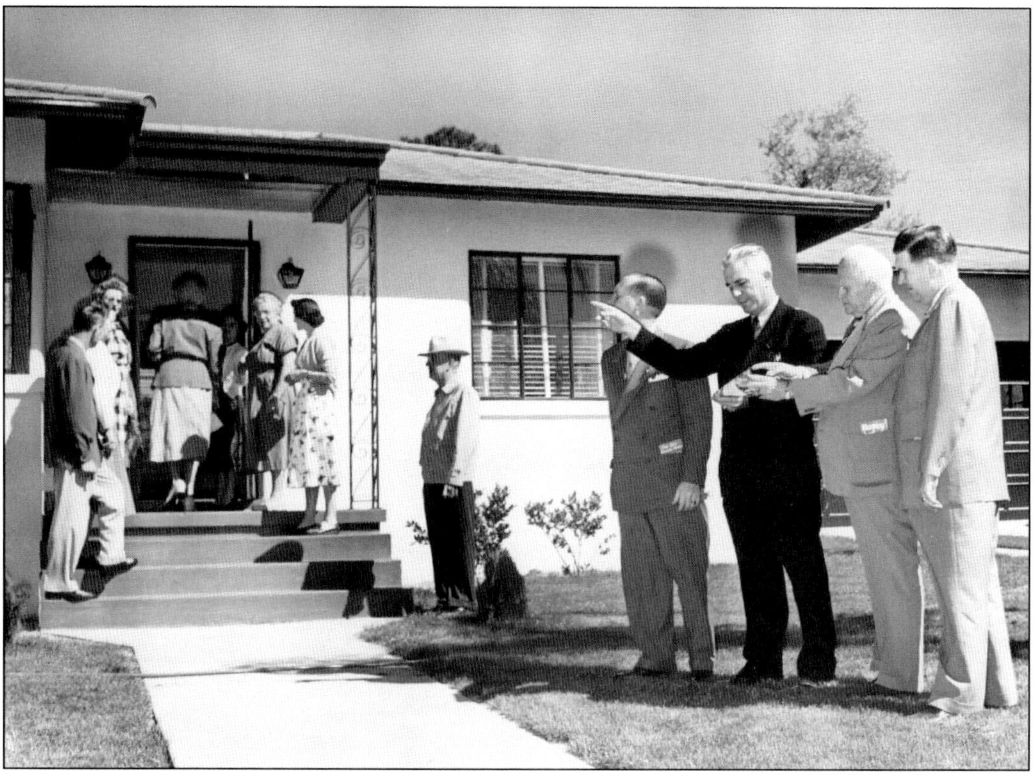

After the coins were tossed, Gov. Fuller Warren and C.V. Griffin officially opened the auction to bidding. Griffin and Hansbrough auctioneers stand before one of the furnished block homes to be auctioned. Prior to the sale, home inspections were encouraged. (HH.)

Ten

Nick Beucher, the Accomplished Visionary

Never has one classified advertisement meant so much to the town of Howey-in-the-Hills. In 1964, Nicholas Francis Beucher responded to a *Wall Street Journal* advertisement for the sale of the Floridan Country Club. Over the years, the golf course had fallen on hard times, as the town's once booming citrus industry went sour with the 1929 stock market crash and a series of grove-damaging freezes.

Beucher recognized the struggling country club as a diamond in the rough. While he described the property as severely neglected, he liked the year-round climate, the proximity to Orlando, and the rare hills throughout the golf course. After a decade of ingenious planning and extensive renovation, the once-simple country club looked more like what Beucher envisioned, an acclaimed golf resort.

Beucher's remarkable accomplishments with Mission Inn Resort were no mistake. This Chicagoan was born on December 9, 1916, and became top salesman for Morton Salt Company at a young age. In 1939, Beucher and friend Tex Bunteen spent 39 days in the saddle riding 1,400 miles from Del Rio, Texas, past Mexico City, a place that inspired the resort's architecture. When Beucher returned to Chicago, Margaret Fortmann accepted his marriage proposal, and the two were married.

Then, in 1942, Nick Beucher began his Chicago-based brokerage business, Packing House By-Products Company. During his commodities career, Beucher became an industry leader and served two terms as president of the National Hide and Leather Association. In 1964, as the trade evolved into more direct sales rather than through brokers, Nick Beucher became enticed by the golf course that William J. Howey developed. By September 1964, Beucher purchased the 168-acre property for $160,000, which included the original clubhouse and golf course. Nick Beucher's future, as well as those of his wife and six children, took a new direction, and his term of being the new leading man in Howey-in-the-Hills began. Over decades, Beucher's vision for the 1,000-acre resort came to fruition with guest, dining, and meeting rooms; two 18-hole golf courses; and hundreds of home sites. Beucher died on May 8, 2005, but his legacy continues in his absence as a family-owned and operated business that he envisioned, Mission Inn Resort and Club.

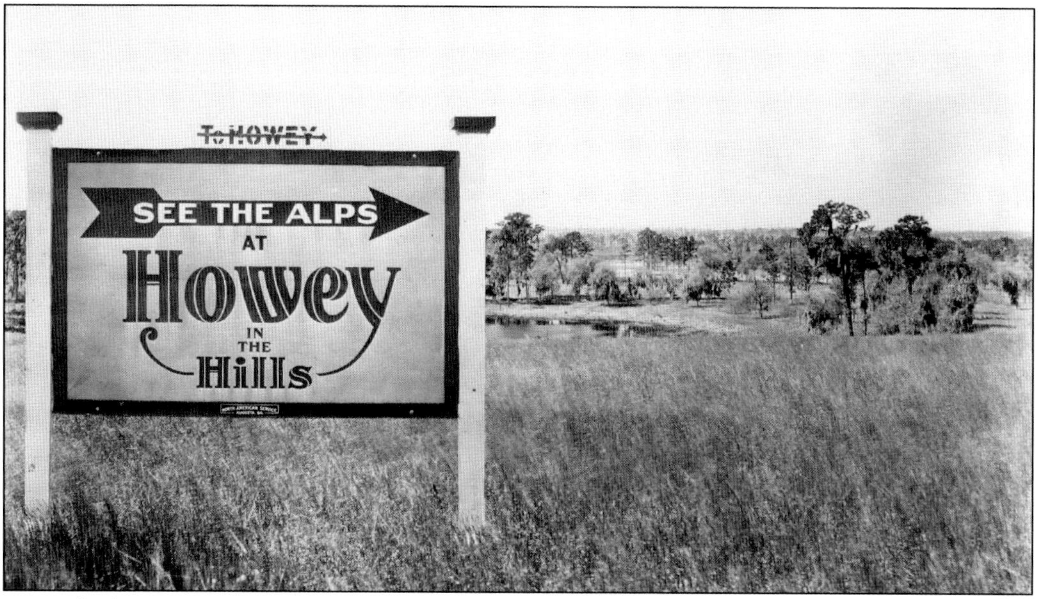

From the beginning, W.J. Howey made certain all signs pointing to Howey brought attention to the "Alps of Florida," as the phrase was coined. This southern Switzerland-like attribute was exactly what attracted Nick Beucher to the property in 1964. As Beucher stood on this exact hilltop location, he envisioned the property's future role as a golf resort destination in the unique Alpine countryside of Central Florida. (LCHM.)

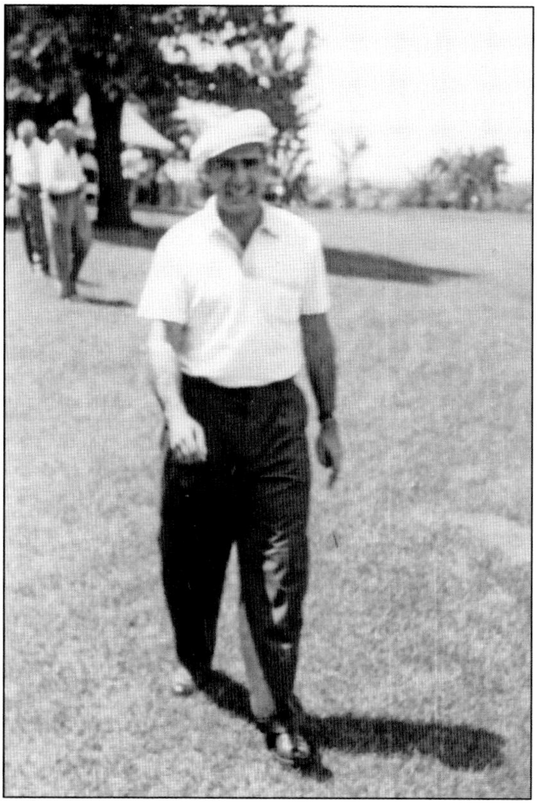

Nick Beucher was eager to make his mark in the Sunshine State hospitality industry when he envisioned the untold opportunity amongst the hills and lakes of his newly acquired golf course. In a matter of a few years, Nick Beucher was recognized for his vision and accomplishments. Beucher served with Arnold Palmer on Florida governor Claude Kirk's prestigious Council of 100 in the 1960s, was made an Honorary Kentucky Colonel in the 1970s, and was named *Golfweek* magazine's "Golf Father of the Year" in 1987, the year prior to Jack Nicklaus. (PBC.)

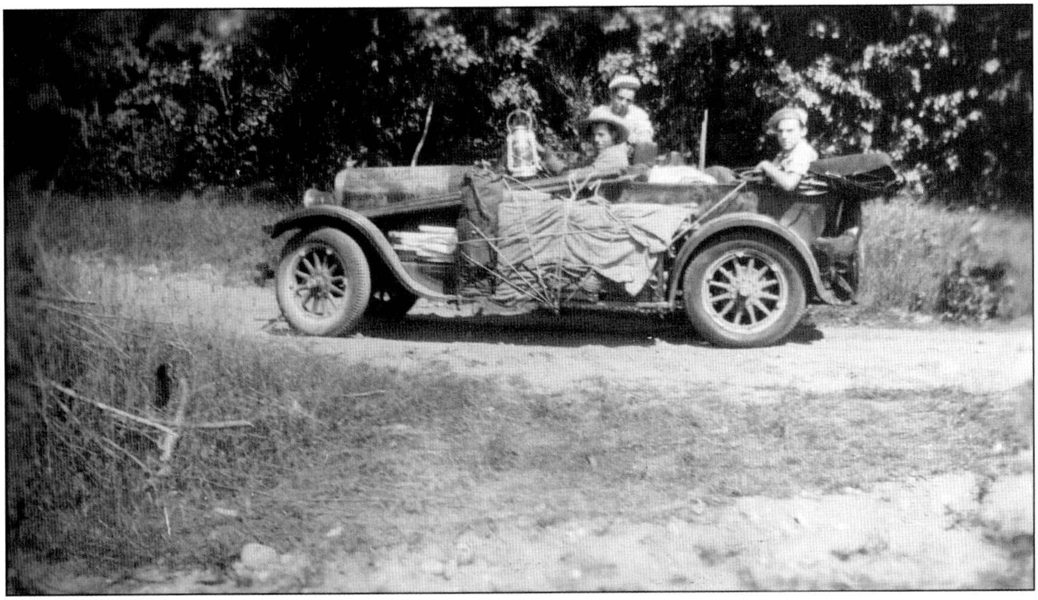

Jesuit priests called on Nick Beucher's parents, Nick and Mary, at their Chicago home and invited their teen to attend the Jesuit's boys' boarding school Campion in Prairie du Chien, Wisconsin, for religious education. Beucher played end on the football team with a leather helmet and graduated from Campion. During one summer break, Nick (back seat), his brother Joe (driving), and friend Jerry Bregenzer (beside Joe) went on an adventure-packed camping trip to Canada. (PBC.)

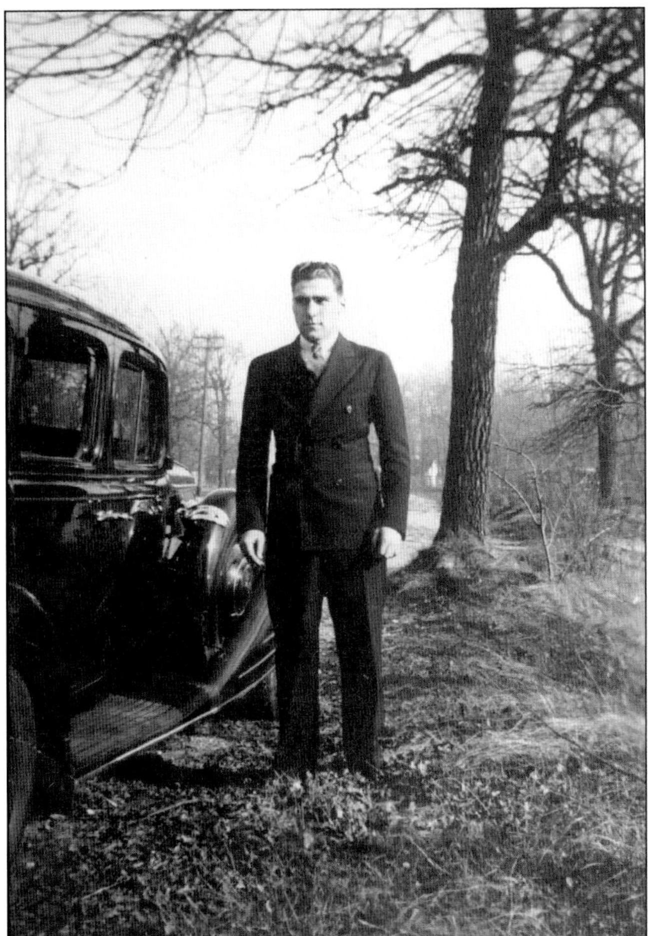

After two years of business classes, Nick Beucher left Chicago's Loyola University eager to go to work. The natural-born salesman lugged beef on his shoulder for $16 a week at his dad's meatpacking company in the interim until 1936, when he went to work for Morton Salt Company. At his $100-a-month job, Beucher became Salesman of the Year for four consecutive years when his sales topped the charts. (PBC.)

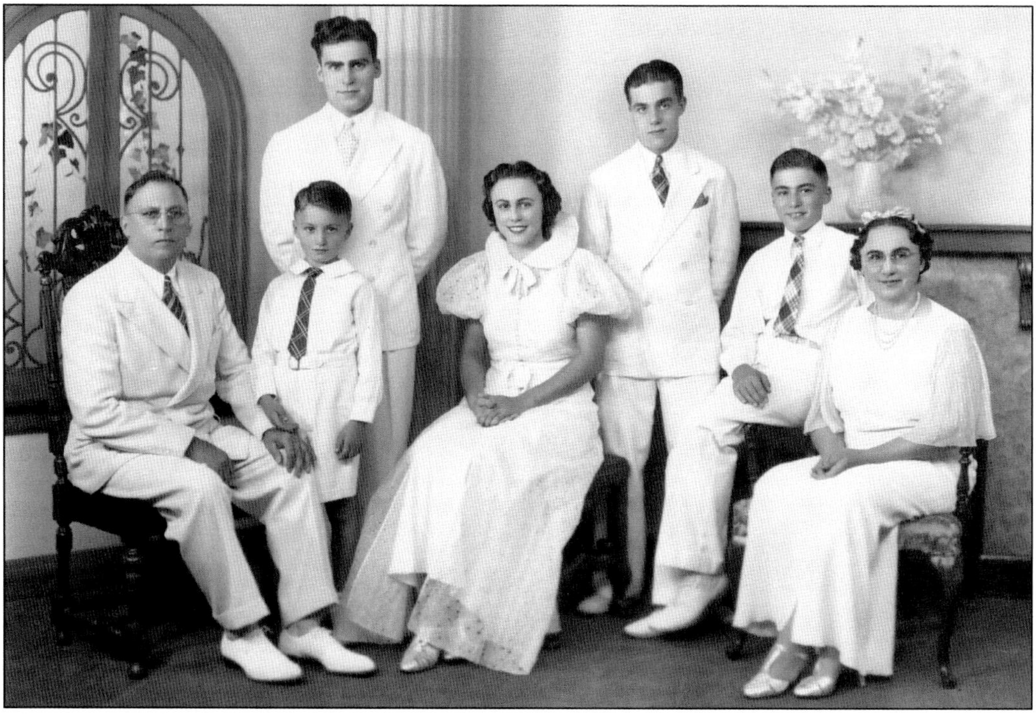

Those pictured in Nick Beucher's family portrait are, from left to right, (first row) his father, Nick; his youngest brother, Ed; his sister, Marie; his brother George; and his mother, Mary; (second row) Nick and his oldest brother, Joe. With a horse-drawn wagon, 16-year-old Nick Sr. started a family company, Nick Beucher & Sons, that eventually shipped hides, tallow, and calfskins worldwide from its Goose Island plant on the Chicago River. (PBC.)

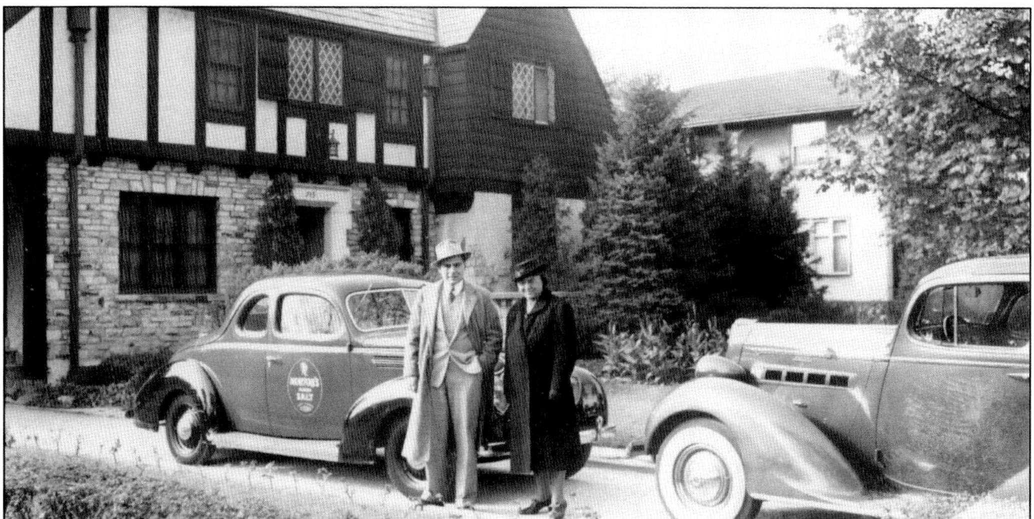

After Nick Beucher's family moved from their Damen Avenue (now Robie Street) home near St. Benedict's in Chicago, where they attended church and school, Nick's parents relocated to the north suburb of Wilmette and this Ashland Avenue home. Nick stands proudly with his mother, Mary, beside his new Morton Salt company car, which he used to help sell salt to western suburban meat markets, grocery stores, bakeries, and feed stores. (PBC.)

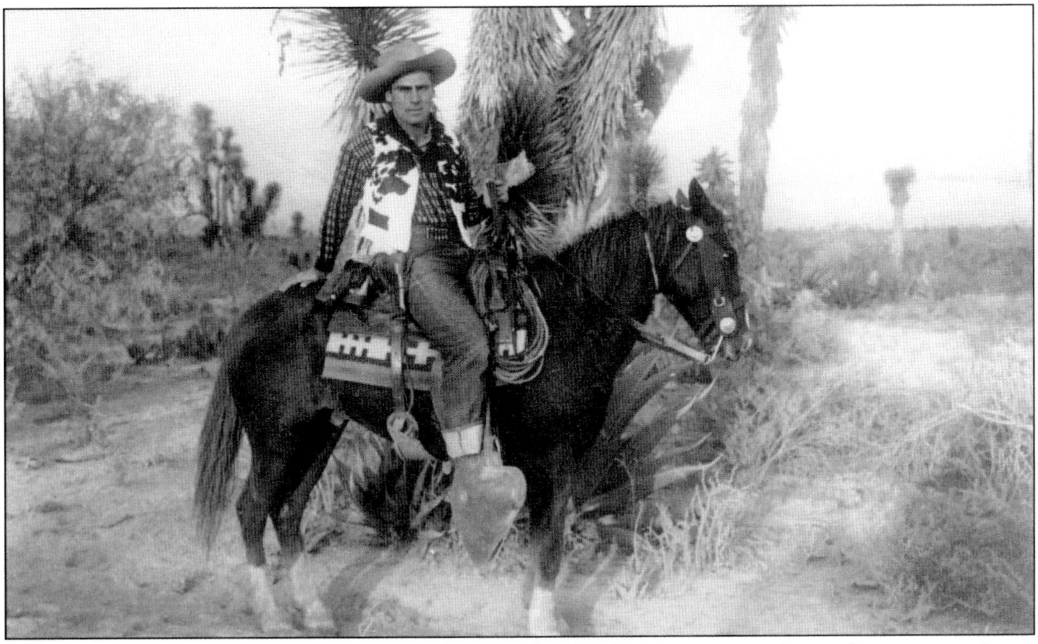

While recuperating in Evanston Hospital from a broken leg encountered barrel racing in a local rodee, Nick Beucher became determined to get back in the saddle and ride the length of Mexico on horseback. He recruited friend Tex Bunteen, a backroom butcher, to take the journey. In 1939, they drove a touring car to Del Rio, Texas, where they broke wild horses and crossed the border into unbridled territory. (PBC.)

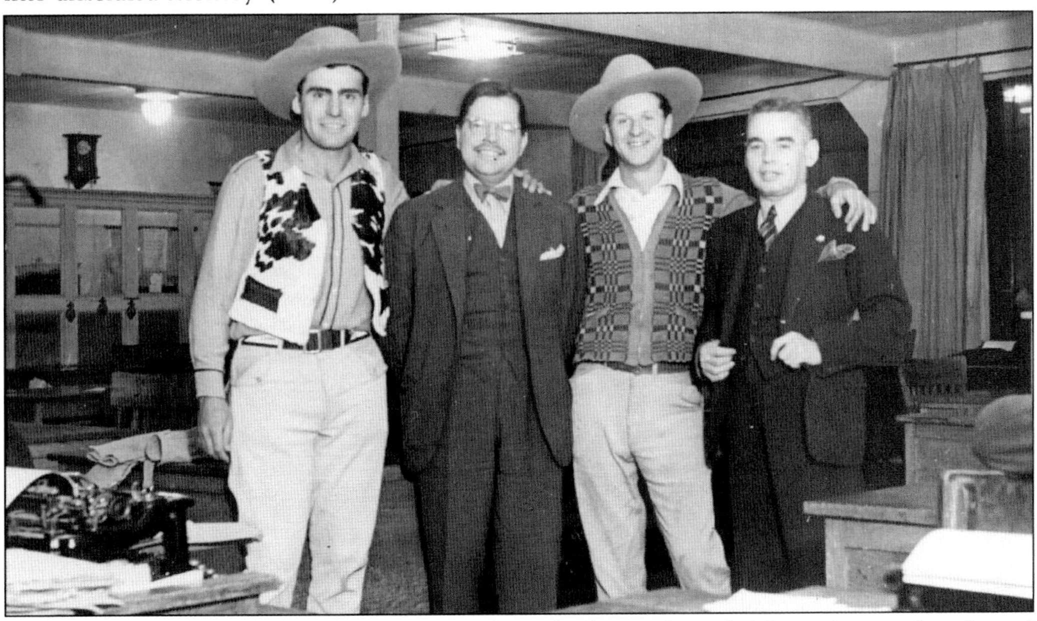

At the trail's end, 39 days after starting their horseback trip through Mexico's rugged, unfenced landscape, Nick Beucher and Tex Bunteen still carried their six-guns. Editors from Mexico City's newspaper the *Excelsior* greeted the American cowboys and ran a front-page story and this photograph in their December 12, 1939, edition. Nick and Tex traveled by bus on the new Pan-American Highway to Del Rio, Texas, and then drove back to Chicago. (PBC.)

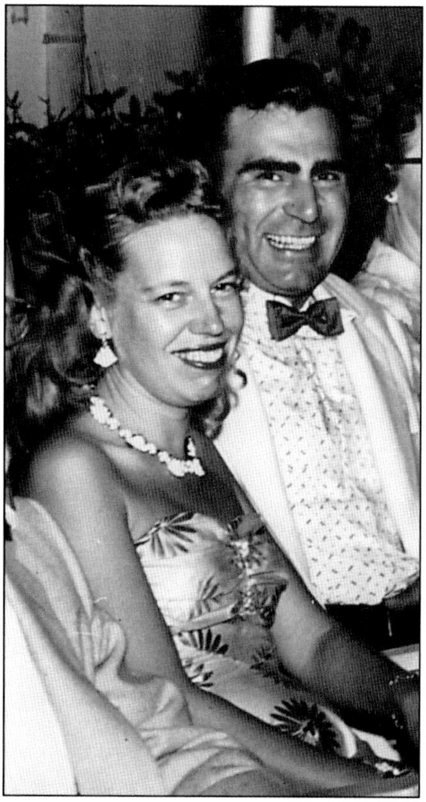

When Nick Beucher returned to Chicago from his horseback trip, he proposed to his sweetheart, Margaret Fortmann of Rogers Park, Illinois. She accepted, and the two exchanged vows at St. Margaret Mary's Catholic Church on June 15, 1940. Over more than 60 years of marriage, they danced often to "Spanish Eyes," went on cruises (including one on their honeymoon), built the business, raised their six children, and thoroughly enjoyed their grandchildren and great-grandchildren. (PBC.)

On March 31, 1942, Nick Beucher received his brokerage license from the City of Chicago, doing business as Packing House By-Products Company. He paid $37.50 a month for his first office, which was downtown in the Mercantile Exchange Building. Nick Beucher is seated at the head of the table, next to secretary Betty Clifford. To the right of Beucher are John Lindquist and broker Edith Olsen Bastgen. Nick's brother-in-law Hank Fortmann is seen standing behind Edith. (PBC.)

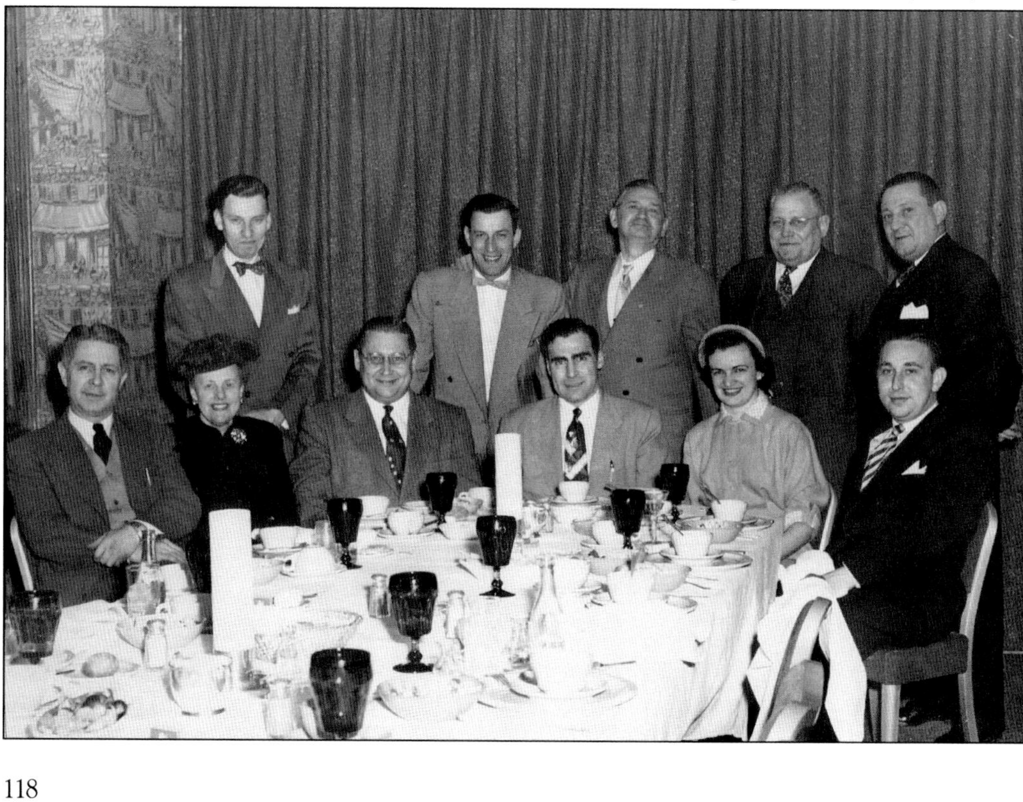

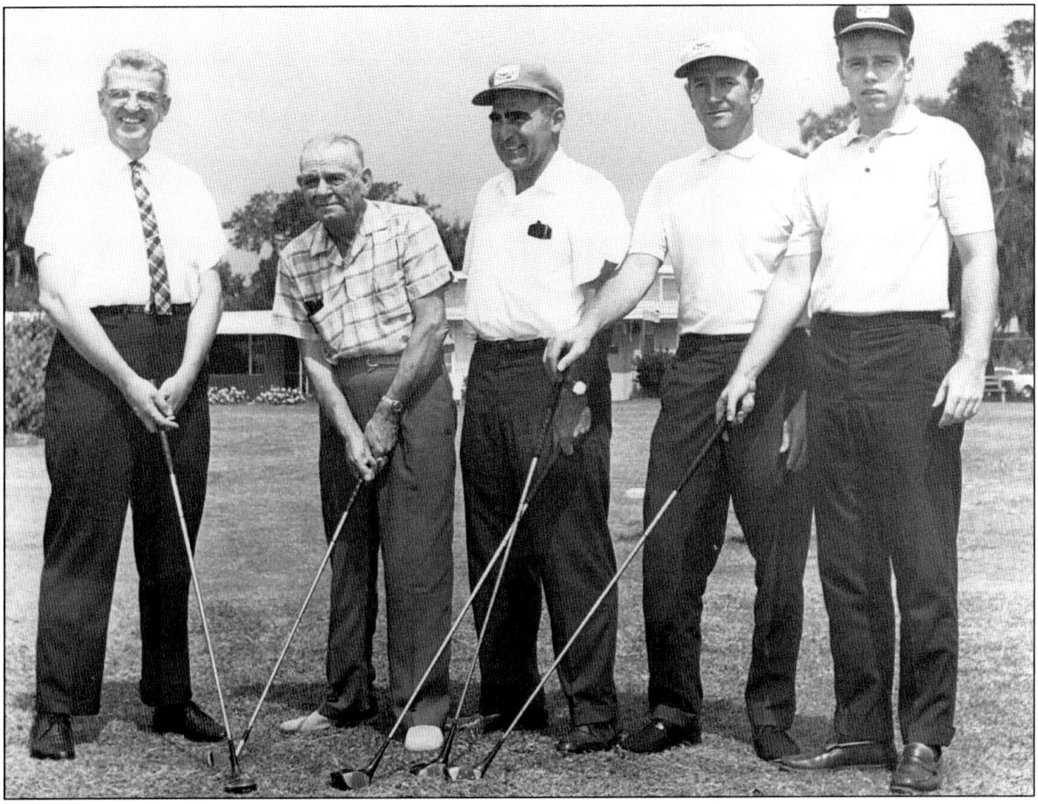

In September 1964, golf club heads changed when Packing House By-Products Company of Chicago purchased the 18-hole, 168-acre facility and clubhouse. Matching clubs to transfer ownership and begin extensive improvements are, from left to right, Frank Fernholz of Chicago, a director and counsel for the firm; Taylor Hunt of Clermont, the former club vice president; Nick Beucher Jr., the chairman of the purchasing firm; Joe Mordini, the new club manager; and Nick's son Bob Beucher, the new president. (EM.)

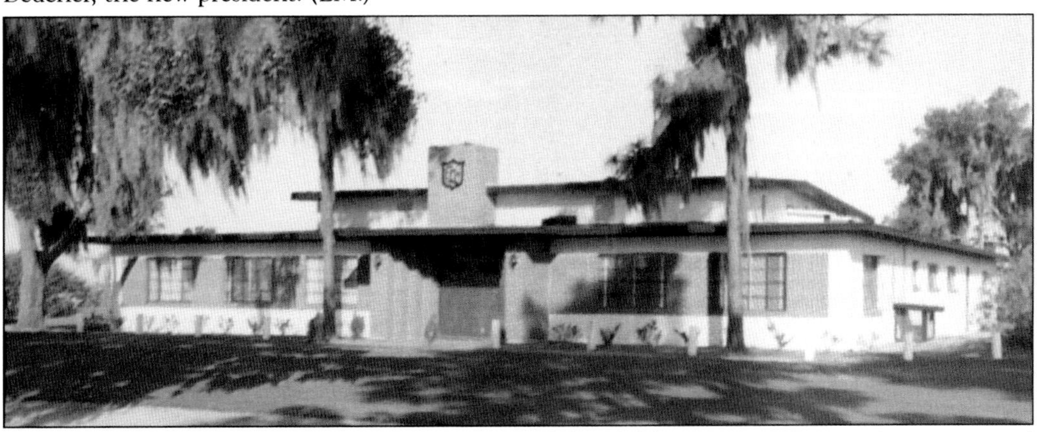

Above the entrance to the Floridan Country Club's clubhouse in 1964 was the recognized three-letter logo of FCC. The raised-roof section was added when the third-floor dance hall of William J. Howey's original Floridan Hotel at the town's south end was removed. This clubhouse stood for decades across from the Howey Mansion until Nick Beucher added the second golf course. (CB.)

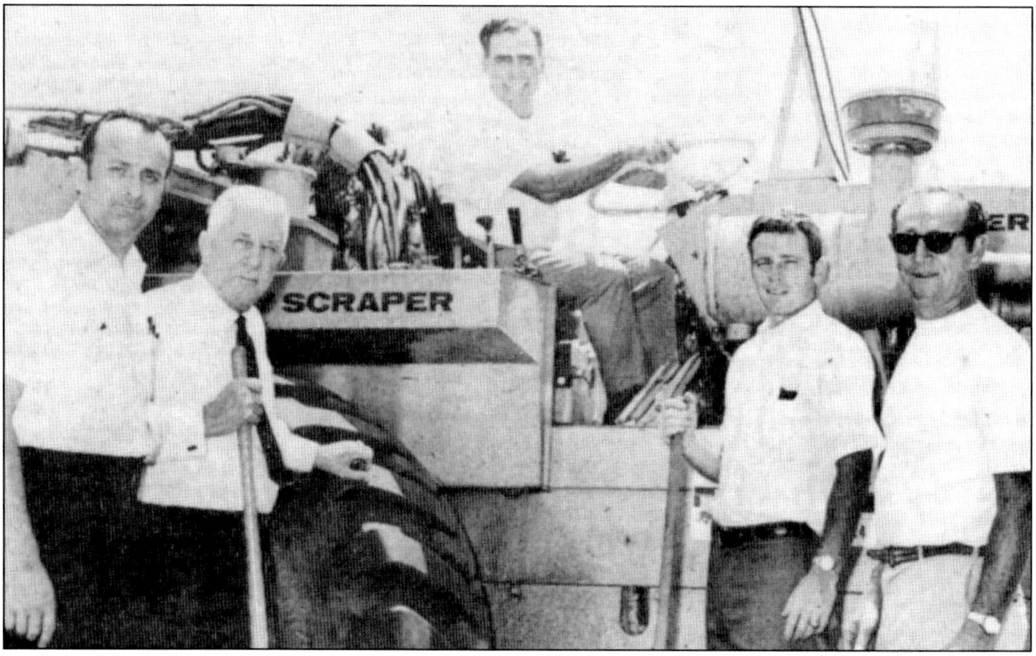

In 1969, Chairman Nick Beucher sits atop the land scraper ready to officially break ground on his first guest accommodations. Next on the left is Jack Matsche, the contractor for the 64-unit, four-story hotel, followed by C.V. Griffin, who sold the additional acreage with golf course frontage to Beucher. Joe Mordini (far right), the new club manager, stands beside Nick's son Bob Beucher, the new president. (PBC.)

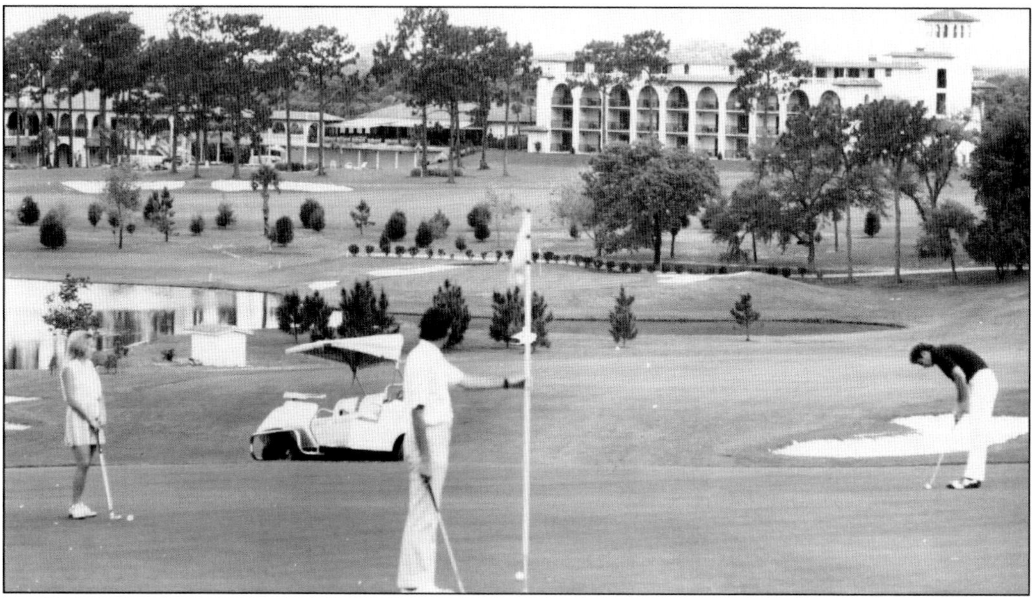

As more guests vacationed at the resort, Nick Beucher expanded guest accommodations and amenities. After the first 64-unit hotel building opened in March 1970, a lobby and swimming pool were added, followed by a two-story restaurant complex with banquet and meeting rooms. The expanded resort facilities and services attracted a broader market that stayed longer in Howey-in-the-Hills. (PBC.)

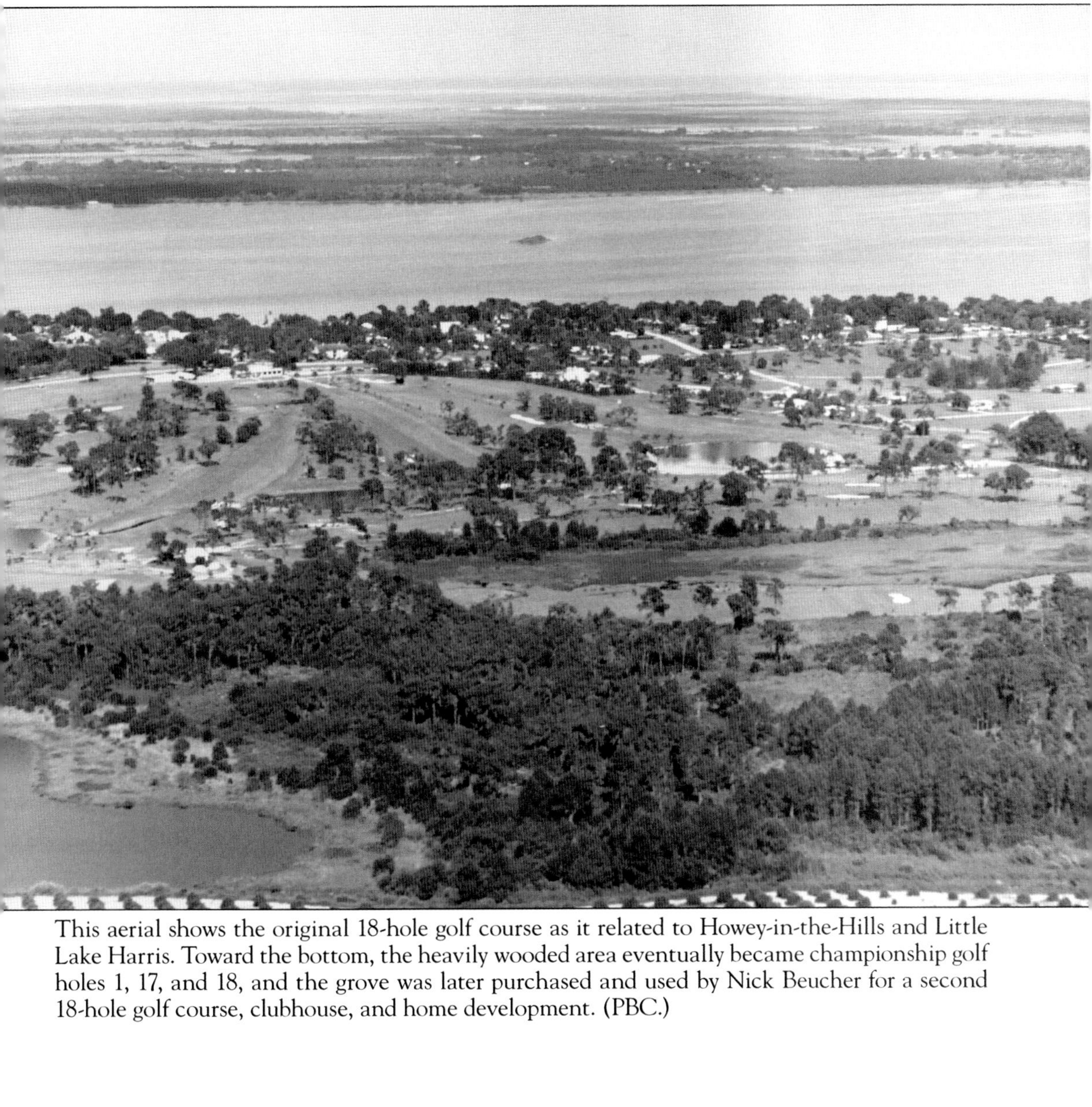

This aerial shows the original 18-hole golf course as it related to Howey-in-the-Hills and Little Lake Harris. Toward the bottom, the heavily wooded area eventually became championship golf holes 1, 17, and 18, and the grove was later purchased and used by Nick Beucher for a second 18-hole golf course, clubhouse, and home development. (PBC.)

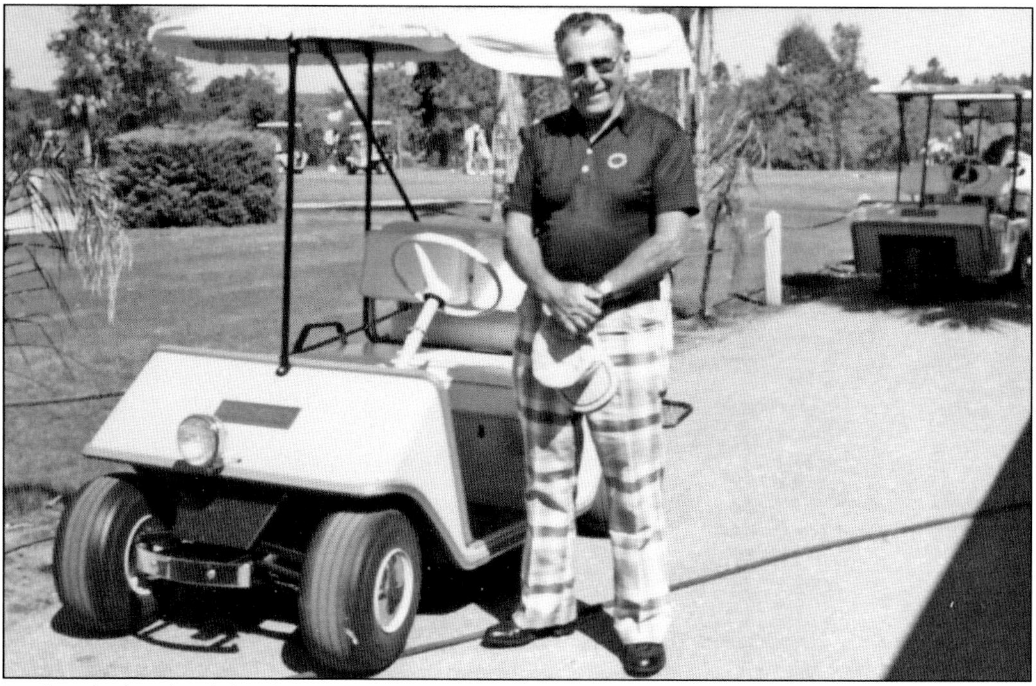

In the plaid style of the day with high-brimmed golf hat, developer Nick Beucher toured every inch of his expanding property on his personal four-passenger cart, with grandchildren, friends, or customers aboard. Reminiscent of the horse-drawn fringed surreys of Howey's era, these fringed carts were a favorite means of transportation around the golfer's paradise in the 1970s. (PBC.)

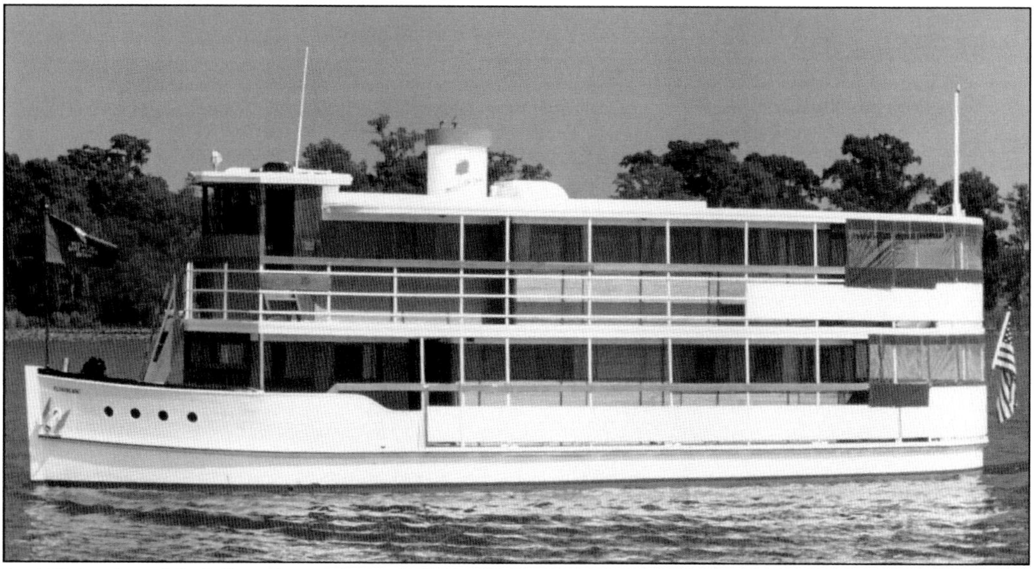

In 1984, when Nick Beucher salvaged the 1930s river yacht, he had it meticulously restored for resort guests to cruise the 13,788-acre Lake Harris. Capt. Noah Tilgman originally crafted *Noah's Ark* for overnight black bass fishing trips along the Palatka River; it had views of the passing cypress-lined waters from every room. Nick renamed the 49-passenger vessel *La Reina*, entertained visitors aboard, and celebrated every birthday afloat, enjoying his favorite dinner with family and friends. (PBC.)

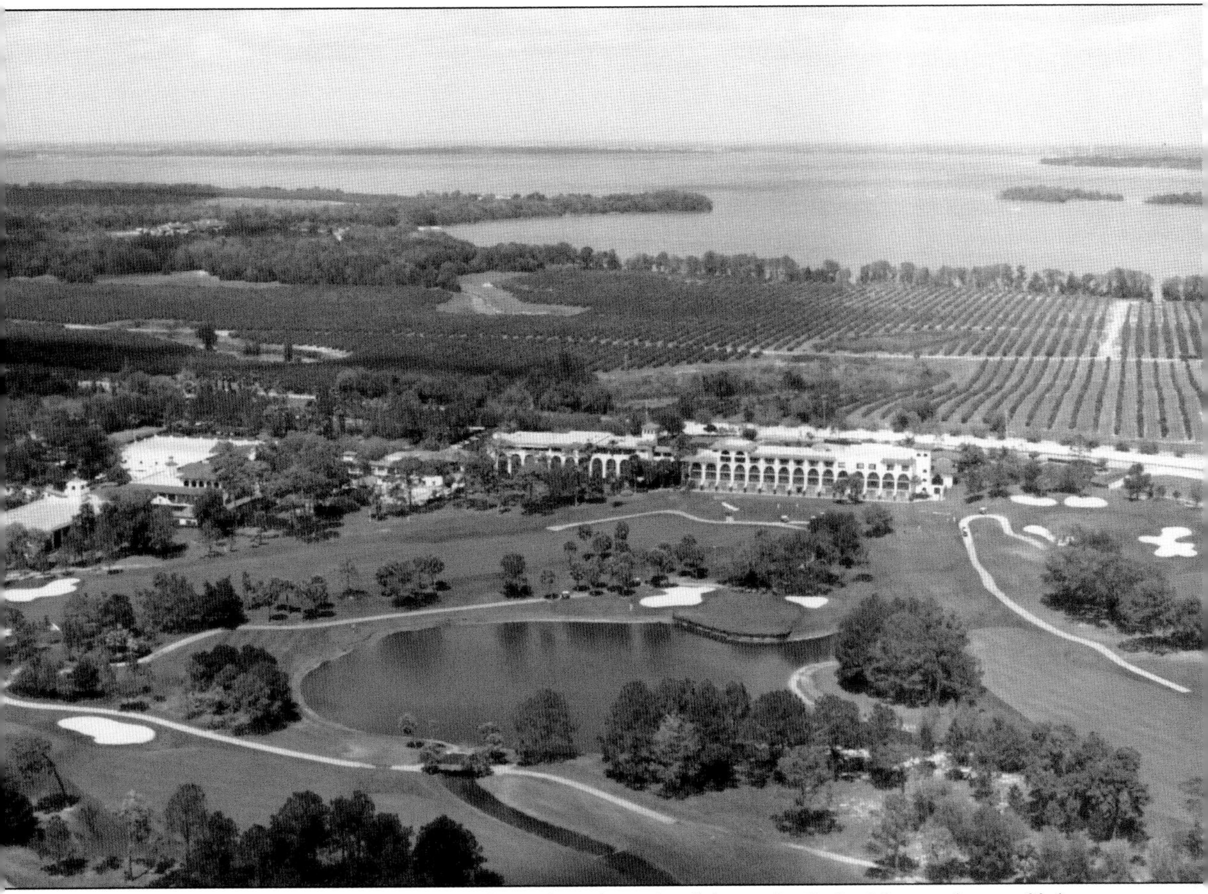

The surrounding groves and golf resort have long benefited from the Lake Harris chain of lakes and endless boating opportunities. Given a few days from the resort's marina, boaters can reach the Atlantic Ocean through Central Florida's network of lakes, rivers, and locks. Unspoiled to this day, these waterways provide a peak into Florida's natural side, much as it was when turn-of-the-century visitors first discovered the Howey land development. (PBC.)

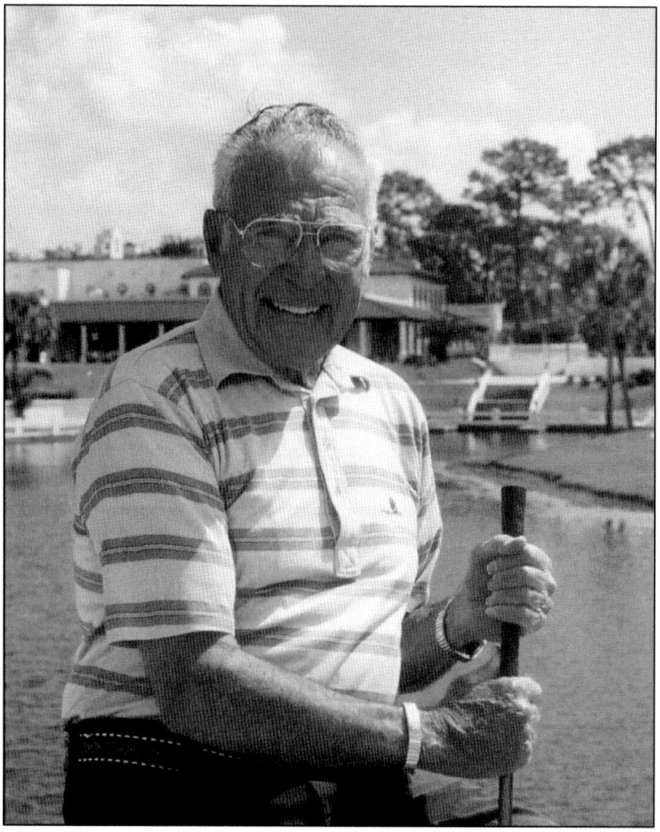

Nick Beucher was proud to be featured on the cover of numerous hospitality and golf magazines. Here, he poses gripping his golf club on the 17th-hole bridge, with resort restaurant La Hacienda across the water in the background. In the 1975, Nick Beucher created holes 17 (the course's hardest), 18, and 1 from dense woods to add length and challenge to the course. (PBC.)

Plaza de la Fontana has become the most photographed setting at the resort and a favorite location for courtyard weddings and special events. Surrounding the landscaped plaza are a 40-unit hotel wing, the 17th hole, and restaurants La Hacienda and El Conquistador. From the tower, turtles, alligators, and sandhill cranes are easily spotted. (PBC.)

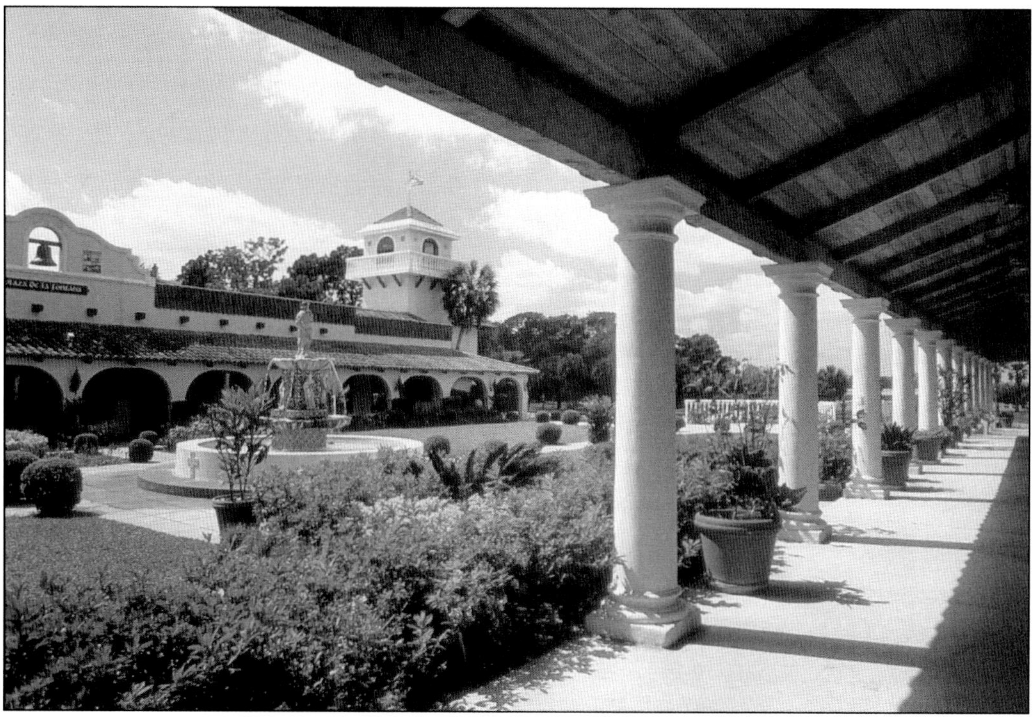

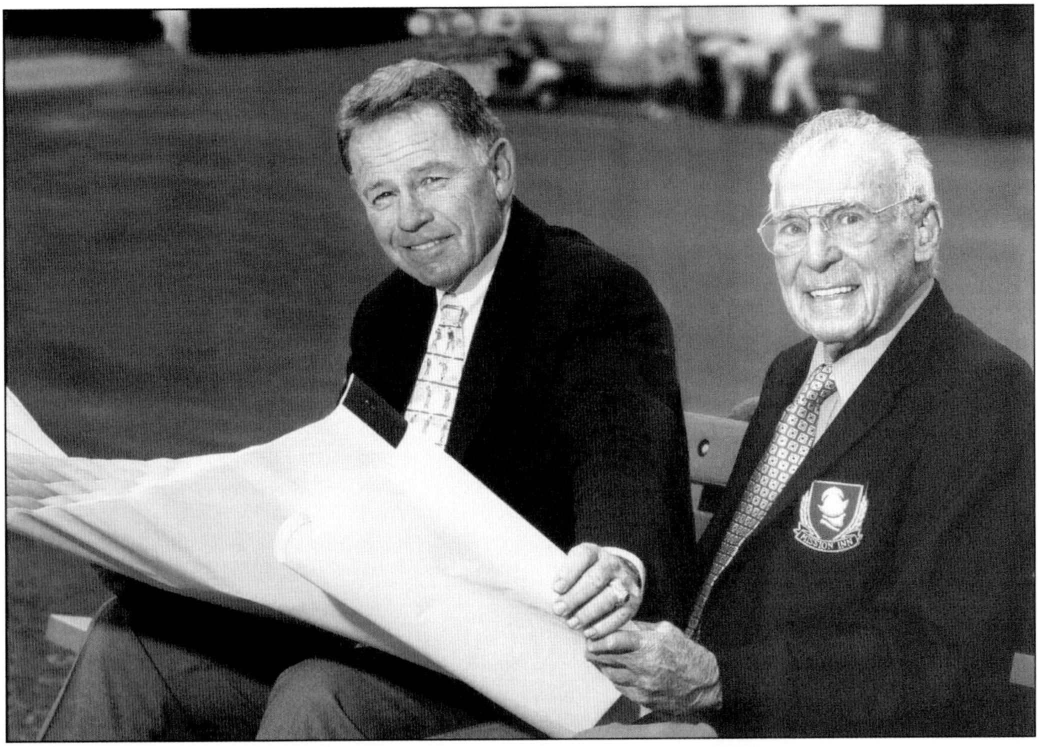

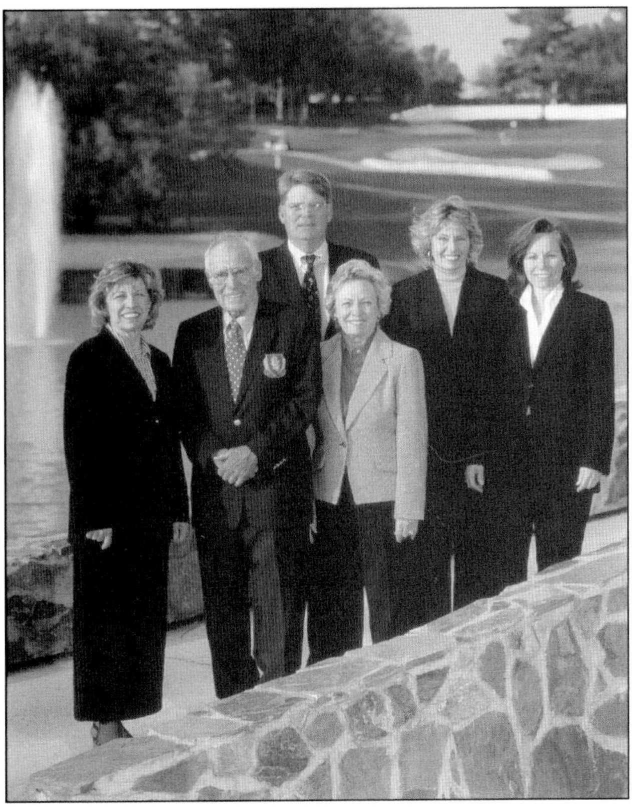

Wearing his sport coat with the resort crest, Nick Beucher poses with his six children in front of the resort for a golf magazine cover and feature. The resort's story and that of the town have received publicity for decades. Beucher always beamed with pride when writers asked him to tell his story. After reminiscing over old plans with son Bob Beucher (above), Nick joined, from left to right in the photograph at right, son and daughters Carol Beucher Kelsey, Bud Beucher, Donna Beucher Line, Michelle Beucher Purser, and Peggy Beucher Clark on a golf course bridge that he had built. Over the years, Nick and Margaret's children moved to Howey-in-the-Hills to manage the business and to raise their families. Nick Beucher was proud to admit that Mission Inn Resort was not the accomplishment of one man but a team effort, much like the Howey Company. (Both, BRP.)

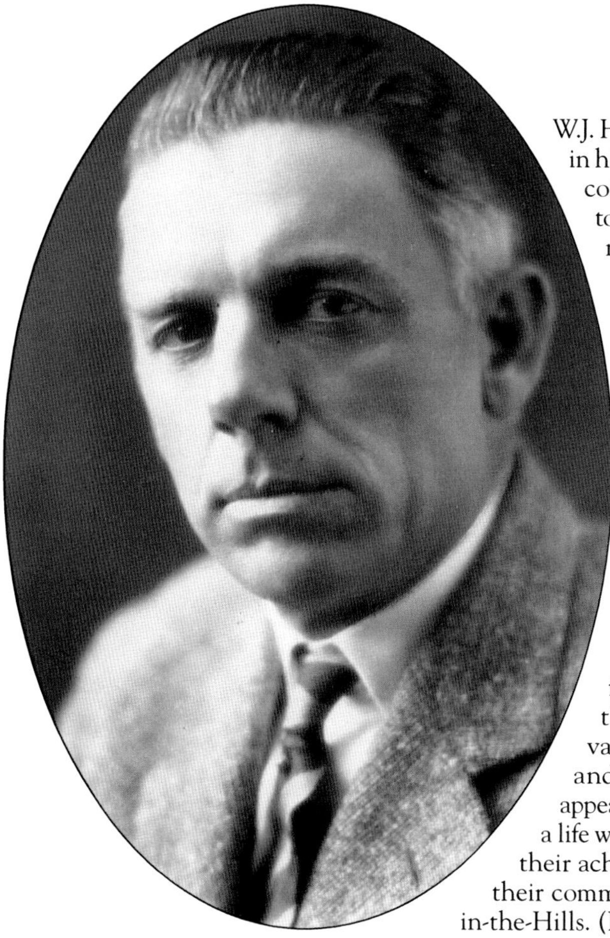

W.J. Howey and the two key men who followed in his footsteps to Howey-in-the-Hills were all coincidentally born in Illinois, committed to commodities, and extremely successful, natural-born salesmen. Each of these visionaries discovered the greatest potential of their day for the Alps of Florida with different outcomes entirely. William J. Howey witnessed a timbered wilderness and foresaw a citrus empire and thriving town sprouting from nothing. C.V. Griffin revived a struggling city economy and dwindling, debt-ridden Howey Company by building a new state bridge, encouraging a flurry of home construction, and creating a college-preparatory academy. Then, in 1964, Nick Beucher rode into town and, from the clubhouse hilltop, envisioned the distressed golf course as a beautiful vacation destination, conference center, and residential community that would appeal to a global audience. The town became a life work for Howey, Griffin, and Beucher, and their achievements stand today as testimony to their commitment to the development of Howey-in-the-Hills. (Both, HH.)

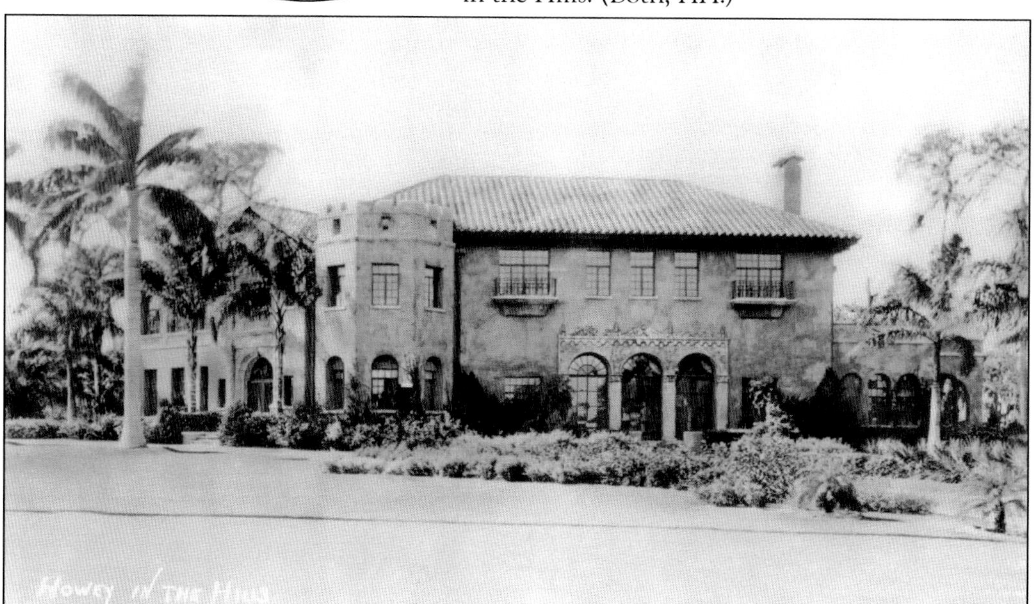

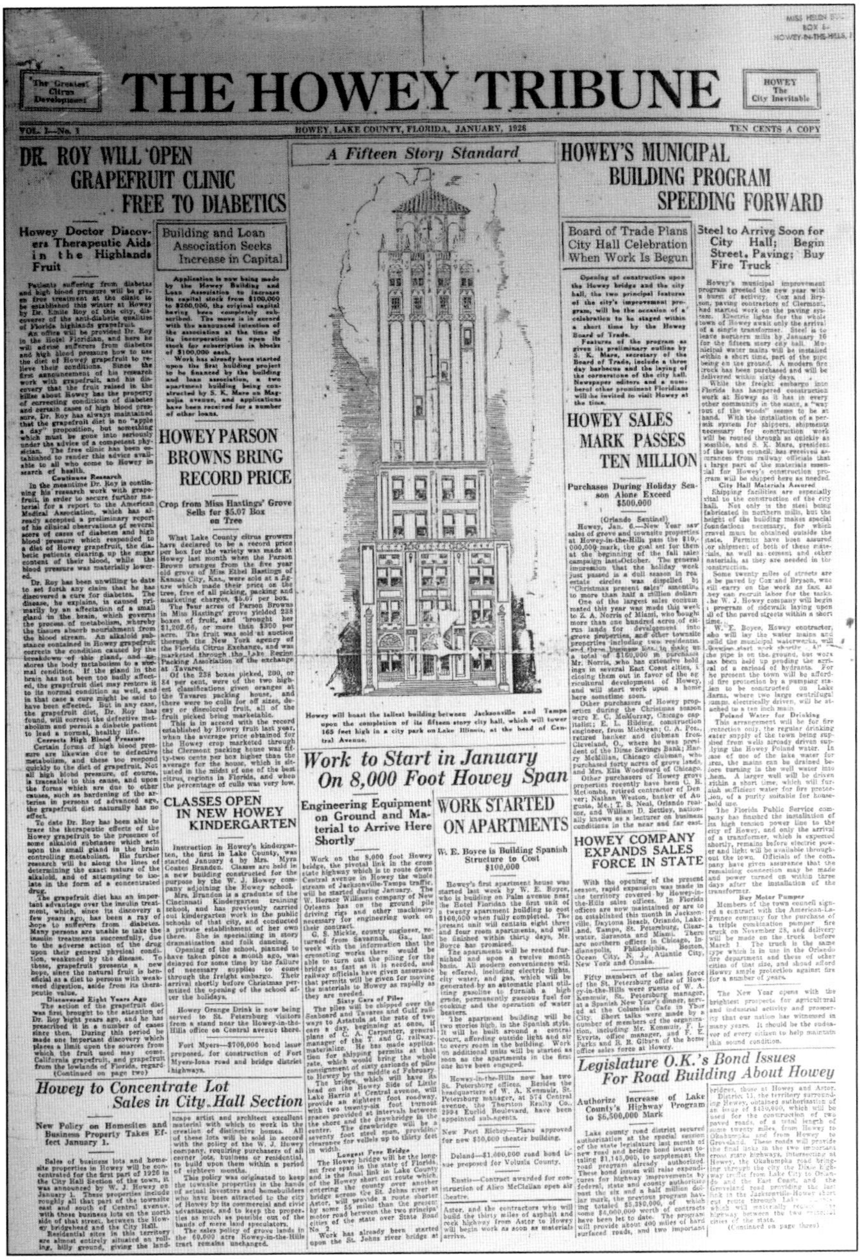

THE HOWEY TRIBUNE

"The Greatest Citrus Development"

HOWEY The City Inevitable

VOL. 1—No. 1 HOWEY, LAKE COUNTY, FLORIDA, JANUARY, 1926 TEN CENTS A COPY

DR. ROY WILL OPEN GRAPEFRUIT CLINIC FREE TO DIABETICS

Howey Doctor Discovers Therapeutic Aids in the Highlands Fruit

Building and Loan Association Seeks Increase in Capital

HOWEY PARSON BROWNS BRING RECORD PRICE

Crop from Miss Hastings' Grove Sells for $5.07 Box on Tree

A Fifteen Story Standard

HOWEY'S MUNICIPAL BUILDING PROGRAM SPEEDING FORWARD

Board of Trade Plans City Hall Celebration When Work Is Begun

Steel to Arrive Soon for City Hall; Begin Street, Paving; Buy Fire Truck

HOWEY SALES MARK PASSES TEN MILLION

Work to Start in January On 8,000 Foot Howey Span

CLASSES OPEN IN NEW HOWEY KINDERGARTEN

Engineering Equipment on Ground and Material to Arrive Here Shortly

WORK STARTED ON APARTMENTS

HOWEY COMPANY EXPANDS SALES FORCE IN STATE

Howey to Concentrate Lot Sales in City Hall Section

Legislature O.K.'s Bond Issues For Road Building About Howey

When Nick Beucher first promoted his Florida golf course and clubhouse in 1964, his Chicago brokerage business mailed brochures to golfing members of Midwestern country clubs, resulting in a customer base from east of the Mississippi. As the resort grew, marketing evolved and attracted a more diverse group to the resort, including meeting groups. Beucher's use of all available media to further broaden the base and entice new customers was also the practice of William J. Howey. One of Howey's most ingenious marketing tools was the *Howey Tribune*, a four-page monthly newspaper of standard size that chronicled past events, current offerings, and predicted crop returns for an annual subscription rate of $1. The social news included local residents and activities and photographs of visiting celebrities and special events. This photograph is of the front page of Vol. 1, No. 1, which premiered in January 1926. (HH.)

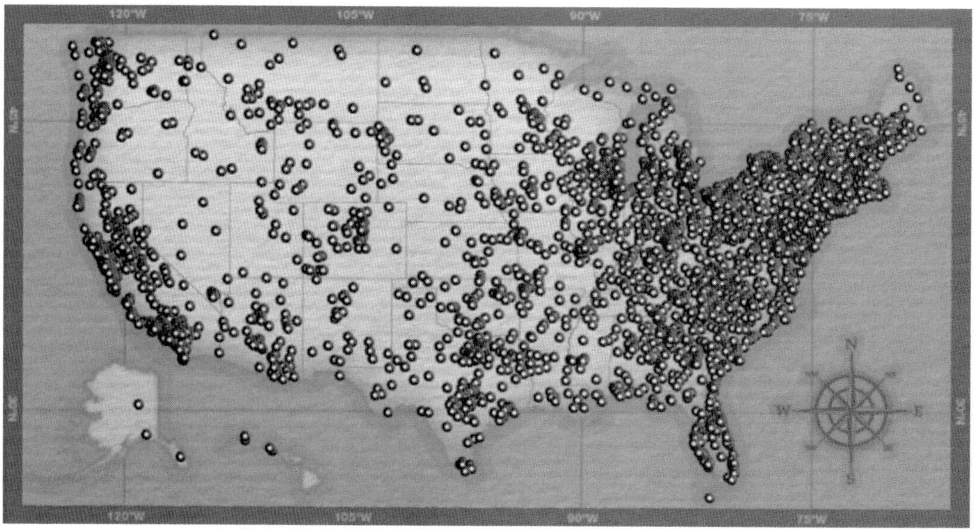

Consistent with our mission to preserve history on a local level, this book was printed in South Carolina on American-made paper and manufactured entirely in the United States. Products carrying the accredited Forest Stewardship Council (FSC) label are printed on 100 percent FSC-certified paper.

MADE IN THE USA